POWERHOUSE
MARKETING PLANS

POWERHOUSE MARKETING PLANS

14 Outstanding Real-Life Plans and What You Can Learn from Them to Supercharge Your Own Campaigns

Winslow "Bud" Johnson

⁂AMACOM

American Management Association

New York • Atlanta • Brussels • Chicago • Mexico City
San Francisco • Shanghai • Tokyo • Toronto • Washington, D.C.

This publication is designed to provide accurate and authoritative information in regard to the subject matter covered. It is sold with the understanding that the publisher is not engaged in rendering legal, accounting, or other professional service. If legal advice or other expert assistance is required, the services of a competent professional person should be sought.

Library of Congress Cataloging-in-Publication Data

Johnson, Winslow.
    Powerhouse marketing plans : 14 outstanding real-life plans and what you can learn from them to supercharge your own campaigns / Winslow "Bud" Johnson.
        p.   cm.
    Includes index.
    ISBN 0-8144-7219-2
    1. Marketing—Management.   I. Title.
HF5415.13.J5878   2004
658.8'101—dc22

                                                                    2004006898

Printing number

10 9 8 7 6 5 4 3 2 1

To my wife and best friend,
Tiffany, with love

Contents

Foreword

"No matter what the field or profession, the 'great ones' always teach." A friend recently shared this thought with me, and the more I contemplated what she'd said, the more I became convinced she was right. In the field of marketing, in my 30 years working to help companies be more innovative marketers, I've met fewer than a dozen "great ones." Bud Johnson makes the short list of great ones. Yes, he is an immensely talented and creative marketer. But he's also a great teacher. And I should know. I was one of Bud's first "students." The first marketing plan I ever developed and wrote (for a new line of fishing tackle) was under the encouraging and creative eye of Bud Johnson. I could have had no better teacher.

And now Bud continues his role as teacher, only on a much broader scale, with the publication of *Powerhouse Marketing Plans*. And, much as when I had the privilege of starting out with Bud, *Powerhouse Marketing Plans*, provides the realest of a real-world education on how to conceptualize, plan, and implement innovative new marketing ventures. What's so wonderful about this book (and a testament to Bud's skill not only as a creative marketer but as a gifted teacher), is that it can be read at many levels, no matter what the reader's business experience, background, talents, or interests.

At one level (the most basic of levels), you can use these sample marketing plans, to guide and model—almost as a template if you will—any marketing plan you have to create. Any (or all) of the fourteen marketing plans will help you make sure you've asked the questions you should be asking, considered all the elements you should be considering, and been clear about the assumptions you're making in your plan. Furthermore, if need be, you can adapt the form and formats of these plans to help you actually write your marketing plan.

On another level, the stories behind the marketing plans can provide inspiration and guidance to the novice and veteran marketer alike, especially when faced with a difficult marketing challenge. Seeing how Bud and his clients solved some of the seemingly insurmountable marketing challenges on the way to developing such marketplace successes as L'eggs pantyhose or Philips long-lasting light bulbs is tremendously helpful, if only in knowing that with enough persistence and creative thought, most problems can somehow be solved. The fact, too, that Bud has intentionally included several less-than-exciting, commodity-type products makes these examples, to my mind, all the more inspiring. Knowing, for instance, that Wooster Brush was able to substantially increase the size of their mini paint roller business with a single, well-executed idea may be a source of hope for the innovation manager charged with developing innovations like laundry detergents, deodorants, or toothpaste. My guess is that many of the marketing challenges that Bud describes in the book, at some level, will not be too very different from the marketing and growth challenges you are now facing or will someday face on your current or future new business ventures.

On a third level, the stories behind the marketing plans are fun to read, while adding to your general business knowledge and education. I like to think of these stories as a kind of Indiana Jones adventure for the marketing mind. As in any new marketing venture, you really have no idea what's going to happen. All you know for sure is that you're in for one hell of a ride.

Specifically, Part One of *Powerhouse Marketing Plans* gives the inside story—literally from wish to launch—of six real-world marketing success stories. Part Two gives eight "sample" marketing plans, disguised for the purposes of client confidentiality, but no less real or instructive than the case studies and marketing plans in Part One. In all fourteen chapters, actual

marketing plans have been selected from scores of alternatives, most of
which Bud has worked on over the years, because of their variety and ability
to elucidate different elements of marketing venture creation within vastly
different industries.

What I find uniquely valuable about *Powerhouse Marketing Plans*, unlike
so many of the other business books I've read over the years, is Bud's ability
to provide the seminal thinking behind the marketing plan: *why* and *how* the
venture was originally conceptualized, the inevitable challenges that come
with creating something new, and ultimately how these challenges were
overcome on the road to business success. As such, I think they provide an
unequaled way to learn about how new business ventures happen in the real
world.

Put another way, the true learning—and value—of *Powerhouse Marketing
Plans* is its exploration of the details of new marketing ventures—and the
interrelationship among these details. In this book, Bud has attended to the
details of all the elements of the marketing mix: from name development
to package creation; from display design to trade dealing, and price/value
tradeoffs; from product positioning to marketing communications; from re-
searching the competitive environment to understanding consumer segments and their unique motivations and interests. As such, we're given a
unique opportunity to look behind the curtain of marketing wizardry to see
both the magic of directed creative thought and the incredibly hard work
that's required to get all the elements of the marketing mix to come together
in an integrated way to create a unique new product with a compelling point
of difference. If more marketing executives would read Bud's book, one can't
help but think that new product failure rates would fall dramatically from
the 80 to 90 percent levels they are at today.

Powerhouse Marketing Plans really has less to do with the actual writing
and format of a marketing plan, and very much more to do with the creative
thinking and problem-solving processes behind literally creating something
out of nothing. Quotes from Dwight D. Eisenhower and my daughter Caroline come to mind as a way to sum up the essence and value of *Powerhouse
Marketing Plans*.

Said Eisenhower about his plans to invade Europe on D-Day: "It's not
the plan, it's the planning."

Said Caroline, dressed in a princess's gown, staring at herself intensely in the mirror: "I have a magic wand, and I'm not afraid to use it."

Bryan W. Mattimore, author of *99% Inspiratio:,*
Tips, Tales and Techniques for Liberating Your Business Creativity

Preface

A business can have a great financial plan, be well capitalized, and have the best products or services in its industry and a talented management team—but it won't survive for long without profitable sales. One of the best publicized examples of this was the large number of dot.com failures. Many of those failed companies had outstanding web sites based on clever business concepts, but they just were not capable of generating sufficient profitable sales.

One of the best ways to ensure that the sales opportunities of a business are realized is through the development of a marketing plan. Ideally this is a written document that spells out, in detail, how the business intends to generate those new and continuing profitable sales. It should be a working document that is adjusted from time to time as the plan is implemented. This book focuses on the development of winning marketing plans. In the book, we'll review the marketing plans of a number of highly successful products, such as L'eggs hosiery, Philips long-life lightbulbs, and EZ Change hearing aid batteries by Energizer. We'll also identify the unique characteristics that differentiate successful from unsuccessful marketing plans. This is the only book that provides you with a series of real examples that can be used as models.

This book also shows a number of ways of significantly improving the odds of developing a successful marketing plan. Many of the successful marketing plans in this book share a number of characteristics. There are similarities in the attitudes of the people who have developed these marketing plans, in the reasons that the marketing plans were developed in the first place, and in the implementation processes employed as these successful business ventures were unfolded. By identifying the common traits in marketing plans that made it, this book provides readers with examples of how to proceed with their own marketing plans.

Who Should Read This Book

Powerhouse Marketing Plans is written for people who are—or would like to be—involved in the development of a marketing plan. The book has been written to be useful both to managers and executives in medium and large-sized corporations and to individuals and small businesses.

Businesses

This book will meet many of the marketing needs of people in established businesses, small and large. For the smaller business, the book will give the CEO or marketing manager a road map that clearly illustrates how to proceed with the development of a marketing plan. For the large business, the book provides in-depth information about critical areas, such as clever ways of evaluating the perceptions of potential customers. The book will also serve as a checklist for these larger businesses, to help them ensure that all the important planning steps have been taken.

Individuals

Entrepreneurs and would-be entrepreneurs are ideal candidates to read this book because it spells out how to create a marketing plan for a potential new venture, even if you are a novice in business or if your new business idea involves a category unfamiliar to you.

All readers will be presented with all the major factors that should be considered when writing a marketing plan—and these factors are surprisingly similar regardless of the size of the business. Readers may choose to go into as much, or as little, depth as they feel is appropriate for their situation and personal background. Because of this, the book will be as useful for someone who is running or would like to start a part-time business as it will be for a marketing team in a *Fortune* 500 company.

Acknowledgments

First, I would like to thank my clients and other individuals from those companies that allowed me to include the stories behind their marketing plans in this book. My thanks to Steven Goldmacher, Director of Corporate Communications, and Joan Emmer, Research and Planning Manager, Strategic Marketing, of Philips Lighting Company for their insight into Philips long-life lightbulbs. I would like to thank the management of the Sara Lee Hosiery Division for its excellent insight into the progress of the L'eggs brand. These executives include Howard Upchurch, President; Barbara Johnson, Director of Public Relations; Nadine Hall, Marketing Director; Angela Hawkins, Marketing Director; Vickie Byrd, Director of Marketing Research; and Larry McAlister, Director Retail Operations/Sales Communications.

From Matrixx Initiatives, Inc., I would like to thank Julie Johannsen, Director of Marketing, and Tim Clarot, Operations Manager, for their insight into the development of the Zicam cold remedy nasal gel. I would also like to thank Scott Rutledge, Vice President of Marketing for the Wooster Brush Company, for providing the details of the Jumbo-Koter marketing plan and Ernie Petrus, Director of Sales and Marketing, Energizer Global Miniature Batteries, for his insight into the development of EZ Change. My thanks also to Joe Sipher, Director of Marketing, Handspring, Inc., for his insight into the development of the Treo mobile phone, web/e-mail device, and organizer.

I would like to thank Jim Gonedes, Vice President of Skin Care North America, Alberto Culver Company, for his insight into how a company can benefit from the development of a platform for growth.

I would also like to acknowledge a number of people who contributed in many different ways to the completion of this book. First I would like to thank my wife, Tiffany Chang, for the inspiration that provided the motivation for me to begin and complete this book. I would like to thank Ed Knappman of New England Publishing for making the book possible by guiding me through the publishing process and by helping me with his unusual sense of what works on paper and what doesn't. My thanks to Ellen Kadin, Senior Acquisitions Editor, AMACOM Books, for her guidance in the structure of this book. I would like to thank Bryan Mattimore for his friendship and for providing me with an excellent writing example in his book *99% Inspiration*. Similarly, I would like to thank Professor Karen Maru from the University of Connecticut for providing me with her broad experience as an author of numerous books on marketing. For a variety of different forms of legal advice, I would like to thank Joseph File, Harriet Wolfe, and Ellen Levine. Thanks to my friends Gilbert LeVasseur, Jr., Edwin V. Clarke, Jr., and Birgit Berry for their advice on a number of business building matters that are reflected in this book. Finally, I would like to thank Dean Robert Dockson from the Marshall School of Business at the University of Southern California and my late friends Elgin Davis and Paul Crane for getting me started in my career.

Introduction

This book will help you write an effective marketing plan by showing you what others have done to make their marketing plans succeed. Whether you're writing a marketing plan for a brand-new business, launching a new product, or branching out into a new product line or market you can learn a great deal from the experience of others.

This book will review some of the key characteristics that differentiate successful marketing ventures from unsuccessful ones. Throughout the book, you will learn the main reasons that marketing ventures, and new products, have succeeded.

Different Types of Marketing Plans

Many of the marketing plans in this book are for something that is being marketed for the first time. Some of them are for totally new products that represent major technological breakthroughs. In other cases, the marketing plan was created for an extension of an existing brand. These line extensions are included because in many cases they were launched in much the same way as a totally new product. Typically, they represented new offerings to the

1

consumer and required their own sales and marketing thrusts if they were to be launched effectively.

This book includes examples of marketing plans from many different types of businesses. In reality, most business ventures have many things in common, whether the venture is a new health food product started by one person or a new electronic product launched by a major corporation. For example, any marketing plan must include a determination of whether or not potential customers will become buyers. A review of the overall market for the venture must be conducted. Legal and financial considerations must always be taken into account. And every marketing plan must also include an internal look at your resources to make sure that you either have or can get what will be required to pull off the mission.

The Best Examples of Marketing Plans Often Relate to New Products

Many of the marketing plan examples included in this book are for highly successful new products. These marketing plans are excellent examples for you to follow, whether your objective is to launch a new product or to engage in some other form of marketing endeavor. Many of the marketing plans included in this book were huge undertakings because the potential reward justified the effort. The complexity of your marketing plan should depend on the scope of your marketing venture.

New product marketing plans are more sophisticated because the profits that can be realized from the launching of a successful new product can be extraordinary. (Depending on the capital requirement, the return on the initial investment required for a new product can be many times greater than the return on almost any other investment. This return can outpace the returns generally realized by acquisitions or even investments in a company's normal operations.)

The Unique Characteristics of Successful Marketing Plans

You can improve your chances of success by understanding the unique characteristics that are common to many successful marketing plans. Your marketing plan may be quite different from other marketing plans that have been launched in the past, but there are many things it will have in common with those other marketing plans. These similarities can give you a significant strategic advantage. If you understand why other marketing plans have succeeded, you may be able to incorporate some of the elements of these successful plans into your own endeavor.

Of course, launching a new product or marketing venture can be risky if it is undertaken without good information. It is the intent of Part 1 of this book to act as your guide in the development of your marketing plan. Many successful marketing plans have been studied for this part of the book, and records have been kept on why these marketing ventures have succeeded. You will see specific examples of things that have been done right, as well as some things that have been done wrong and then corrected.

Having the Correct Positioning

One common denominator of many of the successful new marketing ventures included in this book is that they have positioned the product in a way that was meaningful to their target market. In many cases this positioning has very positively differentiated the product from its competition, giving the product a unique and appealing personality. The positioning of these successful products was clear to potential customers. The developers of these successful marketing plans made sure that there were no major negatives that would prevent people from wanting to buy the product.

Marketing plans often succeed because they demonstrate that the product or service is able to eliminate a significant consumer negative. You may be involved in a product category where existing products seem to meet virtually every consumer requirement, yet careful observation of consumer behavior may reveal an important negative that could enable you to create a critical point of difference for your product. In Chapter 1 you will learn how Energizer has been able to become the fastest-growing brand in the hearing aid battery market by identifying and eliminating a hidden but significant consumer negative.

Meeting Consumer Needs and Desires

Many of the marketing plans that will be discussed in this book succeeded because their developers addressed the needs and/or desires of their potential customers head on. In some cases they helped the customer solve a problem; in other cases they provided consumers with something they felt they definitely needed. Typically, potential buyers clearly recognized the benefits of these successful new products. The products were often the best alternative available at the time they were launched.

Successful marketing plans are often based on the solution of consumer problems. In Chapter 2 you will see the great example of Jumbo-Koter™, a new product that was successful because it solved an irritating consumer problem. In evaluating the marketing plans for your product or service, it is helpful to learn whether your offering solves perceived problems for potential customers. If it does, this is a good indication that they might become buyers. If it is the *only* solution to a major problem, the chances of their buying your product or service is that much better.

With the exception of gifts, people rarely, if ever, buy anything without feeling that the product or service has some specific benefit that is important to them. Many business ventures succeed because they provide meaningful benefits that their customers clearly recognized. In Chapter 3 you will see how Philips Lighting identified the benefits that their customers wanted from their product category, and then wrapped an entire marketing program around those benefits. The results were quite dramatic.

Creating a Comfortable Buying Experience

One factor that many successful marketing plans have in common is that they provide a comfortable and convenient buying experience for their customers. In many of these plans, this was applied to each factor in all channels of distribution, including wholesalers, distributors, retailers, and the final consumer. Often these successful products have been pleasant to purchase because a great deal of attention was placed on the appearance of the product. They simply looked good. The pricing of these successful ventures typically communicated the appropriate image, and all the players on the venture team had the right attitude.

Convenience is more important today than ever because consumers have so many alternatives. If a new product or service is difficult or time-consuming to use, then it is frequently rejected. People want a new product to be easy to buy, and easy to return if something goes wrong. In Chapter 4 you will learn how the Hanes Corporation completed a revolutionary marketing plan to market women's hosiery products in supermarkets and drugstores. This new brand of hosiery, L'eggs, became so successful that it has lasted over 30 years and today is the largest selling brand of pantyhose in the world. This success proved the critical importance of consumer and retailer convenience.

Ensuring Usefulness

As the perceived usefulness of a product or service increases, so does the probability of its success. For example, ideally consumers should have clearly identifiable uses for the product or service. Then the actual effectiveness of the product or service can be a critical factor in its success. Highly successful ventures often saved money or other resources for the users—or simplified some aspect of their lives. Most people want things that are easy to deal with.

Potential customers are generally interested in how effectively a new product or service does its job. If they are convinced that the product will work, they will often buy it. In Chapter 5 you will see how a new product, launched under the brand name Zicam, was successful because its effectiveness lead to repeat purchases. Zicam customers believed that the product really worked and therefore kept buying it over and over again. Many of those customers were so convinced that Zicam worked that they not only used it themselves but told others about it. It is worth asking people why they believe your new concept will do the job it is intended for, and then carefully listening to find out whether they really feel it will be effective.

Timing Is Everything

We have all heard the expression "timing is everything." This can be especially relevant when launching a new product or service. It is not hard to see how timing a new business venture to coincide with trends can lead to success. It is important to determine how your marketing plans fit into the current priorities of your existing and potential customers. Of course, the ultimate timing advantage occurs when a new product or service is preemptive, and is way ahead of the competition.

New products or services that are preemptive are likely to have a greater chance of success. Many new products have jumped years ahead of their competition with ideas that were first in their category and difficult to copy. One such product is the Treo™ from Handspring, Inc., which is discussed in Chapter 6. This was one of the first devices to integrate a mobile phone, a Palm OS organizer, and wireless data applications in one compact, full-color communicator. Use this as an example for your creative thinking. If you can develop a new product or service that is seen by consumers as "the only alternative," you will significantly increase the odds of your success.

This section of the introduction has indicated some of the reasons for the success of marketing plans. The next section deals with the writing of those plans.

Writing Your Marketing Plan

Now that we have discussed the unique characteristics of successful marketing plans, the next big issue is where you should begin in developing your marketing plan.

Your first step should be a thorough review of the market for your products or services, so that you know as many details as possible of the market in which your plan will be operating. Next, you must develop a detailed understanding of the consumers who will be buying your products and services. Then, develop a similar understanding of the retail environment in which the marketing plan will unfold. With an understanding of these fundamentals, you can develop your planning assumptions, objectives, specific elements, and financial projections for the marketing plan.

Part 2 of this book includes a series of detailed successful marketing plans that can serve as examples of what your marketing plan should look like and what it should include. Part 2 also provides you with a number of key information sources for developing a market review and an understanding of consumer and trade attitudes. These sources will help you in gathering the information required to write your marketing plan. The following specific methods of obtaining information are included.

Secondary Research to Develop Market Reviews

If you are faced with the task of writing a marketing plan from scratch, one of the best ways to start is by reviewing the available data. As outlined in

Chapter 7, this includes data written up in secondary sources such as magazines, trade publications, and government publications. This information will generally provide you with a framework of the market and how it breaks down into major market segments. You may want to round out this information with data-gathering field trips such as conducting store checks for the purpose of writing down prices, shelf facings, and other observations about your product category.

Telephone Surveys to Complete Market Reviews

It is not unusual to find that the information on your market that is available from secondary sources alone is insufficient. A good way to develop new information on your market is through a telephone survey. The marketing plan for the Executive Conference Phone in Chapter 8 is a good example of a market review that was done by combining data from secondary sources with a telephone survey. This plan will show you how a market review based on primary and secondary research can be structured.

Market Reviews Completed with Online Surveys

Chapter 9 outlines how the Internet can also be used to gather both primary and secondary marketing information. (Given the global nature of the Internet, this can sometimes be more effective than other methods of gathering information.) One example of this is online surveys. An online survey is similar to a telephone survey, except that rather than answering questions on the telephone, the respondent simply completes a questionnaire on the computer screen.

Focus Groups as the Key to Understanding the Consumer

Focus groups can be very effective in identifying customer practices and attitudes. Chapter 10 explains how focus groups can be used to develop an understanding of consumer usage and attitudes. It also provides some examples of how focus groups can best be done in order to provide a clear understanding of what the consumer is really thinking, as well as some specialized techniques for formulating questions for focus group discussions.

Online Consumer Qualitative Research

Chapter 11 gives you an interesting alternative for conducting qualitative research. When research respondents are sparse or difficult to find because they are scattered in many different locations, Internet qualitative research can be very useful. When the marketing plan for Eagle central air conditioners presented in Chapter 11 was developed, there were very few central air conditioning consumers in Taiwan, and they were located all over the island. Clearly the most efficient research method in this case was over the Internet, as conducting focus groups would have been very difficult. This chapter demonstrates the value of obtaining Internet addresses by region.

Ethnographic Research for Consumer Understanding

In Chapter 12, ethnographic research was used to develop a summary of consumer usage and attitudes in the baby shoe category. The objective was to understand in detail the habits and practices of mothers of infants as related to the purchase and use of baby shoes. The procedure included in-home discussions with respondents about their habits and practices, with videotaped observations of where they kept baby shoes and how they were used. This approach can be very effective for hooking into subtle emotional dimensions that are almost impossible to uncover by simply asking questions.

Trade Research in Marketing Planning

Knowing what the trade is thinking can be critical to the success of your marketing plan. Chapter 13 shows how Zion Housewares Corporation went to great lengths to identify trade practices and attitudes. The process included a series of in-depth face-to-face interviews with retailers. Because these people were quite busy, these interviews took place in the retailer's office. You will see in Chapter 13 that the company conducted these trade interviews through a process outside of the normal sales operations. The interviews were conducted by consultants and marketing managers. This separate interviewing process was used to give importance to the meetings, and to eliminate any political factors related to the ongoing operations.

What to Include in Your Marketing Plan

The completion of the marketing plan is the culmination of all of the research, the conceptualization and testing of ideas, the making of assumptions, the development of objectives, and the preparation of detailed financial plans. It is typically the document that is presented to upper management for final approval of a new marketing venture, or used as the annual plans for the marketing department.

As indicated in Chapter 14, a marketing plan should document the background that led up to the writing of the marketing plan in the first place, all of the research that was done, the key conclusions and objectives based on that research, a description of all the action programs to be implemented in order to achieve the plan's objectives, and financial projections based on those programs. Contingency plans may also be included indicating what the company should do if things do not go exactly as planned. Marketing plans are typically divided into several sections, such as those listed here.

Introduction

The introductory section should clearly state the overall purpose of the marketing plan. It may serve as a table of contents, as illustrated in most of the marketing plans in this book. It may also serve as an executive summary, enabling the reader (including higher management) to quickly grasp the major thrust of the document. As shown in many of the marketing plans in this book, this section may also include a brief description of the steps taken to develop the marketing plan.

Background

The background section of the marketing plan should review the background of the project or past marketing efforts. It should then outline any previous efforts that led to the development of the marketing plan. In some cases this may include a detailed description of the history of the brand or product line. (This may be necessary if there is a complex history that the reader of the plan must know in order to understand the relevance of the new actions planned.) In other cases it may be sufficient to briefly state what led up to the development of the current marketing plan.

Market Review

This section of the marketing plan should present all of the available data relevant to the marketing of the products or services to be included in the plan. The market review should summarize the growth and nature of the market for the related product category. If the company is currently participating in that category, the market review should identify the company's past and projected participation in that market. It should include details such as the size of the market, the market's history and trends, and competitive activity. It may also include things like the number of appropriate retail outlets by trade class and geographic region, product movement through the various retail channels, shares of market by manufacturer, price points by manufacturer and trade class, and industry advertising expenditures by manufacturer and medium.

Consumer Usage and Attitudes

This section of the marketing plan should outline present consumer practices, desires, and expectations concerning your product category in total and, if appropriate, the specific elements of your proposed marketing plan.

Trade Practices and Attitudes

This section of your marketing plan should identify retailer practices related to your product categories, as well as their attitudes toward the distribution aspects of your marketing plan. This is especially important if your plan is designed to obtain new distribution or to achieve improved performance in existing retail outlets.

Planning Assumptions

In this section of the marketing plan, you should present your key conclusions based upon the facts presented in the Background, Market Review, Consumer Usage and Attitudes, and Trade Practices and Attitudes sections of the plan. You should then state the assumptions you used in the development of your specific plans and strategies.

Key Strategic Marketing Objectives

This section should state specifically what you are trying to accomplish with the plan.

Marketing Plan Elements

The following sections of your marketing plan should lay out the specifics of the various actions to be taken to accomplish the Key Strategic Marketing Objectives. The following are examples of the types of marketing plan elements that should be included.

BRAND NAME. This section should state the brand name or names that will be used in the marketing effort described in the marketing plan. If this is a new brand name, such as for a new product, the rationale for using this name should be discussed.

PRODUCT LINE. This section should describe the entire product line included in the marketing plan. If this product line has unique qualities, these qualities should be discussed.

PRODUCT WARRANTIES. Sometimes product warranties can be an important part of a marketing plan. If your product includes warranties, these should be described in this section of your marketing plan.

PACKAGING. Describe the packaging strategy for the products involved in your marketing plan, along with a description of the packaging, in this section. You may also want to include pictures of the artwork.

PRICING STRATEGY. In this section, state the pricing strategy, list the prices of all the products included in the marketing plan, and state the justification for the pricing strategy, if this is appropriate.

SALES AND DISTRIBUTION METHODS. Describe the sales and distribution methods to be used for the products in your marketing plan in this section. In some cases this will simply require a statement that the products will be sold through the normal company sales and distribution organization. In other cases the strategy might be quite different. In those cases the rationale for the strategy should be discussed.

ADVERTISING COPY STRATEGY. If the products in the marketing plan are to be advertised, this section should present the copy strategy.

ADVERTISING MEDIA STRATEGY. If the products are to be advertised, this section should state the advertising media strategy.

SALES PROMOTION. In this section, describe all sales promotion plans, including all consumer discounts, rebates, and trial devices such as coupons. Show the financial implications of these promotions either in this section or in the Financial Projections section. (Several of the marketing plans in this book first discuss the sales promotion plans in this section, then include them in the profit-and-loss statements and leave the detailed calculations for the appendices.)

PUBLICITY. If publicity is to be used in your marketing plan, the publicity strategy and plans should be included in this section.

IN-STORE MERCHANDISING. In this section, outline what will be done to attract consumer attention in the retail store, if this is appropriate for your marketing plan.

INTERNAL STAFFING REQUIREMENTS. If special staffing requirements are necessary for implementing your marketing plan, state these in this section.

TEST MARKETING. If test marketing is planned for the marketing venture, describe it in this section of the marketing plan.

TIMETABLE. Your marketing plan should also include a detailed timetable for the venture.

Financial Projections

This is a key section of your marketing plan. In many cases a "go/no-go" decision on moving forward with your plan will largely depend on the calculations you include here. Because of this, the Financial Projections section of your marketing plan should include detailed calculations on the costs, volume, and pay-out of the plan. It should also include pro forma profit-and-loss statements. In sum, the purpose of this section is to demonstrate the financial viability of the marketing plan.

Contingency Plans

This section should provide plans for retaliating against possible competitive actions. These include competitive product improvements, lower prices from competitors, increased advertising or sales promotion by competitors, and technical changes to the category.

Appendices

Include any background and supporting data for various sections of the marketing plan—including detailed market review data, study questionnaires, a detailed advertising media plan, and the financial assumptions and calculations used in the financial projections—in appendices.

PART 1

MARKETING PLAN SUCCESS STORIES

The marketing plans discussed in Part 1 are real marketing plans from actual companies. Each chapter begins with a narrative that describes the story behind the marketing plan. The purpose of this background is to show you why these marketing plans were conceived, and how the strategies were developed. These stories take you behind the scenes to help you in your own strategic thinking. Each narrative is then followed by a summary of the actual marketing plan. The information in these Part 1 chapters is included with permission from the respective companies.

CHAPTER 1

Successful Marketing Plans Eliminate the Negatives

Example: Energizer® EZ Change™ Hearing Aid Batteries

Great marketing plans often succeed because the product or service is able to eliminate a significant consumer negative. These negatives are not always obvious. Sometimes consumers may not even be aware of negatives that they are actually experiencing every day. Existing products in the product category you are involved in may seem to meet virtually every consumer requirement, yet careful observation of consumer behavior may reveal an important negative that could enable you to create a critical point of difference for your product. In developing your marketing plan, you should search for potential negatives, as these could very well be the keys to success.

By identifying and eliminating a hidden but significant consumer negative, Energizer has been able to become the fastest-growing brand in the hearing aid battery market. In March 1999, Energizer was in last place in this market and was going nowhere. Through some clever research, the company discovered a significant negative that users of hearing aid batteries were unaware of, but that was present every time they changed their hearing aid batteries. This observation resulted in the development of EZ Change, a new product that virtually eliminated this negative. This new product, coupled with a brilliant marketing plan, resulted in an explosion of sales that is rapidly moving Energizer to the number one position in the hearing aid battery category. Sales of Energizer's hearing aid batteries have increased 89 percent since the launch of EZ Change.

A Time for Change

The management of Eveready Battery Company has learned to deal successfully with change. For many years it was a division of Union Carbide. It was acquired by Ralston Purina in the 1980s, and then, approximately three years ago, it was spun off as a separate business under the name Energizer. Throughout all of these changes, the company has held a leadership role in the battery industry. Hearing aid batteries are manufactured and marketed by the Miniature Group, a strategic business unit within Energizer. This group produces miniature batteries for both hearing aids and watch electronics.

Although Energizer is used to a leadership role, in 1999 it had a weak position in the hearing aid battery category. The management of the Miniature Group felt very vulnerable and did not like the way things were going. It had tried several traditional marketing techniques to improve the company's position, but nothing seemed to work. It had tried advertising on the radio and had tried bonus packs, such as including a free battery caddy for hearing aid batteries. The company's market share did not increase. It became obvious that Energizer really needed to do something different to strengthen its position in the marketplace.

The decision was made to create a new product that would represent a true breakthrough in the hearing aid battery marketplace—something that would clearly set Energizer apart from all the other manufacturers. A venture team was assembled that included key people within the company, along with a group of outside suppliers who were experts in various appropriate fields. A budget was allocated for this project, and a development timetable was agreed upon.

Creativity Based on Solid Consumer Research

The project was given the name "Gamebreaker." This was indicative of the team's mission, which was to break all of the rules of the current game and come up with something truly revolutionary. The key internal players included the director of marketing, the head of market research, and experts from the plant that would have to implement the production side of the venture. External players included the advertising agency, consultants, and a design group.

An initial step was to learn something about the behavior of the core consumer group. The distribution of hearing aid battery consumers is heavily skewed toward the aging population. Approximately 70 percent of these consumers are seventy-five years of age or older. A form of observational research was conducted in assisted living centers. Hearing aid users were brought into a room in each assisted living center for this research. A moderator asked questions and guided their activities while key members of the team observed.

Respondents were asked numerous questions about their hearing aid batteries. They were asked what they liked and disliked about these batteries. They were asked specifically how they went about changing the batteries. They were asked what they felt was important to them in hearing aid batteries. They were then asked to actually change their hearing aid batteries while the team watched. As this process unfolded, the team began to develop ideas and new product concepts.

A series of store checks were conducted to help stimulate creative ideas. As members of the venture team visited different types of retail stores, they looked at products from a broad variety of different product categories, paying particular attention to all of the types of packaging and in-store merchandising that were used. They looked at breath fresheners, health and beauty aids, and food and nonfood products. If a unique package provided a solution, or just stood out, the product was purchased and brought back for further analysis. The idea was to maintain a creative environment and to think outside of the box.

The results of all this research were brought into a series of brainstorming sessions for the purpose of coming up with ideas covering the whole area of hearing aid batteries and packaging. The idea was to find solutions to any negatives that could be identified, and to leverage existing ideas from other categories. These brainstorming sessions involved the company's internal people, an audiologist, and some key people from outside the company with different backgrounds and skills.

At this point a series of focus groups were held with hearing aid users to learn more about their behavior, to identify the details of any problems they might be having, and to test some of the key concepts developed thus far. These groups were held in several cities, such as Tampa and Phoenix, that had a sizable elderly population. Concepts were refined as the researchers went from one group to another. A total of twenty different hearing aid concepts were tested with consumers during these focus groups.

It Is Not a Battery; It Is a Solution

A key finding from the observational and focus group research was that hearing aid batteries were difficult for the user to change, although this was an unarticulated problem. Users of hearing aids dealt with this problem all the time, so when they were asked if they had a problem changing their hearing aid batteries, they typically said no. It was a different story, however, when they were asked to describe or demonstrate the process.

Respondents frequently made comments like, "I always do it at the kitchen table, and I lay out a towel because I know I am going to drop the battery." They told stories about how many batteries they had lost in their pocket or purse. They described how they dropped hearing aid batteries because the oils on their hands made them slippery. There were several respondents who told how the battery slipped out of their hands, then added that once it was in the carpet, it was very difficult to find. Observations of people changing hearing aid batteries confirmed this difficulty.

For many of these elderly consumers, the difficulty of changing this very small battery was compounded by poor dexterity and poor eyesight. Some who had diabetes had lost the feeling in the tips of their fingers, which further complicated the problem. These people used the spin pack because they had no choice. It was obvious, however, that there was a need for a packaging solution that would assist the user in getting the battery from the package into the hearing aid.

The winning concept presented to respondents in focus groups was a package for a hearing aid battery that would make it very easy for them to change the battery. The solution that changed everything and separated Energizer from the competition was a revolutionary new dispenser that would help the user achieve precise placement of the battery every time without even touching the battery. What the research revealed was that it was not a different battery that was needed, it was a solution to a hidden but significant consumer negative.

A New Product Is Born

At this point, a design firm was retained to turn the winning new hearing aid battery concept into a reality. The difference between this new product and other traditional hearing aid batteries was to be in the application system. The user would simply use the applicator to put the battery into the hearing aid. The applicator would be magnetized so that there would be no risk of the battery's dropping on the ground.

The actual design turned out to be a circular delivery system that had the batteries sealed. This was similar to the familiar traditional hearing aid packaging, although it was much better because it actually installed the batteries for the user. The user would simply rotate the device to a fresh battery, then push it off of a tabbing material onto a magnet. The magnet then held it so that the user could put it right into the hearing aid. It was a very simple process that Energizer was able to patent.

One of the problems with hearing aid batteries is that they are activated by the oxygen in the air through a small pinhole. If you handle these batteries, the oil on your hand can get into the pinhole and affect the performance of the battery. The new design kept the batteries sealed until the user was ready to use one, and would peel the tab off and insert the battery without the user ever touching the battery.

This new design also had significant advantages for audiologists. Traditionally these professionals had to do a dexterity test on users to see what size battery they could handle. An audiologist might not be able to prescribe the best hearing aid for an individual situation or the smallest hearing aid if the user did not have the dexterity to handle the small battery. This prevented some people from using almost invisible hearing aids. The new product design addressed that situation and gave audiologists the latitude to recommend any hearing aid.

"EZ Change" Became the Ideal Name

Coming up with an appropriate name for the new hearing aid battery was one of the most difficult parts of the project. The venture team came up with hundreds of names. Some of these names came from internal marketing people and other people within Energizer. Other names came from the advertising agency. The list of potential names was culled down to two favorite alternatives: "EZ Load" and "EZ Change." Focus groups helped management select the better name.

During one of the focus groups, a respondent determined that the magnet on the dispenser could help the user remove the existing battery as well as load the new battery. The respondent then made the comment that this new dispenser does more than just make it easy to load the new battery. It makes it easy to both load and unload the battery, or to change the battery. This made it obvious to the venture team that it was really making it easy for the user to do the entire changeover, so the team settled on the name EZ Change.

A Very Simple Incremental Product Line

A total of only four products were included in the EZ Change product line. In the hearing aid battery market, there are four battery sizes that account for 100 percent of the sales. EZ Change included one product, or stock-keeping unit (SKU), for each of these sizes. For each of the three smaller hearing aid batteries, Energizer provided an eight-pack, and then it provided a six-pack for the largest size.

It was decided that the old Energizer hearing aid battery product line would not be discontinued. Prior to EZ Change, Energizer had had a line of hearing aid batteries in the traditional spin-pack packaging. There were a total of eleven different items (SKUs), including four-packs, eight-packs, and twelve-packs. The market research indicated that EZ Change would appeal to over 50 percent of the marketplace, but it would not appeal to everybody. Because of this, there was still going to be a need for hearing aid batteries in traditional spin packs.

Larger Packaging That Opens with Bigger Type and Pictures

One of the important findings of the consumer market research was that consumers knew very little about the hearing aid batteries they were using on a regular basis. They also could not read the material on the package because the card size was so small. All the information on the traditional cards was in very small print that was impossible for many of these elderly users to read.

The decision was made to go with a much larger card, two and a half times the size of the traditional packaging. This larger card size enabled the designers to use larger fonts to communicate with this elderly crowd, and it enabled them to use a lot of pictures. The pictures were very effective in explaining how the device works. The card included a picture of the device that was about to be inserted into the hearing aid. To enable even more communication, the new package opened up to provide room for printing on four different surfaces.

Production in the United States of America

All Energizer hearing aid batteries have traditionally been made in Bennington, Vermont, and the company is proud to continue this tradition with EZ Change. Although a few parts for the dispenser are made by an Energizer plant in China, the company has kept hearing aid battery production in the United States. The idea is to maintain jobs for loyal employees. Some of the Energizer employees' families have been with the company for generations. Energizer feels that as long as it can keep bringing in innovations and remain competitive, it is going to keep production in Vermont.

A Premium-Priced Product

The pricing sensitivity studies conducted as part of the EZ Change market research clearly indicated that this new product had to be priced within a narrow range if it was to be successful. Because hearing aid batteries are bought continuously, consumers—especially the current user base of elderly consumers—are sensitive to price. When the baby boomers enter the market in a few years, the market may become a little less price-sensitive because these people are more interested in convenience and premium brand names.

Because of its unique advantages and higher cost to produce, it was decided to sell EZ Change at a retail price that represented a premium to other brands. At the time of this writing, the consumer was paying about $7.99 for a traditional spin pack of eight units. The initial price structure resulted in a retail price of approximately $8.99 for an eight-pack of EZ Change.

In the focus groups, many respondents said that they would pay an extra dollar for a product with all of the advantages of EZ Change. Naturally, the smaller the price gap between EZ Change and traditional hearing aid batteries, the more people would buy it. The consumers in the focus groups understood that it would cost more to make EZ Change. They could see that there was a lot of difference in the components, and therefore the cost to manufacture EZ Change, compared with a traditional spin pack of hearing aid batteries.

A Coordinated Sales Effort

For the developers of EZ Change, one of the advantages of being part of a large battery company was that the product could be sold through the regular Energizer retail distribution system. The new product would be introduced to the larger retailers by the Energizer sales force, and in some cases could receive attention at retail by the Energizer in-store detailing force. Specialty distributors would be used to sell the product to audiologists. EZ Change representatives would also attend trade shows aimed at audiologists in order to communicate directly with them about the benefits of EZ Change.

The Advertising Message: "Precise Placement Every Time"

A number of alternatives were evaluated as potential advertising slogans for EZ Change. The research showed that seniors don't want to hear about negatives like dropping batteries or fumbling. They resist this because they are sensitive about the insinuation that they have a problem. "Precise placement every time" tested out to be the best message for clear communication. This statement clearly tells the consumer about the benefits of the new product without getting into any sensitive areas. This slogan was to be used in all advertisements and on the packaging.

A secondary point to be made in the advertising was that EZ Change batteries work in all styles of hearing aids. That was a very difficult point to communicate because there are a lot of different hearing aid styles and designs, and it is very difficult to demonstrate all of them in a thirty-second television commercial. The advertising agency developed five different ways to communicate the EZ Change message in storyboards. The winning commercial ended up demonstrating the use of the product in three different hearing aid styles at the same time. The hope was that the consumer would see something that matched the product that he or she used. The final point in the advertising was to reinforce the Energizer name because the research showed that branding is important.

Television Would Be the Primary Advertising Medium

A key objective of the media plan was to visually show the product and give the hearing aid user the motivation to buy this new solution. This is a very visual product, and it was decided to use videos to show its benefits. Television was selected as the primary advertising medium for EZ Change. The hearing aid category had never been advertised on a broad-scale basis on television before, so EZ Change would be implementing a totally new way to communicate with users of hearing aid batteries. The goal was to reach 90 percent of all hearing aid users with the TV advertising once, and to reach 65 percent of the target audience three times.

Senior citizens are fairly easy to reach through television because they frequently watch network news and game shows. They also watch programs like those on the History Channel. The media plan targeted these shows, which was less costly than trying to cover many different types of television programming. The plan was for EZ Change to become a consistent advertiser on these types of television programs. The television advertising would be shown more on national than on local programs.

Television would be supplemented with print media. The print media would include magazines such as *Reader's Digest* and the AARP's *Modern Ma-*

turity. Parade and Sunday supplements would also be used. Newspaper advertisements would be included through retailer promotions. The plan assumed that EZ Change would have to keep advertising on television and in print because it would take a long time to develop the brand and change the behavior of these aging consumers. Hearing aid users traditionally were not very brand-conscious and often were not even very aware of what brand they actually bought.

Off-Shelf Displays Would Highlight EZ Change

It was decided that corrugated off-shelf displays would be used to facilitate rapid distribution of EZ Change during the initial launch of the product. There would be several versions of these displays, including a counter display and a wing rack. These displays would also help the company communicate with consumers by highlighting the new hearing aid battery solution at the point of purchase. Each preloaded display would provide brochures to help educate the consumer on how this innovate new product works. In many cases a one-dollar in-store coupon would be included during the initial product launch. It was envisioned that many retailers would use these displays until they were able to put EZ Change into their normal plan-o-gram.

Many of the larger retailers have a full battery section, and they locate hearing aid batteries in these sections as well as in the pharmacy. They often have a separate display in the pharmacy department just for hearing aid batteries. Counter displays of hearing aid batteries in the pharmacy department are often permanent, and it was felt that the EZ Change counter displays would become permanent in some of these stores. Hearing aid batteries tend to get lost in an in-line section; therefore, the ideal situation would be a permanent EZ Change counter display.

Total Guaranteed Customer Support

The EZ Change marketing plan provided a clear link from the manufacturer to the consumer to ensure complete customer satisfaction. There was to be an 800 number on the package that would link to a customer hot line where EZ Change representatives would help customers with any problems that they might be having with the product. There would also be a web address printed on the package along with the statement, "To learn more about the dispenser and to see it in action, visit our web site at www.energizer-ezchange.com." The web site would include a video on how EZ Change works.

EZ Change would also guarantee complete satisfaction to the consumer. There would be a simple guarantee printed on the back of each package: "Energizer guarantees all our hearing aid batteries and dispensers to be free from all defects in materials and workmanship. If you are not completely satisfied, call this toll-free number for a replacement battery or dispenser." It was recognized that some consumers might bring EZ Change back to the retailer. Because of this, arrangements for handling this situation were made in advance with the retailers. Energizer would always stand behind its products.

Launching in a Diversified Market

To visualize the opportunity for a new breakthrough hearing aid product, it is necessary to understand this consumer segment. Hearing aid batteries are sold to consumers through three different types of retail distribution channels. One is the professional channel, where consumers buy their hearing aid batteries from audiologists. The second is through major retail stores, where sales are measured by A. C. Nielsen & Co. with scan data. These include most supermarkets, drugstores, and mass merchants. The third is through direct mail or through retailers that don't report their sales to Nielsen, such as warehouse clubs.

There are approximately 12,500 audiologists in the United States, and many older consumers prefer to buy their hearing aid batteries from these professionals. Many of these people had purchased their hearing aids from these audiologists, and they simply feel comfortable going back to them for their batteries. It is difficult to estimate the exact size of this segment of the market because these professionals do not report their sales data to an organization such as A. C. Nielsen.

The 70,000 retail stores measured by Nielsen make up the largest segment of the total hearing aid battery category. This is also the segment that is the best understood because frequent scan data measurements provide very accurate sales information. It is also the fastest-growing segment because as younger consumers enter the market, they prefer to buy from these stores because of their convenience. Consumers who buy from these stores do not believe that there is any difference between the hearing aid batteries bought in these stores and those bought from audiologists.

Most drugstores carry hearing aid batteries, as do the pharmacy departments of most supermarkets and mass merchants such as Kmart and Wal-Mart. Drugstores make up the largest portion of the retail segment. These stores generally have a battery section that includes a selection of different brands of hearing aid batteries. Most stores carry the Energizer and Duracell brands along with private-label batteries. Some also carry the Ray-O-Vac brand, although this brand is more frequently sold through audiologists.

A small but significant segment of the market is the direct mail and Internet business. Seniors do quite a bit of "surfing" over the Internet. They are especially interested in doing medical research over the Internet. Although they tend to look for information rather than buy products over the Internet, the amount of purchases through this channel is significant and is growing. Seniors also frequently buy hearing aid batteries through magazines such as AARP's *Modern Maturity*. Sales information for this channel is not readily available.

EZ Change Was Thoroughly Tested Before It Was Launched

One of the tests done to make sure that EZ Change was really practical from a user standpoint was a series of in-home usage trials. Energizer felt that it was important to see how consumers reacted to the new product when they were really using it in their homes. The members of a panel of consumers were given an EZ Change package containing eight new hearing aid batteries. They were told to read the directions and change the batteries in their hearing aids every day, even though the batteries obviously lasted longer than one day. Then they were asked to fill out a diary every day describing their experience. The results of these tests were very positive.

The final test before the launch of EZ Change was a quantitative test through BASES®. This is a procedure in which the complete marketing plan is subjected to a process that is designed to determine the success of the new product. The input for this model includes a number of factors such as consumers' intent to purchase based on market research, pricing of the new and existing products, distribution estimates, and each element of the marketing plan, including the amount of advertising planned. It also includes detailed information on the market. Based on all of this input, the BASES model predicts the impact that the new product will have on the category.

EZ Change Was Launched Based on Several Positive Assumptions

Energizer management assumed that EZ Change would result in a significant increase in the company's sales of hearing aid batteries. The results of the BASES model indicated that, with the advertising planned for the product, EZ Change would double Energizer's sales of hearing aid batteries.

Management assumed that customers would like this solution because they had clearly said so in the consumer research. This whole venture was based on feedback from consumers. All of the focus groups and observational research indicated that there was a real need for an improved hearing aid battery. When EZ Change was showed to consumers, most of them loved it. Many of them made comments such as, "Somebody is finally thinking about us."

Management believed that retailers would take on this new hearing aid battery, even though it used a bigger card size for the packaging. This was based on a belief that retailers realized that communication with consumers was important in this category, and that they generally wanted to be part of innovative new solutions to consumer problems. Management also felt that retailers would be interested because of the heavy television advertising planned for EZ Change.

A final major assumption was that the hearing aid battery category would not change during the initial period following the launch of EZ Change. This seemed like a reasonable assumption because this was not a category that had seen a lot of product innovations in the past. However, this assumption turned out to be incorrect. At the same time that Energizer launched EZ Change, its biggest competitor, Duracell, launched another solution: a longer tab for hearing aid batteries. Duracell called its product Easy Tab.

The Goal Was to Become Number One

Energizer had three primary objectives in launching EZ Change. First, it wanted to become the number one brand of hearing aid batteries. Prior to EZ Change, Energizer was number three in a three-way race, and it wanted to completely change that positioning. Second, it wanted to separate itself from the competition by providing a solution that would give the company a leadership place in the hearing aid battery category. Third, it wanted to strengthen the overall franchise of the entire Energizer brand. The hundred-year-old company had developed the first flashlight battery and had introduced numerous innovations in portable power. A major driver was to continue this tradition.

An Exciting Eighteen Months

The development of EZ Change began in March 2000. After completing the consumer research, developing the product, completing the marketing plan, and testing the overall venture, the company launched the product in September 2001. The emotions within the company shifted at various times during this period. In the beginning there was the excitement of a new venture. Then, about six months before the launch, people could not wait to get EZ Change into the marketplace. As the venture neared the launch date, the concern was about getting the retailers to execute their responsibilities by the time the advertising began. The company did not want to be advertising before EZ Change was on the shelves. It was an exciting time.

EZ Change Was an Unqualified Success

As predicted by BASES, Energizer has almost doubled its sales of hearing aid batteries in the Nielsen-measured marketplace since the launch of EZ Change. Through advertising, point-of-purchase impact, and repeat purchase, it has created a demand for EZ Change, so that consumers are now looking for it and buying it over and over again. Many retailers also strongly support the revolutionary new product, and those that support EZ Change are now seeing faster growth in their hearing aid battery sales than other retailers.

It also appears that Energizer's goal of becoming number one in the hearing aid battery category is being reached. Energizer's sales of hearing aid batteries have increased 89 percent since the launch of EZ Change, and the trend is still positive. Naturally Energizer's market share has also increased substantially, and the shares of both of Energizer's main competitors have declined. In the short reporting period prior to this writing, Energizer's share of the overall hearing aid battery market is just slightly above its competitors'.[1] It appears that this lead will widen over time, and that Energizer will take a solid number one position in the market.

Competitors' Reactions Have Been Ineffective

One of the initial responses of Energizers' competitors in the hearing aid battery market to the introduction of EZ Change was aggressive promotion and price cutting. These actions have not been effective. Consumers have demonstrated that they want the EZ Change solution no matter how much competitors promote the alternatives. The sales of EZ Change have continued to grow and its exposure at retail has continued to expand in spite of heavy promotional spending by competitors.

Another competitive action was the introduction of Easy Tab by Duracell. Energizer found out about this new competitive hearing aid battery in March 2001, Just six months before the time that EZ Change was launched. The consumer reaction to Easy Tab has not been strong enough to affect the sales of EZ Change. Energizer management feels that there are three reasons for this. First, the Easy Tab card size is very small, making it difficult for the consumer to read. Second, the EZ Change focus groups indicated that hearing aid users really do not like tabs, which are the basis of the new Duracell product. Finally, the Easy Tab batteries come in a rectangular package, which

[1] Source: A. C. Nielsen.

is different from the package that hearing aid battery users are accustomed to.

Lessons: Pay Attention to the Consumer and Think Outside the Box

One of the lessons to be learned from the success of EZ Change is to listen to your consumers and carefully observe their actions. Look for negatives that they may be experiencing in your category, as these might be the keys to identifying an innovation that could substantially improve your position in the market. As the EZ Change research showed, consumer needs and wants are not always obvious from simply asking questions. Hearing aid users typically said that they did not have a problem changing their batteries. Observing their behavior, however, showed otherwise. The identification of this unarticulated need resulted in a major marketing success.

Another important lesson from EZ Change is that you should allow yourself to think outside the box. A year before the launch of EZ Change, many industry experts would have argued that Energizer would fail if it were to try to introduce a hearing aid battery on a large card that would take up much more space than traditional cards in the crowded battery section. Energizer would also have been criticized for attempting to advertise a small specialty category like hearing aid batteries on television. The company's success shows that these critics would have been wrong. Good consumer communication proved to be one of the reasons for the success of EZ Change.[2]

---

[2] Energizer and EZ Change are trademarks of Eveready Battery Company, Inc., and are used with permission.

Summary Marketing Plan for:
Energizer EZ Change Hearing Aid Batteries
Eveready Battery Company, Inc.[3]
2000

MARKETING PLAN SUMMARY

1. **BACKGROUND.** In March 1999, Energizer was in last place in the hearing aid battery market and was going nowhere. Through some clever research, the company discovered a significant negative that users of hearing aid batteries were unaware of, but that was present every time they changed their hearing aid batteries. This observation resulted in the development of EZ Change, a new product that virtually eliminated this negative. This new product, coupled with a brilliant marketing plan, resulted in an explosion of sales that is rapidly moving Energizer to the number one position in the hearing aid battery category. Sales of Energizer's hearing aid batteries have increased 89 percent since the launch of EZ Change.

2. **MARKET REVIEW.** Hearing aid batteries are sold to consumers through three different types of retail distribution channels. One is the professional channel, where consumers buy their hearing aid batteries through audiologists. The second is through major retail stores, where sales are measured by A. C. Nielsen & Co. with scan data. These include most supermarkets, drugstores, and mass merchants. The third is through direct mail or through retailers that don't report their sales to Nielsen, such as warehouse clubs. There are approximately 12,500 audiologists in the United States. The 70,000 retail stores measured by Nielsen make up the largest segment of the total hearing aid battery category. A small but significant segment of the market is the direct mail and Internet business.

3. **CONSUMER USAGE AND ATTITUDES.** The distribution of hearing aid battery consumers is heavily skewed toward the aging population. Approximately 70 percent of these consumers are seventy-five years of age or older. A key finding from the observational and focus group research was that hearing aid batteries were difficult for the user to change, although this

---

[3] Energizer and EZ Change are registered trademarks of Eveready Battery Company, Inc and are used with permission.

was an unarticulated problem. Users of hearing aids dealt with this problem all the time, so when they were asked if they had a problem changing their hearing aid batteries, they typically said no. It was a different story, however, when they were asked to describe or demonstrate the process.

4. **PLANNING ASSUMPTIONS.** Energizer management assumed that the introduction of EZ Change would result in a significant increase in the company's sales of hearing aid batteries. The results of the BASES model indicated that, with the advertising planned for the product, EZ Change would double Energizer's sales of hearing aid batteries. Management also assumed that customers would like this solution because they had clearly said so in the consumer research. When EZ Change was showed to consumers, most of them loved the product. Management further believed that retailers would take on this new hearing aid battery. This was based on a belief that retailers generally wanted to be part of innovative new solutions to consumer problems. Management also felt that retailers would be interested because of the heavy television advertising planned for EZ Change. A final major assumption was that the hearing aid battery category would not change during the initial period following the launch of EZ Change.

5. **KEY STRATEGIC MARKETING OBJECTIVES.** Energizer had three primary objectives in launching EZ Change. First, it wanted to become the number one brand of hearing aid batteries. Prior to EZ Change, Energizer was number three in a three-way race, and it wanted to completely change that positioning. Second, it wanted to separate itself from the competition by providing a solution that would give the company a leadership place in the hearing aid battery category. Third, it wanted to strengthen the overall franchise of the entire Energizer brand. The hundred-year-old company had developed the first flashlight battery and had introduced numerous innovations in portable power. A major driver was to continue this tradition.

6. **MARKETING PLAN ELEMENTS**

   A. *Brand name.* The brand name selected for the new hearing aid batteries was EZ Change. During one of the focus groups, a respondent determined that the magnet on the dispenser could help the user remove the existing battery as well as load the new battery. The respondent then made the comment that this new dispenser does more than just make it easy to load the new battery. It makes it easy to load and unload the battery, or to change the battery. This made it obvious to the venture team that it was really making it easy for the user to do the entire changeover, so the team settled on the name EZ Change.

B. *Product line.* The product itself was based on a revolutionary new dispenser that would help the user achieve precise placement of the battery every time without even touching the battery. A total of only four products were included in the EZ Change product line. In the hearing aid battery market, there are four battery sizes that account for 100 percent of the sales. EZ Change provided one product, or stock-keeping unit (SKU), for each of these sizes. For each of the three smaller hearing aid batteries, Energizer provided an eight-pack, and then it provided a six-pack for the largest size.

C. *Packaging.* The EZ Change packaging used a much larger card, two and a half times the size of traditional packaging. This larger card size enabled the designers to use larger fonts to communicate with the elderly market, and it enabled them to use a lot of pictures. The pictures were very effective in explaining how the device works. The card included a picture of the device that was about to be inserted into the hearing aid. To enable even more communication, the new package opened up to provide room for printing on four different surfaces.

D. *Pricing strategy.* Because of its unique advantages and higher cost to produce, it was decided to sell EZ Change at a retail price that represented a premium to other brands. At the time of this writing, the consumer was paying about $7.99 for a traditional spin pack of eight units. The initial price structure resulted in a retail price of approximately $8.99 for an eight-pack of EZ Change. In the focus groups, many respondents said that they would pay an extra dollar for a product with all of the advantages of EZ Change.

E. *Sales and distribution methods.* EZ Change was to be sold through the regular Energizer retail distribution system. The new product would be introduced to the larger retailers by the Energizer sales force, and in some cases could receive attention at retail by the Energizer in-store detailing force. Specialty distributors would be used to sell the product to audiologists. EZ Change representatives would also attend trade shows aimed at audiologists in order to communicate directly with them about the benefits of EZ Change.

F. *Advertising copy strategy.* "Precise placement every time" tested out to be the best message for clear communication. This statement clearly tells the consumer about the benefits of the new product without getting into any sensitive areas. This slogan was to be used in all advertisements and on the packaging. A secondary point to be made in the advertising was that EZ Change batteries work in all styles of hearing aids.

G. *Advertising media strategy.* A key objective of the media plan was to visually show the product and give the hearing aid user the motivation to buy this new solution. Television was selected as the primary advertising medium for EZ Change. The goal was to reach 90 percent of all hearing aid users with the TV advertising once, and to reach 65 percent of the target audience three times. Television would be supplemented with print media. The print media would include magazines such as *Reader's Digest* and the AARP's *Modern Maturity. Parade* and Sunday supplements would also be used. Newspaper advertisements would be included through retailer promotions.

H. *Customer support.* The EZ Change marketing plan provided a clear link from the manufacturer to the consumer to ensure complete customer satisfaction. There was to be an 800 number on the package that would link to a customer hot line where EZ Change representatives would help customers with any problems that they might be having with the product. There would also be a web address printed on the package along with the statement, "To learn more about the dispenser and to see it in action, visit our web site at *www.energizer-ezchange.com.*" The web site would include a video on how EZ Change works. EZ Change would also guarantee complete satisfaction to the consumer.

I. *In-store merchandising.* It was decided that corrugated off-shelf displays would be used to facilitate rapid distribution of EZ Change during the initial launch of the product. There would be several versions of these displays, including a counter display and a wing rack. These displays would also help the company communicate with consumers by highlighting the new hearing aid battery solution at the point of purchase. Each preloaded display would provide brochures to help educate the consumer on how this innovative new product works. In many cases a one-dollar in-store coupon would be included during the initial product launch

J. *Test marketing.* The final test before the launch of EZ Change was a quantitative test through BASES. This is a procedure in which the complete marketing plan is subjected to a process that is designed to determine the success of the new product. The input for this model includes a number of factors, such as consumers' intent to purchase based on market research, pricing of the new and existing products, distribution estimates, and each element of the marketing plan, including the amount of advertising planned. It also includes detailed information on the market. Based on all of this input, the BASES model predicts the impact that the new product will have on the category.

K. *Timetable.* The development of EZ Change began in March 2000. After completing the consumer research, developing the product, completing the marketing plan, and testing the overall venture, the company launched the product in September 2001.

7. **FINANCIAL RESULTS.** As predicted by BASES, Energizer has almost doubled its sales of hearing aid batteries in the Nielsen-measured marketplace since the launch of EZ Change. Energizer's sales of hearing aid batteries have increased 89 percent since the launch of EZ Change, and the trend is still positive. Energizer's market share has also increased substantially, and the shares of both of Energizer's main competitors have declined.

CHAPTER 2

Successful Marketing Plans Often Solve Consumer Problems

Example: Jumbo-Koter™ by Wooster Brush

Many successful marketing plans are based on solutions to consumer problems. In evaluating the marketing plans for your product or service, it can be helpful to find out whether your offering solves perceived problems for potential customers. If potential customers really see your product or service as the solution to their problems, this is a good indication that they might become buyers. If your product or service provides the only solution to a major problem, the chances of consumers' buying it is even better. Make sure, however, that this is really their perception and not just an assumption on your part. Jumbo-Koter is an example of success based on a new product that offers the solution to an irritating customer problem.

One of the objectives in painting a wall is to get the paint spread evenly where the ceiling and the wall come together and in the corners where one wall meets the other. Many painters use a roller to paint most of the wall because a roller is much faster than a brush for applying large amounts of paint. They then typically use a brush to apply paint in the corners because a traditional roller is too big to do that job. The problem with using a roller on the wall and a brush in the corners is that the paint sometimes looks different in the corners and around the edge of the wall. To solve this problem, painters often use mini-rollers because these rollers can get closer than a traditional roller. A mini-roller is less than half the size of a traditional roller, which makes it easier to control.

Here is where the consumer problem comes in. Many painters have problems with their mini-rollers. Because these rollers are smaller than traditional rollers, they are great for getting paint into tight places and corners. On the other hand, the small size of the roller sometimes causes it to stick after a certain number of uses. Painters often become frustrated when they have to drag a stuck mini-roller down a wall. This consumer problem led to a whole new product line called the Jumbo-Koter, and to a marketing plan that effectively leveraged the strengths of the Wooster Brush Company.

Wooster Brush Decided to Compete Through Innovation

The paint applicator industry is made up of a relatively small number of companies, and it changes only slightly from year to year. This is partly because painters tend to be very steadfast in terms of the type of paint applicators they use. The Wooster Brush Company is one of the larger factors in this industry and has been around for 151 years. With its long history, Wooster Brush has been in an excellent position to watch and benefit from trends as they have developed in this industry.

Over the past few years, Wooster Brush had been manufacturing a small-diameter roller-cover system. As the company watched the use of this mini-roller, it noticed that the roller really didn't perform as well as it could. It didn't always roll up the wall well. It might just slide up the wall when it was filled with paint, and it would not always turn as freely as it should. The company also noticed that users of competitive mini-rollers often experienced similar problems.

Another trend identified by Wooster Brush was the influx of foreign competition into the mini-roller market. Because of the effectiveness of using a mini-roller for detail painting jobs, the market for these small rollers was growing. As this was happening, several manufacturers were importing mini-rollers from China and other offshore sources. Wooster Brush was being forced to compete with these lower-priced imports. The company concluded that its best response would be to innovate. It would make substantial improvements to its existing mini-roller.

For many years Wooster Brush had been a leader in traditional roller covers (9 inches long, 1½ inches in diameter). It also produced an excellent cage frame that was very well accepted in the marketplace. The company decided to shrink all of that down to a small diameter. The engineering department was challenged to come up with a very tiny cage frame and a small, low-priced roller cover that would consistently roll on the wall without slipping. To meet competitive costs, mini-roller covers would be developed in a variety of professional-quality fabrics that would be more affordable than traditional small-diameter covers.

The engineers were able to develop a system that turned more freely. The old mini-roller contained a free-floating retaining band that was hard to line up with the wire handle and that often caused friction between the frame and the roller cover. This made it hard to roll. The new system is actually a separate cage system and a cover. The cover has nothing to do with the rolling of the frame. There are no works inside. The cover is easy to slide on and off. It will withstand the abuse of a professional painter and still allow for constant rolling day in and day out. The system will also keep the cover from walking off as you paint up the wall. In sum, the best technology from the large Wooster Brush frames was used in the development of Jumbo-Koter.

Like most successful new products, Jumbo-Koter was not created overnight. Six years earlier the company had noticed the need for an improvement in mini-rollers. At that time Wooster Brush had made an initial attempt to create a small caged cover system. The company succeeded technically, but the product was not very attractive. Finally Wooster Brush pushed the button on a major development effort that took eighteen months to complete. It took another three months to achieve the initial national distribution. At the time of this writing, Jumbo-Koter has been in national distribution for one year and is considered by current users to be a major innovation in the paint applicator category.

Market Research Confirmed a Major New Product Opportunity

Wooster Brush used an observation tracking system to identify the extent to which mini-rollers were being used across the United States. Interviews were conducted with managers of paint and hardware stores to determine their impressions of trends in the sales of mini-rollers. Personal observations of the back of contractors' trucks were then conducted to see what inventory the contractors were carrying. Specifically, these observations noted the extent to which mini-rollers were present in the trucks. This system of store interviews and personal observations enabled Wooster Brush management to determine that mini-rollers were gaining market share and were eroding paintbrush usage more and more.

Wooster Brush management believed that painting contractors were the key to success in launching a new paint applicator. Consumers represent the bulk of the unit sales; however, they tend to buy what is available and recommended in paint and hardware stores, and these stores typically display and recommend what is used by professional contractors. Before launching Jumbo-Koter, therefore, Wooster Brush felt that it was necessary to determine whether painting contractors would consider this new mini-roller to be a true improvement over the current products available in the market.

For research projects of this type, Wooster Brush has established an extensive panel of painting contractors located throughout the United States. Each of these contractors has completed a survey indicating the type of painting done. For example, contractors indicated the extent to which they use brushes or rollers and whether they typically paint commercial or residential facilities. There is also detailed demographic information on each of these contractors. The respondents in this sample of contractors have also stated that they would be willing to try new products from Wooster Brush.

Prototype products were sent to a sample of contractors that matched the typical user of mini-rollers. These contractors were given a chance to use the prototype products and then asked to provide their feedback on a survey questionnaire that was included with the samples. A subsample of these people was contacted by telephone to obtain their perceptions on a qualitative basis. The purpose of these one-on-one interviews was to determine exactly how the new mini-rollers were being used and to probe the respondents' perceptions of any perceived advantages or disadvantages.

The quantitative and qualitative research enabled Wooster Brush to obtain feedback on the reactions to the new mini-roller that they might expect in a variety of different regions across the United States. It was learned that Jumbo-Koter was generally perceived as a significant improvement over the mini-rollers that were currently available. A substantial number of the respondents who tried the new product felt that they would definitely purchase it on an ongoing basis. They liked how smoothly the cage frame rolled, and they liked how close the redesigned covers were able to get to the corner of walls and other tight places. The results of this research were so strong that Wooster Brush management made the decision to launch the program.

Planning Assumptions Were Developed Based on History and Research

Prior to launching Jumbo-Koter, the management of Wooster Brush made a series of assumptions regarding the outcome of the implementation. These planning assumptions were based on a long history of things that had happened during the launch of previous new products from Wooster Brush. The following is a list of the key planning assumptions made by the Wooster Brush Company:

1. Paint and hardware stores will generally accept distribution of Jumbo Koter because of the success these retailers have had with previous new products from Wooster Brush and the fact that they know that Wooster Brush will stand behind problem-solving products that it introduces. In the past, when Wooster Brush innovations have been introduced, they have achieved widespread distribution.

2. The fabric on Jumbo-Koter rollers will be accepted by professionals and consumers because it is the same fabric that has been successfully used on the professional big rollers.

3. Professional painters will want to use Jumbo-Koter mini-rollers because a sample of these professionals found the new product highly satisfactory in the panel test.

4. Pricing on Jumbo-Koter will be accepted as long as the price points are similar to those of the low-priced mini-rollers currently on the market. This was based on competitive data available at the time of the product launch. Jumbo-Koter is a superior product, and it should be well received if it is offered at the lower price points currently available. It is

likely to be perceived as a more affordable system than the domestic systems that are currently on the market.

5. Should Jumbo-Koter not be successful, Wooster Brush will still be able to capture a share of the mini-roller market with its current mini-roller system. The current system will not be discontinued. It will be sold side-by-side with the Jumbo-Koter system.

6. Over the next few years, Jumbo-Koter could make it possible to eliminate the old mini-roller system.

Specific Marketing Objectives Were Set for the New Product

Based on these planning assumptions, the management of Wooster Brush set up a series of specific key strategic marketing objectives for the Jumbo-Koter venture. These objectives covered marketing communication goals, sales goals, distribution objectives, inventory planning, and the overall time-table for the launch of the venture. The following are the key strategic marketing objectives set by the management of the Wooster Brush Company:

1. To entice consumers and professionals to purchase a mini-roller system that is not interchangeable with other mini-roller systems. This is a superior system because it utilizes a cage frame that does not stick over time the way current systems do. However, users must purchase a new frame and covers that will work only with the Jumbo-Koter system. The goal is to get Jumbo-Koter frames into the hands of users, and then motivate them to repeat purchases of Jumbo-Koter covers.

2. To get the majority of the twenty-four different Jumbo-Koter rollers and two frames into broad-scale distribution. To maximize consumer sales, the goal is to have the full product line available in as many retail stores as possible.

3. To time the expansion of distribution so that production is able to keep up with retail sales. A key goal is not to run out of product at any time during the launch of the Jumbo-Koter product line.

4. To achieve specific sales volume objectives that will enable the venture to pay back the investment in new equipment within a specific time

frame. The Jumbo-Koter product line required new equipment for manufacturing and packaging. A key goal was to cover the investment in this equipment in a timely manner.

5. To launch the Jumbo-Koter line nationally in the initial distribution targets within three months.

6. To overcome the potential objection by retailers and customers that the Jumbo-Koter covers do not have a fabric covering on the end of the rollers. One of the improvements included in the Jumbo-Koter covers is that the professional-style fabric does not go over the end of the cover. This enables the roller to get closer to the corner. An important goal is to communicate this benefit, because retailers and users now expect all Wooster Brush rollers to have fabric on the end of the cover.

The New Mini-Roller Was to Be Called Jumbo-Koter

The new mini-roller system was launched under the overall brand name Wooster Jumbo-Koter. This name appeared on all packaging and display header signs. Also, seven additional names were used to differentiate the different types of covers: Super Fab™, Pro Doo-Z™, Mohair Blend™, 50/50™, Super Twist™, Painter's Choice™, and Pro Foam™.

On each package, the description name (Pro Doo-Z, etc.) was in the largest type. This was intended to be what would catch the customer's attention. In many cases this name and the graphic appearance of the bag were the same as those of the well-established nine-inch Wooster Brush rollers that could be found down the aisle in the same store. The idea was to establish a link between the new mini-rollers and other Wooster Brush products now used by professional painters.

The name Wooster® was in the next largest type size on all Jumbo-Koter packaging. The Wooster name is not well known by the average consumer; however, it is very well known by retailers and professional painters. The Wooster name included on the packaging was to signal professional painters and the trade that these are high-quality mini-rollers. Jumbo-Koter was in the smallest type size. This name communicates that this is a new product, but it was not intended to be the key element in driving sales.

The overall brand name strategy was to leverage the power of the current Wooster Brush image. Most of these names, or parts of names, have been previously used by the Wooster Brush Company. The name *Wooster* helps establish that this is a professional small-diameter system. The name *Koter* has been used on previous Wooster Brush products, but it has not been linked with the word *Jumbo*. Previous examples were Magi-Koter™ and Mini-Koter™. The names Pro Doo-Z and Super Fab were taken from the nine-inch roller program to help establish a connection to a well-established product line.

A Comprehensive Product Line Was Developed

Jumbo-Koter is a comprehensive line of twenty-four different mini-rollers and two different frames. The short-handle frame has a 14-inch handle, and the long-handle frame has a $26^{1}/_{2}$-inch handle. Both of these are cage frames, which turn much better than the traditional wire frames. Both the short-handle frame and the long-handle frame have a 4-inch arm, even though there are $4^{1}/_{2}$- and $6^{1}/_{2}$-inch roller covers. A unique button on the end of the $6^{1}/_{2}$-inch roller covers plugs into the frame, enabling the frame to be used with both the $4^{1}/_{2}$- and the $6^{1}/_{2}$-inch roller covers. The fabrics used for the roller covers vary and are differentiated by brand name, pile, and width. Most of the covers are packed two per package, although some are packed six per package. Specifically, the line includes the following products:

No.	Brand	Fabric	Pile (inches)	Width (inches)	Pack
1	Super Fab	Knit	$^{3}/_{8}$	$4^{1}/_{2}$	2
2	Super Fab	Knit	$^{1}/_{2}$	$4^{1}/_{2}$	2
3	Super Fab	Knit	$^{3}/_{8}$	$6^{1}/_{2}$	2
4	Super Fab	Knit	$^{1}/_{2}$	$6^{1}/_{2}$	2
5	Pro Doo-Z	Woven	$^{3}/_{8}$	$4^{1}/_{2}$	2
6	Pro Doo-Z	Woven	$^{1}/_{2}$	$4^{1}/_{2}$	2
7	Pro Doo-Z	Woven	$^{3}/_{8}$	$6^{1}/_{2}$	2
8	Pro Doo-Z	Woven	$^{1}/_{2}$	$6^{1}/_{2}$	2
9	Pro Doo-Z	Woven	$^{3}/_{8}$	$4^{1}/_{2}$	6
10	Pro Doo-Z	Woven	$^{3}/_{8}$	$6^{1}/_{2}$	6

No.	Brand	Fabric	Pile (inches)	Width (inches)	Pack
11	Mohair Blend	Mohair	$1/4$	$4^1/_2$	2
12	Mohair Blend	Mohair	$1/4$	$6^1/_2$	2
13	50/50	Blend	$1/2$	$4^1/_2$	2
14	50/50	Blend	$1/2$	$6^1/_2$	2
15	Super Twist	Fabric	N/A	$4^1/_2$	2
16	Super Twist	Fabric	N/A	$6^1/_2$	2
17	Super Twist	Fabric	N/A	$4^1/_2$	6
18	Super Twist	Fabric	N/A	$6^1/_2$	6
19	Painter's Choice		$3/8$	$4^1/_2$	2
20	Painter's Choice		$3/8$	$6^1/_2$	2
21	Painter's Choice		$3/8$	$4^1/_2$	6
22	Painter's Choice		$3/8$	$6^1/_2$	6
23	Pro Foam		N/A	$4^1/_2$	2
24	Pro Foam		N/A	$6^1/_2$	2

Production Would Be in Ohio to Maintain Tight Control

The decision was made to produce the majority of the Jumbo-Koter line in the Wooster Brush Company factories in Ohio. One of the reasons for this was to maintain tight control of the timing of the production. It was felt that manufacturing would have to keep up with distribution in order to maintain in-store inventories. Wooster Brush did not want any out-of-stock situations in the retail stores. The manufacturing facilities in Ohio were somewhat self-contained, so that control could be managed more easily than with offshore manufacture and importing.

There were several reasons for not manufacturing any of the Jumbo-Koter line in China, even though inexpensive production was available there. First, Wooster Brush did not have any established roller-producing contacts in China. Management felt that working in an environment without established contacts could present potential quality problems. Second, paint rollers have a lot of air space, which increases the cost of shipping. This detracted from the advantages of Chinese production. Third, Wooster Brush management was worried about releasing the rights to use certain fabrics that were the exclusive property of the Wooster Brush Company.

A few unique roller covers were imported from Germany for the Jumbo-

Koter product line. Management felt that it needed to offer these unique covers with a closed end (fabric on the end). This was to meet anticipated objections by a few current customers. The company had dealt with people in Germany before and had been comfortable with the consistency in quality from this organization.

The Wooster Brush Traditional Sales and Distribution Methods to Be Used

The Wooster Brush Company basically sells its products through a national network of distributors and buying groups. It does have some direct accounts; Lowe's and Home Depot, for example, are direct accounts. Most of its sales, however, go through distributors. These are typically traditional stocking distributors that take orders and then make shipments to the retailers. Very few rack jobbers are used. The Jumbo-Koter product line was to use this standard method of distribution.

Jumbo-Koter was to be sold into national distribution by the Wooster Brush Company sales force and network of service personnel. The company maintains its own staff to help retailers set stores. When a new account is established, this detail force works with the distributor and retailer to set up Wooster's product lines, then trains them on how to communicate the benefits of the products to customers. This sales and servicing force is a competitive advantage for the Wooster Brush Company.

The Pricing Strategy Was to Meet the Low-Priced Imports

The Jumbo-Koter product line was set up with a different price point for each of the different products in the line. The pricing strategy was to hit the price points of the low-priced imported competition. Wooster Brush management did not feel that the company had to match competitors' prices exactly because Jumbo-Koter was a different type of product with unique advantages, such as easier-turning rollers. The Jumbo-Koter rollers were also longer and larger in diameter. Management felt that if Jumbo-Koter's prices were within a few pennies of those of the low-priced imports, it would have the advantage. Jumbo-Koter mini-rollers were launched at lower prices than domestic products, including other Wooster Brush mini-rollers.

When the program was launched, a 10 percent introductory allowance was offered on the entire line. The line was also launched with incentives to use a display with the Jumbo-Koter line. These discounts were to be offered at pro shows and at distributor shows. A consumer discount was also offered upon introduction of the program. A premium pack that included a frame and six roller covers in a box was to be sold during the product launch. It was to be put on a counter or on the rack. The consumer bought the six covers and got the frame free. Getting the frame into customers' hands without their having to make a perceived investment was felt to be crucial, because they were likely to hang onto that frame for the next five years and keep on buying replacement covers.

A pricing contingency plan was set up in case the competition decided to lower its prices in response to this program. Wooster Brush management decided that it would not reduce the Jumbo-Koter prices if that were to happen. Management felt that by the time the competition was able to implement a price reduction, Wooster Brush would have established the Jumbo-Koter line as a viable one in the market. It felt that most customers would continue to purchase Jumbo-Koter products at the initially established price.

In-Store Displays Were Used to Attract Consumer Attention

It was felt that a key to success in getting the full Jumbo-Koter product line into retail stores was an in-store display program. The cornerstone of this program was a two-foot freestanding merchandiser that included the full Jumbo-Koter product line. Wooster Brush would give the rack free to retailers. Management felt that this would be a good way to make sure that the whole product line was displayed together. Often stores will fragment product lines and scatter the different products in the line around the store. The rack encourages stores to keep all the products in the line together. Also, once retailers get the rack in, they will tend to keep the whole product line even if some items sell better than others.

Retailers were given three display options. First, they could use the freestanding rack, which typically goes at the end of an aisle. Second, they could decide not to use the freestanding display, but take the full contents of the Jumbo-Koter rack and display them on pegboard. In this case, they would be given a detailed plan-o-gram on how the display was to be set up. All of the necessary hardware and signage would be included with the in-line display. Wooster Brush would even send out people to help retailers set up the display. The third option was for the retailer to simply buy Jumbo-Koter products without the freestanding or in-line display.

A piece of literature for the consumer was included with either display option. This was an 8½- by 11-inch sheet of paper folded in half that described the complete program. It told the consumer what each of the different mini-rollers should be used for. It also talked about the types of paint that each of these covers was best suited for. This literature was also to be passed out at trade shows at the time the display options were being demonstrated.

The display program was primarily intended for paint and hardware stores. It was felt to be unlikely that Wooster Brush would get all twenty-six Jumbo-Koter products into a mass merchandiser such as Home Depot, as there typically is not room in these stores for the full program. It was felt that in these stores, perhaps a dozen products would be accepted into distribution upon introduction, and these products would be displayed in the store's paint applicator section. If the stores were satisfied with the initial sales of these products, they might add a few additional items.

The Advertising Copy Strategy Was to Sell the Improvement

The objective of the Jumbo-Koter advertising was to communicate to paint and hardware stores that a new improved mini-roller was coming on the market and that this mini-roller would be available only from the Wooster Brush Company. The magazine advertising described the professional grip on the frame, which is important to the professional painter because the frame will not unthread itself when it is used with a Wooster professional extension pole. The advertising explained that the cage frame was new to mini-rollers and was important to painters because it rolls freely. It also explained that use of the cage frame actually costs less than the use of the mini-rollers currently on the market because it is not necessary to buy expensive refill covers with all of the works inside.

Wooster used trade advertisements that took advantage of the strong reputation of the Wooster Brush Company name. These advertisements explained that the new Jumbo-Koter mini-rollers used the Wooster fabrics that professional painters already knew and loved to use. They emphasized that these new mini-rollers rolled smoothly and required fewer trips to the paint bucket because they held more paint and did not stop rolling. The net result was less cost to the painter.

The Advertising Media Strategy Was Directed to the Trade

Jumbo-Koter advertising was designed to be run in trade publications such as *Do-It-Yourself Retailing* and other magazines targeted to paint and hardware stores. There was no consumer advertising of Jumbo-Koter. One- and two-page spreads were placed in these magazines at the time of the product launch. The advertising was not actually placed until Wooster Brush was confident that there was enough product in the warehouse to satisfy retailer demand. The advertisements initially ran in conjunction with the initial launch. Further flights of these same advertisements were to be run every three or four issues, in rotation with the regular Wooster Brush advertising campaign.

Public relations was also used to introduce Jumbo-Koter. A press release was sent to all of the key trade publications prior to placement of the print advertising. Wooster Brush Company management anticipated that a significant number of articles would result from this press release because Wooster Brush was a regular advertiser in all of these magazines. The press release introduced Jumbo-Koter as a new product from the Wooster Brush Company and included the major points from the advertising copy.

Product Warranties Were Unnecessary Due to Wooster's Strong Reputation

There was no formal warranty on the Jumbo-Koter product line. The Wooster Brush Company does not have a formal warranty on any of its products. The company will, however, replace any returns involving normal and proper use. If a consumer has a problem with any product from the Wooster Brush Company, he or she can bring it back to the store and the store will replace it. Wooster Brush will then compensate the retailer. The Wooster Brush Company always stands behind its products 100 percent of the time.

Internal Staffing Maintained a Lean Organization

The marketing of the Jumbo-Koter product line was implemented through the normal Wooster Brush Company organization. The management of the company believes that one of the keys to its success and longevity (the company is 151 years old) is its ability to operate with a lean organization. The company has no product managers and does not use separate sales or marketing organizations for its different brands.

In most cases the Wooster Brush sales force introduced the Jumbo-Koter product line to distributors and trained them in the advantages of these new mini-rollers. The distributors' sales force then obtained retail distribution and trained the dealers on how to sell the new product line to their customers. A few outside sales representatives were used to contact distributors in remote areas. National accounts were contacted by an internal national sales force operating from the company's national headquarters in Ohio.

Conservative Financial Projections Were Prepared

The engineering department prepared an estimate of the expenses that were anticipated for the Jumbo-Koter venture. These included the up-front investment in new equipment. The marketing department then prepared an initial and multiyear sales forecast, as well as forecasted profit and loss statements. The purpose of these financial projections was to show that the Jumbo-Koter venture would produce a satisfactory return on investment, assuming that the project unfolded as expected.

The financial projections were conservative in that they did not include any estimates of sales from the large national accounts such as Lowe's or Home Depot. Only sales from paint and hardware stores were included. The reason for this was to add stability to the forecasts. Wooster Brush management felt that it could confidently predict potential sales from the traditional paint and hardware stores, based on a long history with these accounts. Predictions for the large national accounts were much less reliable. Management did not want to develop production capacity based on speculative assumptions.

Innovation Is a Good Way to Maintain Market Presence

The Jumbo-Koter venture is a good example of the development of a successful new product by solving a consumer problem. The Wooster Brush Company identified the difficulty that painters were having because their mini-rollers were sticking after a few uses. The new Jumbo-Koter mini-rollers solved that problem by using a smooth-turning cage frame. Wooster Brush further improved these mini-rollers by using high-quality fabrics from its highly successful nine-inch rollers. Finally, by not extending fabric over the end of the new mini-rollers, Jumbo-Koter enabled the painter to get into tighter spaces than with traditional mini-rollers. This also prevented paint from spinning off onto another surface.

One lesson to be learned from the Jumbo-Koter program is that innovation is a good way for a company to maintain its presence in the marketplace. The Wooster Brush Company has made a notable effort to continue to innovate, developing truly beneficial products in a very stodgy, old-fashioned business for many years. The Jumbo-Koter product line is a good example of this. This continuous innovation has enabled the company to compete successfully without participating in industry price wars. At the time of this writing, the Wooster Brush Company was in the process of developing additional new products to meet the paint application needs of its customers.

> *Summary Marketing Plan for:*
> Wooster Jumbo-Koter™
> Wooster Brush Company[1]
> 2002

MARKETING PLAN SUMMARY

1. **BACKGROUND.** Many painters have problems with their mini-rollers. Because these rollers are smaller than traditional rollers, they are great for getting paint into tight places and corners. On the other hand, the small size of the roller sometimes causes it to stick after a certain number of uses. Painters often become frustrated when they have to drag a stuck mini-roller down a wall. This consumer problem led to a whole new product line called the Jumbo-Koter, and to a marketing plan that effectively leveraged the strengths of the Wooster Brush Company.

2. **MARKET REVIEW.** The paint applicator industry is made up of a relatively small number of companies, and it changes only slightly from year to year. A trend identified by Wooster Brush was the influx of foreign competition into the mini-roller market. Because of the effectiveness of using a mini-roller for detail painting jobs, the market for these small rollers was growing. As this was happening, several manufacturers were importing mini-rollers from China and other offshore sources. Wooster Brush was being forced to compete with these lower-priced imports.

3. **CONSUMER USAGE AND ATTITUDES.** A program of store interviews and personal observations enabled Wooster Brush management to determine that mini-rollers were gaining market share and were eroding paintbrush usage more and more. Consumers represent the bulk of the unit sales; however, they tend to buy what is available and recommended in paint and hardware stores, and these stores typically display and recommend what is used by professional contractors. Through quantitative and qualitative research, Wooster Brush

---

[1] Wooster and Jumbo-Koter are trademarks of The Wooster Brush Company, and are used with permission.

learned that painting contractors generally perceived Jumbo-Koter as a significant improvement over the mini-rollers that were currently available in the market.

4. **PLANNING ASSUMPTIONS.** Prior to launching Jumbo-Koter, the management of Wooster
   Brush made a series of assumptions regarding the outcome of the implementation. The
   following is a list of the key planning assumptions made by Wooster Brush Company:

   A. Paint and hardware stores will generally accept distribution of Jumbo-Koter because of
       the success these retailers have had with previous new products from Wooster Brush.

   B. The fabric on Jumbo-Koter rollers will be accepted by professionals and consumers.

   C. Professional painters will want to use Jumbo-Koter mini-rollers.

   D. Pricing on Jumbo-Koter will be accepted as long as the price points are similar to those
       of the low-priced mini-rollers currently on the market.

   E. Should Jumbo-Koter not be successful, Wooster Brush will still be able to capture a
       share of the mini-roller market with its current mini-roller system.

   F. Over the next few years, Jumbo-Koter could make it possible to eliminate the old mini-
       roller system.

5. **KEY STRATEGIC MARKETING OBJECTIVES.** Based on the above planning assumptions, the
   management of Wooster Brush set up a series of specific key strategic marketing objectives
   for the Jumbo-Koter venture. The following are the key strategic marketing objectives set by
   the management of the Wooster Brush Company:

   A. To entice consumers and professionals to purchase a mini-roller system that is not
       interchangeable with other mini-roller systems.

   B. To get the majority of the twenty-four different Jumbo-Koter rollers and two frames
       into broad-scale distribution.

   C. To time the expansion of distribution so that production is able to keep up with retail
       sales.

   D. To achieve specific sales volume objectives that will enable the venture to pay back the
       investment in new equipment within a specific time frame.

   E. To launch the Jumbo-Koter line nationally in the initial distribution targets within three
       months.

F. To overcome the potential objection by retailers and customers that the Jumbo-Koter covers do not have a fabric covering on the end of the rollers.

6. **MARKETING PLAN ELEMENTS**

A. *Brand name.* The new mini-roller system was launched under the overall brand name Wooster Jumbo-Koter. This name appeared on all packaging and display header signs. Also, seven additional names were used to differentiate the different type of covers: Super Fab™, Pro Doo-Z™, Mohair Blend™, 50/50™, Super Twist™, Painter's Choice™, and Pro Foam™. The overall brand name strategy was to leverage the power of the current Wooster Brush image.

B. *Product line.* Jumbo-Koter is a comprehensive line of twenty-four different mini-rollers and two different frames. The short-handle frame has a 14-inch handle, and the long-handle frame has a 26½-inch handle. Both of these are cage frames, which turn much better than the traditional wire frames. Both the short-handle frame and the long-handle frame have a 4-inch arm, even though there are 4½- and 6½-inch roller covers. A unique button on the end of all of the 6½-inch roller covers plugs into the frame, enabling the frame to be used with both the 4½- and the 6½-inch roller covers. The fabrics used for the roller covers vary and are differentiated by brand name, pile, and width. Most of the covers are packed two per package, although there are some covers that are packed six per package.

C. *Pricing strategy.* The Jumbo-Koter product line was set up with a different price point for each of the different products in the line. The pricing strategy was to hit the price points of the low-priced imported competition. Management felt that if Jumbo-Koter's prices were within a few pennies of those of the low-priced imports, it would have the advantage. Jumbo-Koter mini-rollers were launched at lower prices than domestic products, including other Wooster Brush mini-rollers. When the program was launched, a 10 percent introductory allowance was offered on the entire line.

D. *Sales and distribution methods.* The Wooster Brush Company sells its products through a national network of distributors and buying groups. It does have some direct accounts; Lowe's and Home Depot, for example, are direct accounts. Jumbo-Koter was to be sold into national distribution by the Wooster Brush Company's sales force and network of service personnel.

E. *Advertising copy strategy.* The objective of the Jumbo-Koter advertising was to communicate to paint and hardware stores that a new improved mini-roller was coming on the market and that this mini-roller would be available only from the Wooster Brush Company. Wooster used trade advertisements that took advantage of the strong reputation of the Wooster Brush Company name. These advertisements emphasized that these new mini-rollers rolled smoothly and required fewer trips to the paint bucket because they held more paint and did not stop rolling. The net result was less cost to the painter.

F. *Advertising media strategy.* Jumbo-Koter advertising was designed to be run in trade publications such as *Do-It-Yourself Retailing* and other magazines targeted to paint and hardware stores. There was no consumer advertising of Jumbo-Koter. One- and two-page spreads were placed in these magazines at the time of the product launch.

G. *Sales promotion.* The line was launched with incentives for retailers to use a display with the Jumbo-Koter line. These discounts were to be offered at pro shows and at distributor shows. A consumer discount was also offered upon introduction of the program. A premium pack that included a frame and six roller covers in a box was to be sold during the product launch. It was to be put on a counter or on the rack. The consumer bought the six covers and got the frame free.

H. *Publicity.* Public relations was also used to introduce Jumbo-Koter. A press release was sent to all of the key trade publications prior to placement of the print advertising. Wooster Brush Company management anticipated that a significant number of articles would result from this press release because Wooster Brush was a regular advertiser in all of these magazines. The press release introduced Jumbo-Koter as a new product from the Wooster Brush Company and included the major points from the advertising copy.

I. *In-store merchandising.* It was felt that a key to success in getting the full Jumbo-Koter product line into retail stores was an in-store display program. The cornerstone of this program was a two-foot freestanding merchandiser that included the full Jumbo-Koter product line. Wooster Brush would give the rack free to retailers. A piece of literature for the consumer was included with the display.

J. *Timetable.* After Wooster Brush pushed the button on a major development effort, it took eighteen months to complete. It took another three months to achieve the initial national distribution. At the time of this writing, Jumbo-Koter has been in national distribution for one year.

7. **FINANCIAL PROJECTIONS.** The financial projections were conservative in that they did not include any estimates of sales from the large national accounts such as Lowe's or Home

Depot. Only sales from paint and hardware stores were included. The reason for this was to add stability to the forecasts. Wooster Brush management felt that it could confidently predict potential sales from the traditional paint and hardware stores, based on a long history with these accounts. Predictions for the large national accounts were much less reliable. Management did not want to develop production capacity based on speculative assumptions.

8. **CONTINGENCY PLANS.** A pricing contingency plan was set up in case the competition decided to lower its prices in response to this program. Wooster Brush management decided that it would not reduce the Jumbo-Koter prices if that were to happen. Management felt that by the time the competition was able to implement a price reduction, Wooster Brush would have established the Jumbo-Koter line as a viable one in the market. It felt that most customers would continue to purchase Jumbo-Koter products at the initially established price.

CHAPTER 3

Benefits Must Be Perceived by Customers

Example: Philips Long-Life Lightbulbs

Except for gifts, people will rarely buy a new product or service unless they feel that it has some specific benefits that are important to them. Many business ventures have succeeded because they provided meaningful benefits that were clearly recognized by their customers. This chapter provides an example of how Philips identified its product's most significant benefit and created something new around that benefit, and then how the company used positioning to communicate this benefit. You should always make a point of finding out what benefits potential customers feel they will get from your product or service. You want to know specifically what these benefits are and why they are important to your customers.

Philips Lighting Company, headquartered in Somerset, New Jersey, is the U.S. lightbulb division of Philips Electronics North America Corporation. In 1998 the management of Philips Lighting Company decided to try to make a significant impact on the consumer lightbulb market. It began this effort by doing some serious market research to see what was really important to consumers of lightbulbs. The idea was to find out what benefits consumers wanted, then provide those benefits and wrap an entire marketing program around them. The result was an incredibly successful marketing plan.

Philips Decided to Become the Long-Life Lightbulb Company

The results of Philips's market research clearly indicated that long life was the most important feature that consumers would like to have in a lightbulb. Many consumers indicated that they simply did not want to have to climb up a ladder every two months to change a lightbulb. The management at Philips found this believable because of Philips's long history with long-life lightbulbs. A major problem uncovered by this research, however, was that there was a lot of consumer confusion concerning the category. For example, although the expected number of hours was printed on lightbulb packaging, people had no idea how many hours a lightbulb should last.

Philips decided to provide the consumer with long-life lightbulbs and at the same time take away the consumer confusion. It would do this by offering a series of new long-life lightbulbs. This would involve a good, better, best strategy. DuraMax would be the good lightbulbs, with a guaranteed life of one year (twice as long as the average lightbulb). Halogena would be the better lightbulbs, with a guaranteed life of two years. Marathon would be the best lightbulbs, with a guaranteed life of five to seven years.

This long-life strategy took over the entire Philips consumer incandescent lightbulb product line. As of this writing, Philips has become the only company whose whole consumer line is long life. It has become the long-life company. In fact, long life has become a worldwide strategy for Philips lightbulbs. The current Philips worldwide marketing vision statement is, "Philips is the brand of lightbulbs that helps to enhance the quality of your life. Philips delivers a full line of long-lasting lightbulbs that satisfy your lighting needs and are guaranteed to perform." In the United States, this was brought down to "light bulbs that last."

This long-life strategy has been very successful for Philips. The company is achieving strong consumer sales of all three of its new product lines: DuraMax, Halogena, and Marathon. It has also been very successful from a retail distribution standpoint. Philips has been able to show retailers its consumer research, which indicated total confusion at the point of purchase. Philips has then been able to explain to the retailer how it has been able to take the confusion out of the lightbulb business with its good, better, best strategy.

This has resulted in broad-scale distribution in Home Depot and many other major retailers of consumer lightbulbs.

History Shows Long Life as the Number One Attribute for Lightbulbs

Over the past thirty years, long life has come up several times as the number one attribute that consumers look for when buying a lightbulb. In 1983, Philips substantially expanded its lightbulb business in the United States by purchasing all of the lamp divisions of the Westinghouse Electric Corporation. One of the things that came along with that acquisition was a product line that had a longer-life strategy. Prior to that, Westinghouse had had several successes with long-life lightbulbs.

In 1977, Westinghouse had launched a major venture selling long-life lightbulbs through grocery stores. The venture was called Turtle-Lite. Turtle-Lite was based on a wealth of consumer market research obtained from 1972 to 1977 that indicated that consumers wanted lightbulbs that lasted longer than current offerings. Turtle-Lite was a long-life lightbulb that was unconditionally guaranteed to provide the consumer with two years of service. Turtle-Lite lightbulbs were sold off of a unique freestanding in-store merchandiser and were supported with heavy consumer advertising and promotion.

Turtle-Lite successfully achieved distribution in most of the grocery stores in the western United States. The program was successful in generating substantial consumer sales in each of the stores in which it operated. This proved that consumers were interested in purchasing long-life lightbulbs. The program was eventually discontinued as a result of competitive pressure. Strong competitive couponing brought the price of standard incandescent lightbulbs down so low that Turtle-Lite became uncompetitive. This was coupled with the movement of the grocery trade away from freestanding displays.

When Westinghouse was acquired by Philips, its lightbulb product line included a uniquely shaped long-life lightbulb called T-Bulb. This lightbulb enabled consumers to get about a third longer life than the standard incandescent lightbulb without a significant reduction in lumen (light) output. That was the premier product when Philips acquired the Westinghouse lightbulb division. Philips kept this product in its line for several years. From 1992 to 1996, however, Philips concentrated mainly on the industrial and commercial side of the market. As a result, the long-life product kind of faded away. Even the unique shape of the T-Bulb was discontinued because of its cost.

In reviewing the past history of lightbulbs, Philips identified a number of products providing different consumer benefits. Some focused on the quality of the light given off, some focused on energy usage, and some focused on environmental issues. Long life surfaced as the most consistently well received consumer benefit. Energy was very popular at times, such as in California when energy was scarce. Nothing, however, ever moved long life away from the top spot.

The Project Began with a Thorough Review of the Market for Lightbulbs

As part of the overall strategy development process conducted in 1998, Philips completed a thorough review of the overall lightbulb market. By this time the company had become very fact-based and had an excellent market research department. The research department provided a review of all of the available data on the lightbulb market, as well as data from several custom studies. Store checks and interviews with retailers were also conducted to provide a hands-on view of the current marketplace.

The consumer market for incandescent lightbulbs has five retail distribution segments: grocery stores, hardware and home center stores, mass merchandisers, drugstores, and a category labeled "other." Grocery chains had previously been the dominant source of lightbulbs, but by 1998, this dominance had shifted dramatically to the home centers and mass merchandisers. The grocery segment was declining, and the mass merchandiser and home center segments were increasing.

Consumers saw that stores like Home Depot carried one hundred feet of lightbulbs, including every type of lightbulb they might need for the home. In comparison, a grocery store would carry maybe twelve to sixteen feet of lightbulbs and certainly did not have every type of lightbulb. Home Depot alone sold one out of every five lightbulbs. Purchases in grocery stores now tended to be those where the consumer was shopping in the store and re-membered that one of his lightbulbs had burned out, so he bought a four-pack just to make sure. However, if the consumer was doing a lighting proj-ect and was buying fifteen or twenty lightbulbs at one time, she would do this at a home center.

GE was the dominant player in the grocery chains and mass merchan-disers. Philips was the dominant player in home centers because Philips was the primary supplier of lightbulbs to Home Depot, which sold 20 percent of all the lightbulbs sold in the United States. Sylvania was number three among the major brands. The other factor was private label. Some retailers were selling lightbulbs imported from the Far East under their own private label. Some imported lightbulbs were also being sold under the Westing-house brand name, which was licensed from Viacom (the current owner of the trademark).

Sophisticated Qualitative Market Research Used to Pinpoint Key Benefit

In 1998 Philips conducted a series of market research projects to determine consumer perceptions of the most important benefits related to lightbulbs. This research began with a series of consumer focus groups held in various parts of the United States. Psychographic screening questionnaires were used to bring in males and females who demonstrated the ability to deal effectively with abstract concepts. This initial qualitative research was fol-lowed by a series of in-depth one-on-one interviews with consumers of vari-ous brands of lightbulbs.

During the initial focus groups, respondents engaged in a brainstorming session on their idea of an ideal lightbulb. This brainstorming generated a long list of perceived benefits of lightbulbs, which respondents then evalu-ated with the help of several highly sophisticated projective techniques. Ben-efit chains were used to stimulate the respondents' ability to create lists of alternative benefits. Forced relationships were then used to help respondents compare current lightbulbs. For example, respondents were at times asked to imagine what type of animal different types of lightbulbs might be and then describe their attributes based on the animal they selected. The following are two examples:

> "That major-brand lightbulb reminds me of
> a dog, which is man's best friend. So many
> families have them. It's a comfort—a big name
> that you are comfortable with, and you know
> they probably will be good."

> "That generic-brand lightbulb is a turtle. Turtles
> are relatively unimportant and in the background.
> Nobody is paying attention to them."

Concept statements created in the focus groups were presented to consumers during lengthy in-person interviews. As the series of interviews progressed, the concepts were modified to reflect consumer attitudes. The concepts included a number of the most popular benefits identified during the focus groups. Different facts about lightbulbs were also presented to respondents to determine their believability.

Long Life Identified as the Only Lightbulb Benefit Worth a Premium

The consumer focus groups revealed that a typical consumer perception was that lightbulbs burn out too soon. Consumers wanted long-life lightbulbs, but they thought that current claims of long life were not believable. They felt that a better lightbulb would be one that lasted longer, and that this was the only benefit that would be worth a premium. They felt that long-life lightbulbs would be less annoying and safer, and could save money in the long run. Many respondents also felt that a guarantee would add credibility to claims of long life.

The personal in-depth interviews with consumers refined their perceptions of the long-life benefit. Many of the consumers included in this research felt that a full line of long-life lightbulbs would be more credible than one new long-life lightbulb. Respondents liked the full-line concept because they would be able to choose the ideal lightbulb type for different locations. For example, they would be able to buy expensive, very-long-lasting lightbulbs for some locations and other, less-expensive lightbulbs for other locations.

Philips Assumed That Its Customers Would Accept a Long-Life Strategy

On completion of the market review and market research, Philips decided to proceed with the launching of a major strategic effort to transform itself into the "long-life company." It made assumptions about the likely reactions of consumers and retailers to the strategy. It made assumptions about the planned pricing for the new products, and even about the technical design of the new long-life lightbulbs. The following are Philips's key planning assumptions:

1. A long-life strategy would effectively differentiate Philips's lightbulbs from those of the competition.

2. As previous long-life products by Westinghouse and Philips had shown, and as indicated by the market research, consumers would buy into the long-life lightbulb idea.

3. The long-life strategy would help Philips's retailers compete with their competitors. Philips believed that retailers were tired of seeing the same products advertised in a Sunday circular at different prices. For example, Home Depot would see Wal-Mart, in a Sunday ad, cutting its price on the same GE lightbulbs that Home Depot was carrying. Philips believed that many retailers were not happy about this and wanted to differentiate their products, but did not know how to do so. Philips believed it had the answer.

4. Premium pricing on a line of superior products would be acceptable to retailers and consumers. Philips did not want to compete on the basis of price because it knew that it could not be the low-cost leader. With the long-life strategy, the company would be bringing out a line of products that could not be compared directly with competitive lightbulbs. Philips would have a different product that would last longer. It would take

Philips out of the direct comparison situation, such as matching the price of its four-pack with that of GE's.

5. The Philips engineering department had identified the proper line between life and light, so that it could provide the consumer with a series of lightbulb products that would be ideal for home use.

Marketing Plan Written with Two Primary Objectives

Based on these assumptions, the new marketing plan had two primary objectives. First, Philips would introduce a series of lines of long-life lightbulbs that would be significantly different from the lightbulbs offered by the competition. Second, because they were superior, these new product lines would be sold at premium prices, which would generate higher margins for Philips and for Philips's retail partners.

The New Corporate Long-Life Strategy Included Three Brand Names

Philips Marathon was the name used for the longest-lasting or "best" lightbulbs (guaranteed for five to seven years), Philips Halogena was the name used for the second-longest-lasting or "better" line of lightbulbs (guaranteed for two years), and Philips DuraMax was used for the entry-level or "good" line of lightbulbs (guaranteed for one year). Marathon and Halogena became available in 2000, and DuraMax was added two years later.

The name Halogena was given to the U.S. operation by Philips's European operation, as this name had been previously used in Europe. Marathon and DuraMax were developed in creative sessions involving Philips management and Philips's advertising and public relations agencies. A series of names were tested among consumers, and those two names were picked as suggesting reliability and long life.

The Long-Life Lightbulb Formula Is Tricky

It is the coil and some of the chemicals inside that make one lightbulb last longer than another. There is a mix of inert gases, such as carbon, krypton, argon, and neon, inside of a lightbulb. The coil that is used in an incandescent lightbulb is made of tungsten, and if the coil were stretched out, it would be quite long. The thickness of the coil and the number of turns are part of the science of making a lightbulb. It is the combination of the differences in the coil and the slight differences in the gases that fill the vacuum that differentiate one lightbulb from another.

The long-life formula is tricky. If you put too much life into a lightbulb, the light output goes down. A lot of imported lightbulbs have tried too hard to maximize life. For example, a company would come out with a three-year incandescent lightbulb, but the light output from these lightbulbs would drop dramatically. The life of a lightbulb is important, but the quality of the light is also important. You can't just bring out a long-life lightbulb; it also has to have sufficient light output. The trade-off between life and light has to be optimized.

The challenge at Philips was to develop an incandescent lightbulb that would last at least one year. Consumer research showed that consumers might accept a six-month life, but Philips felt that at least one year would represent an improved product. This was the "good" lightbulb. Philips then added halogen technology to create a "better" lightbulb with a two-year life. Finally, Philips used fluorescent technology to create the "best" lightbulb, with a life of between five and seven years. Management felt that this would take Philips lightbulbs out of the commodity class and make them products with real value-added qualities.

DuraMax Lightbulbs Last One Year

DuraMax was the line of "good" light bulbs, which would have a minimum life of one year. These were incandescent lightbulbs that were comparable to GE incandescent lightbulbs, which typically had a life of six months. Depending on the particular lightbulb, this longer life was achieved through the use of a larger coil, a different gas, or a combination of the two. DuraMax had a full line of different incandescent lightbulbs.

Although DuraMax lightbulbs had twice the life of a traditional incandescent lightbulb, they were designed to have the same perceptible light output. For example, if a GE incandescent lightbulb had a light output of 880 lumens for a sixty-watt lightbulb, the DuraMax light bulbs might have 860 lumens for that same sixty-watt lightbulb. That difference would not be perceptible to the human eye. Philips knew that if it were to use an even thicker coil and reduce the light output to 800 lumens, that would be perceptible, so the company did not do that. It was a trade-off that was very carefully done.

Halogena Lightbulbs Last Two Years

Halogena was the line of "better" light bulbs, with at least a two-year life. Halogena was a product line that had been made by Philips in Europe for several years, but had never been introduced into the United States. It was added to the mix to fill in the good, better, best strategy.

Halogen technology was a little different. It had an incandescent coil in a quartz glass container. Instead of argon or neon, it used a halogen gas. Halogen gases replace the tungsten in a burning coil constantly. When an incandescent lightbulb heats up, little bits of tungsten flake off. Eventually the coil gets a weak spot because too much tungsten has flaked off. Then when you flip the switch, you hear that "pop" and the bulb burns out. That happens because the coil has been weakened at that one spot. This happens more slowly with halogen technology, which is why Halogena lightbulbs last two years.

There are several other advantages to Halogena lightbulbs. The light from these lightbulbs is actually whiter and brighter than that from standard incandescent lightbulbs. An incandescent light bulb usually generates fifteen to seventeen lumens per watt, whereas a Halogena lightbulb can go up to twenty-five lumens per watt, making it more efficient. Halogena bulbs do not burn hotter because their shape keeps the inner burner far away from the bulb wall, so that the heat does not really affect the outer wall.

Even though they are based on a different technology, Halogena lightbulbs are practical for home use. Halogena lightbulbs can be screwed into any incandescent lightbulb socket. They are even dimmable, just as incandescent lightbulbs are.

Marathon Lightbulbs Last Five to Seven Years

Marathon would be the "best" lightbulbs. They would have a minimum life of five to seven years, depending on the particular lightbulb selected. These lightbulbs are based on a technology that is very different from that of an incandescent lightbulb. They use fluorescent technology, where most of the energy is captured as light and not heat. That is a huge difference. Philips invented compact fluorescent lightbulbs back in the 1970s. When they first came out, compact fluorescent lightbulbs were designed for commercial use, where companies wanted to save electricity because they had to keep their lights on all the time. With Marathon, these lightbulbs were adapted for home use.

It took a lot of years to get a compact fluorescent to mimic the look of an incandescent lightbulb. Philips had to get these compact fluorescents to burn in the same yellow color range as incandescent lightbulbs to make them look like the other lightbulbs in the home. Now the Marathon lightbulb can go anywhere in any home and look exactly like incandescent lightbulbs. Philips has a demonstration room where, in a simulated bedroom, it asks you to tell which is the incandescent and which is the Marathon. Maybe one out of fifty people will figure it out. You can't tell the difference.

In addition to the much longer life, a major advantage of Marathon lightbulbs is that they save a lot of money on electricity. To get the amount of light you are used to from a sixty-watt incandescent lightbulb, you have to use only fifteen watts with a Marathon lightbulb. That is four times more energy-efficient. The reason for this is that you are not losing energy to heat, as most of the energy is going to light output. Because they have been made very compact, Marathon lightbulbs can do anything regular incandescent lightbulbs can do. They can dim, they can be three-way, and they can fit into any socket.

Traditional Lightbulb Shapes Were Used Except for Decorative Bulbs

During the development stages of this marketing plan, Philips discovered that the design of a lightbulb (the shape of the bulb) is very important to consumers. Research was done with different shapes, and consumers said that they wanted their lightbulbs to have a traditional shape, except when they were using them for decorative purposes. This became the basis for the design of Philips's lines of long-life lightbulbs.

Marathon was the most difficult. From a design standpoint, Philips had to make a fluorescent lightbulb look like an incandescent lightbulb. In the past that had always been one of the barriers to fluorescent technology. People were used to the shape of an incandescent lightbulb. When Philips had come out with bulbs that looked like little fluorescent bulbs, it had had difficulty selling them. Because of this, many of the Marathon lightbulbs were designed to hide the fluorescent tubing and to look exactly like an incandescent lightbulb.

DuraMax lightbulbs were based on traditional incandescent technology and had the traditional lightbulb shape. Halogena, however, departed somewhat from tradition. Because of the beauty of the light from a Halogena lightbulb, many consumers wanted to use these bulbs for decorative purposes. Therefore, the shape of these lightbulbs was designed to be more artistic, so that they would be appropriate in a fixture that showed the lightbulb.

Vibrant New Packaging Was Created

Philips felt that this marketing effort gave the company an opportunity to create vibrant new packaging that told a better story to the consumer. It wanted to create packaging that would help sell the product off of the shelf without confusing the consumer. Philips felt that with its old packaging, and with the packaging of GE and Sylvania, the consumer had trouble figuring out which lightbulb was better and why. The company felt that, in addition to advertising, the good, better, best story would have to be told on the packaging.

On the new packaging Philips designed, wattage was the most prominent number, and how long the lightbulbs would last was the second most prominent number. Philips felt that consumers could not relate to life represented in hours, so it stated the life in years. It also gave the guarantee on the packaging: The lightbulbs were guaranteed for one year, two years, five years, or seven years. Finally, the packaging visually showed the consumer the shape of the lightbulb and where it should go in the home. The idea was to simplify the shopping process.

A Local Production Strategy Was Implemented to Ensure High Quality

Philips decided to manufacture the consumer product line in its own factories. Philips has enormous production capacity. The total consumer and industrial Philips product line includes over three thousand different types of lightbulbs. Philips has seven factories in the United States, one in Canada, and one in Mexico. It also has additional production facilities in Europe. By producing all of the lightbulbs internally, Philips believed that it would be able to maintain much better quality than if it imported the lightbulbs from the Far East. The company felt that this would represent an advantage over some of the competition.

Sales and Distribution Strategy Was Based on Heavy Trade Involvement

At the time this marketing effort was being planned, except for the private-label lightbulbs, there was mostly one brand per retail outlet. There were some exceptions. For example, at Home Depot, GE and Philips were the two major lightbulb brands, and then there were six other brands on the shelves, including Panasonic, Toshiba, and Westinghouse. ABCO licensed the Westinghouse brand name from Viacom and put it on imported lightbulbs from China.

The Philips factories generally shipped lightbulbs from the factory warehouse to a Philips combination warehouse, where all of the different types of lightbulbs were brought together. The retailer's regional depot orders would come into these facilities, and the products ordered would go to the retailer's regional warehouses. The retailer would then generally distribute the lightbulbs to the stores. There were some exceptions where Philips would ship directly from its combination warehouse to a retail store. Usually, however, Philips would deliver to a chain's warehouse for store-level distribution.

Philips did a lot of research with the retail trade in preparation for this major new marketing strategy. The sales force was involved in this research, but so were a lot of marketing people. A lot of the higher-level meetings were not limited to a salesperson, but included a vice president of marketing, the category leader for the products, and sometimes even the president. Philips presented to retailers what its research had shown, and explained how the new Philips product line would differentiate the retailer's offering. Category management suggestions were an important part of these meetings. Philips showed retailers how they could earn substantially more money from the same amount of shelf space with the new line of Philips lightbulbs because of the premium pricing of these superior products.

The long-life strategy worked well. Home Depot eventually made Philips its exclusive major brand of lightbulbs. This was significant because Home Depot sold one out of every five lightbulbs in America at that time. Home Depot felt that the new Philips strategy would help it differentiate its lightbulbs from those sold by Wal-Mart and other competitors. Other retailers also switched their lightbulb brand from their previous source to Philips. Wegmans, for example, switched to Philips because it is a store that likes to sell better products, and it saw that switching to Philips fit its overall strategy.

Premium Prices Resulted in Substantial Hidden Savings for Consumers

The pricing strategy for DuraMax and Marathon light bulbs was to provide the consumer with a longer-life lightbulb, and to enable the consumer to save money at the same time. The strategy for Halogena was different. Halogena was to be sold at a premium price because of its longer life and the uniqueness of the lightbulbs. Halogena lightbulbs provided a refreshingly whiter light that was unavailable with traditional incandescent lightbulbs. The Halogena lightbulbs were also useful as decorative bulbs because of their attractive shape and glass.

The price of a sixty-watt incandescent lightbulb from GE varied from store to store, but was often about fifty cents. This lightbulb typically had a useful life of six months. A Philips DuraMax lightbulb with the light output of a sixty-watt bulb would also cost approximately fifty cents, yet it would have a life of one year. A Philips Halogena lightbulb with the light output of a sixty-watt lightbulb would have a two-year life and would cost about four dollars. The Philips Marathon lightbulb with the light output of a sixty-watt bulb would have a life of five years and would sell for approximately nine dollars.

There was a substantial additional hidden savings with Philips Marathon lightbulbs. Over the five-year life of this lightbulb, the owner would save approximately thirty-five dollars in electricity costs. Naturally this would vary depending on where the consumer lived. The financial comparison with a sixty-watt GE lightbulb is very interesting. Over five years the consumer would have paid approximately five dollars for ten GE lightbulbs with a six-month life each. Over the same five years, the consumer would have paid nine dollars for a single Philips Marathon bulb, or an extra four dollars. However, the consumer would have saved thirty-five dollars in electricity costs, for a net profit of thirty-one dollars.

The Advertising Message Was "Light Bulbs That Last"

To introduce consumers to the new Philips long-life strategy, an advertising campaign called "light bulbs that last" was created. Philips's advertising agency came up with a number of humorous television and radio commercials and magazine advertisements depicting situations in which a lightbulb had burned out. These advertisements were run in eight- to ten-week flights on introduction, and then periodically for about two years. The campaign was successful and won numerous advertising industry awards.

The Halogena television commercial showed a young man on a ladder that he had made out of a couch and a chair. His friend walked into the room and explained to him that if he replaced that lightbulb with a Halogena bulb, he would not have to go back up on that ladder for two years—guaranteed. This advertisement was quite humorous and emphasized the two-year guarantee.

The Marathon television advertisements talked about the five-year guarantee. One commercial opens on an empty room from the vantage point of a ceiling lamp. Then you see a young man arriving at college, accompanied by his parents. They're carrying moving boxes. Next, you see the family walk into the empty dorm room. The overhead light is flicked on, and the bulb burns out. The father pulls a Philips Marathon bulb out of its box and screws this new bulb into the lamp fixture. As the commercial develops, you see the young man studying, at a sports victory party, playing his guitar, and slow dancing—always from the vantage point of the bulb. Finally, you see him on graduation day in his empty dorm room, unscrewing the bulb to take it with him. The copy says, "He finished up in four . . . the bulb is on the five-year plan. The Marathon bulb by Philips."

As a second Marathon television commercial opens, you see a man in his mid-thirties climbing up a scenic mountain trail. He arrives at a rustic cabin at dusk. He then goes to turn on the overhead light and the bulb burns out. He is noticeably displeased. The man then checks a message on an old answering machine and sets down his old manual typewriter. During the commercial, he is directed by the phone message to various storage areas to check on amazing quantities of supplies.

> "Hi, it's Gayle. Hope you found the place OK.
> Use the cabin for as long as it takes to finish the book.
> You'll find plenty of toilet paper in the closet . . .
> 400 pounds of dried beef in the cellar . . .
> loads of canned goods in the pantry . . . that should do it.
> Oh, yeah, there's a five-year supply of light bulbs in the top left drawer.
> Call me.

It's getting a bit darker as time goes by, and the man is visibly concerned about the lack of light inside. Finally, when he is directed to the drawer in the kitchen, you see one bulb. Eventually light is restored to the cabin, and all is well. A voice-over says: "The Marathon bulb by Philips. Good for five years. Guaranteed. That should be long enough. Philips. Light bulbs that last."

Philips Halogena Light Bulbs Tied Into Times Square Publicity

In addition to advertising, the Philips long-life lightbulb strategy was the basis of a highly successful public relations campaign. The campaign centered around Philips Halogena lightbulbs. When Philips heard that a new ball was being created for the Times Square New Year's Eve celebration in New York City, it called the organization responsible and offered to work with that organization on including Halogena bulbs. The result was that Halogena became the official Times Square lightbulb for five years, including the huge millennium celebration. This formed the basis of the public relations campaign.

Philips began the campaign with a press conference, then implemented a broad national publicity tour. The most watched event of the millennium New Year's celebration was the dropping of the ball in Times Square. Because of its use for this, Halogena lightbulbs were broadly publicized in print and on television, including the *Today* show. The end result was a three-inch book full of press clippings. Retailers also participated in the event. Home Depot, for example, provided an end aisle display of Halogena lightbulbs for the six weeks surrounding New Year's Eve. All of this resulted in the sale of a lot of Halogena lightbulbs.

Individual In-Store Merchandising Done for Retailers

Philips worked with each retailer to help that retailer customize the in-store displays for its light bulbs. A lot of retailers were very conscious of the look of their stores, and they wanted manufacturers to work within their framework. In most categories, things were done on an individual basis. For example, Philips found that Wegmans and Walgreens had very different requirements, and special solutions had to be developed for each of these important chains.

Home Depot had a whole wall of lightbulbs, and Philips provided the chain with a detailed plan-o-gram and recommendations to help it help its customers to find what they needed quickly. For example, Philips suggested educational materials to quickly direct people to the right lightbulbs. Philips provided signs and operating samples of products.

Philips also provided occasional off-shelf displays. The company suggested that the best way to sell some of these lightbulbs was to cross-merchandise them with other products. For example, if the retailer was selling fixtures, it was told that it should sell lightbulbs with them. Retailers were told that if someone is buying a chandelier that needs decorative bulbs, the right bulbs should be next to the chandeliers. There were also several other places within the store where lighting products could be cross-merchandised with whatever the retailer was selling.

All Philips Long-Life Lightbulbs Were Guaranteed

If a lightbulb failed to last as long as Philips said it would last, the customer would be able to mail it back to Philips for a prompt refund. No questions would be asked. The customer would simply have to send the product back with a proof of purchase or register receipt. In sum, Philips was not only saying that the light bulbs would last one, two, five, or seven years, but also guaranteeing it.

It took a little effort to sell this extensive guarantee policy internally at Philips. Everybody finally agreed, however, that if the company really believed in the product, it should stand behind it. This seems to have been the right strategy at the right time. Consumers and retailers liked the idea of a guaranteed life. At this point, Philips has seen only a handful of returns come in on a daily basis, which is very small compared to how many lightbulbs it sells.

Detailed Financial Projections Were Prepared for Management Approval

A detailed financial plan was created for the overall long-life strategy. Documentation on all of the planned expenditures and expected sales was presented to senior Philips management for approval prior to launching the program. These documents were then updated from time to time as the plan unfolded. Thus far the numbers on Marathon and Halogena are holding as planned. Consumers are definitely trading up to these premium products in large numbers. DuraMax was only launched in 2001, which is too recent to make a final judgment on its success, but it looks very good so far.

No Competitive Reactions to Long-Life Strategy Expected

Philips's largest competitor is the General Electric Company. Philips does not believe that GE will come out with a major effort on long-life lightbulbs.

Philips believes that GE would hurt itself if it focused on long life because it would shrink the incandescent market, of which it has an enormous market share. Philips feels that GE is likely to react by providing something other than long life, leaving the long-life niche to Philips.

Wrap Your Marketing Strategy Around Benefits Your Customers Want

The main lesson to be learned from the success of Philips's long-life light-bulbs is to pay attention to the needs of your customers. This applies to both the consumer and the retailer. It is easy to simply look inside your company for the answers. Philips succeeded because it did a lot of consumer and trade research right at the beginning of this marketing effort. It found out what was really important to its customers regarding its product category. It identified what benefits its customers wanted, then provided those benefits and wrapped an entire marketing program around them. The results were very successful.

> *Summary Marketing Plan for:*
> Philips Long-Life Lightbulbs
> Philips Lighting Company[1]
> 2001

MARKETING PLAN SUMMARY

1. **BACKGROUND.** In 1998 the management of Philips Lighting Company decided to try to make a significant impact on the consumer lightbulb market. It began this effort by doing some serious market research to see what was really important to consumers of lightbulbs. The results of this market research clearly indicated that long life was the most important feature that consumers would like to have in a lightbulb. Philips, therefore, decided to provide the consumer with long-life lightbulbs and at the same time take away the consumer confusion concerning this category. It would do this by offering a series of new long-life lightbulbs. As of this writing, Philips has become the only company whose whole consumer line is long life. It has become the long-life company.

2. **MARKET REVIEW.** The consumer market for incandescent light bulbs has five retail distribution segments: grocery stores, hardware and home center stores, mass merchandisers, drugstores, and a category labeled "other." GE was the dominant player in the grocery chains and mass merchandisers. Philips was the dominant player in home centers because Philips was the primary supplier of lightbulbs to Home Depot, which sold 20 percent of all the lightbulbs sold in the United States. Sylvania was number three among the major brands. The other factor was private label. Some retailers were selling lightbulbs imported from the Far East under their own private label. Some imported lightbulbs were also being sold under the Westinghouse brand name, which was licensed from Viacom (the owner of the trademark).

3. **CONSUMER USAGE AND ATTITUDES.** Consumer focus groups revealed that a typical consumer perception was that lightbulbs burn out too soon. Consumers wanted long-life light-

---

[1] The long-life lightbulbs Philips Marathon, Philips Halogena, and Philips DuraMax are trademarks of Philips Lighting Company, and are used with permission.

bulbs, but they thought that current claims of long life were not believable. They felt that a better lightbulb would be one that lasted longer, and that this was the only benefit that would be worth a premium. Many respondents also felt that a guarantee would add credibility to claims of long life. Many of the consumers included in this research felt that a full line of long-life lightbulbs would be more credible than one new long-life lightbulb. Respondents liked the full-line concept because they would be able to choose the ideal lightbulb type for different locations.

4. **PLANNING ASSUMPTIONS.** Philips decided to proceed with the launching of a major strategic effort to transform itself into the "long-life company." The following are Philip's key planning assumptions:

   A. A long-life strategy would effectively differentiate Philips's lightbulbs from those of the competition.

   B. Consumers would buy into the long-life lightbulb idea.

   C. The long-life strategy would help Philips's retailers compete with their competitors.

   D. Premium pricing on a line of superior products would be acceptable to retailers and consumers.

   E. Philips's engineering department had identified the proper line between life and light.

5. **KEY STRATEGIC MARKETING OBJECTIVES.** Based on these assumptions, the new marketing plan had two primary objectives. First, Philips would introduce a series of lines of long-life lightbulbs that would be significantly different from the lightbulbs offered by the competition. Second, because they were superior, these new product lines would be sold at premium prices, which would generate higher margins for Philips and for Philips's retail partners.

6. **MARKETING PLAN ELEMENTS.**

   A. *Brand names.* The new corporate long-life strategy included three brand names. Philips Marathon was the name used for the longest-lasting or "best" lightbulbs (guaranteed for five to seven years), Philips Halogena was the name used for the second-longest-lasting or "better" line of lightbulbs (guaranteed for two years), and Philips DuraMax was used for the entry-level or "good" line of lightbulbs (guaranteed for one year).

   B. *Product line.* The challenge at Philips was to develop an incandescent lightbulb that would last at least one year. This would be the "good" lightbulb. Philips then added halogen technology to create a "better" lightbulb, with a two-year life. Finally, Philips used fluorescent technology to create the "best" lightbulb, with a life of between five and seven years. Management felt that this would take Philips lightbulbs out of the commodity class and make them products with real value-added qualities.

C. *Packaging.* On the new packaging Philips designed, wattage was the most prominent number, and how long the light bulbs last was the second most prominent number. Philips felt that consumers could not relate to life represented in hours, so it stated the life in years. It also gave the guarantee on the packaging: The lightbulbs were guaranteed for one year, two years, five years, or seven years. Finally, the packaging visually showed the consumer the shape of the lightbulb and where it should go in the home. The idea was to simplify the shopping process.

D. *Pricing strategy.* A Philips DuraMax lightbulb with the light output of a sixty-watt bulb would cost approximately fifty cents, yet would have a one-year life versus a six-month life for GE lightbulbs. A Philips Halogena lightbulb with the light output of a sixty-watt lightbulb would have a two-year life and would cost about four dollars. The Philips Marathon lightbulb with the light output of a sixty-watt bulb would have a life of five years and would sell for approximately nine dollars. There was a substantial additional hidden savings with Philips Marathon lightbulbs. Over the five-year life of this light bulb, the owner would save approximately thirty-five dollars in electricity costs.

E. *Sales and distribution methods.* Philips's factories generally shipped lightbulbs from the factory warehouse to a Philips combination warehouse, where all of the different types of lightbulbs were brought together. The retailer's regional depot orders would come into these facilities, and the products ordered would go to the retailer's regional warehouses. The retailer would then generally distribute the lightbulbs to the stores. However, there were some exceptions where Philips would ship directly from its combination warehouse to a retail store.

F. *Advertising strategy.* To introduce consumers to the new Philips long-life strategy, an advertising campaign called "light bulbs that last" was created. Philips's advertising agency came up with a number of humorous television and radio commercials and magazine advertisements depicting situations in which a light bulb had burned out. These advertisements were run in eight- to ten-week flights on introduction, and then periodically for about two years.

G. *Publicity.* In addition to advertising, the Philips long-life lightbulb strategy was the basis for a highly successful public relations campaign. The campaign centered around Philips

Halogena lightbulbs. Halogena became the official Times Square lightbulbs for five years, including the huge millennium celebration. The most watched event of the millennium New Year's celebration was the dropping of the ball in Times Square. Because of its use for this, Halogena light bulbs were broadly publicized in print and on television, including the *Today* show. Retailers also participated in the event. Home Depot, for example, provided an end-aisle display of Halogena lightbulbs for the six weeks surrounding New Year's Eve.

H. *In-store merchandising.* Philips worked with each retailer to help that retailer customize the in-store displays for its lightbulbs. Home Depot, for example, had a whole wall of lightbulbs, and Philips provided the chain a detailed plan-o-gram and recommendations to help it help its customers to find what they needed quickly. Philips provided signs and operating samples of products. Philips also provided occasional off-shelf displays. The company suggested that the best way to sell some of these lightbulbs was to cross-merchandise them with other products. For example, if the retailer was selling fixtures, it was told that it should sell lightbulbs with them.

I. *Product warranties.* All Philips long-life lightbulbs were guaranteed. If a lightbulb failed to last as long as Philips said it would last, the customer would be able to mail it back to Philips for a prompt refund. No questions would be asked. The customer would simply have to send the product back with a proof of purchase or register receipt. In sum, Philips was not only saying that the light bulbs would last one, two, five, or seven years, but also guaranteeing it.

7. **FINANCIAL PROJECTIONS.** A detailed financial plan was created for the overall long-life strategy. Documentation on all of the planned expenditures and expected sales was presented to senior Philips management for approval prior to launching the program. These documents were then updated from time to time as the plan unfolded. Thus far, the numbers on Marathon and Halogena are holding as planned. DuraMax was only launched in 2001, which is too recent to make a final judgment on its success.

8. **CONTINGENCY PLANS.** Philips's largest competitor is the General Electric Company. Philips does not believe that GE will come out with a major effort on long-life lightbulbs. Philips believes that GE would hurt itself if it focused on long life because it would shrink the incandescent market, of which it has an enormous market share. Philips feels that GE is likely to react by providing something other than long life, leaving the long-life niche to Philips.

CHAPTER 4

Consumer and Retailer Convenience Is Critical

Example: L'eggs® Hosiery

In today's world, convenience is more important than ever. People want it to be easy to buy a new product and to return it if something goes wrong. It's not that we have become lazy; it is just that marketers have spoiled us in many ways by making it very easy to buy their products and services. It is easy to fall in love with your own inventions. The temptation is to think that what you have developed is so great that everyone will want it, no matter how hard it is to find or buy. Don't you believe it. People have a lot of options, and they will not do business with you unless you make it very easy for them.

The importance of convenience is paramount from a trade as well as a consumer standpoint. When you are selling in retail stores, you must make it easy for retailers to carry your product. You must then make it easy for the consumer to buy from those retailers. If you are selling directly to end users, you must also make it easy for them to buy from you.

In the fall of 1969, the Hanes Corporation completed a historic marketing plan covering the selling of women's hosiery products in supermarkets and drugstores. The strategy was to make it easy for women to buy hosiery by selling this high-volume product in these conveniently located stores. There were no major brands of hosiery in the supermarket and drugstore channels at the time. These stores sold only private-label or unbranded hosiery. No brand had more than a 4 percent share, and pricing was the main form of competition. In short, the keystone of the strategy was convenience. This was to be the only widely available, premium-priced, heavily advertised brand of hosiery in these stores.

This new brand of one-size stretch stockings and pantyhose became so successful that it has lasted more than thirty years and today is the largest-selling brand of pantyhose in the world. The brand is called L'eggs. The revolutionary marketing plan was based on the application of packaged goods marketing, sales, and distribution techniques to a degree that had not previously been attempted for women's hosiery. The marketing plan created such strong points of difference and benefits to the consumer and the trade that it skyrocketed to national prominence. Its success proved the critical importance of consumer and retailer convenience.

L'eggs Began with a Series of Exploratory Research Projects

The L'eggs venture began in May 1969 with the implementation of a series of research projects designed to identify the supermarket and drugstore opportunity for hosiery products. Hanes had no experience with the food and drug distribution channels, and there were many questions that it had to answer before it proceeded with a venture of this magnitude—questions like: Who is the hosiery consumer in these channels? How does this differ between pantyhose purchasers and purchasers of stockings? What are the attitudes, opinions, and beliefs about hosiery as they relate to the supermarket and drugstore? Is selling hosiery through the supermarket a viable concept? To whom should advertising be directed? What should the advertising say?

The research began with a national profile study of the hosiery market throughout the United States. This was coupled with a series of store checks conducted in supermarkets and drugstores in key markets throughout the country. Key retail accounts were called on for the purpose of obtaining information on current hosiery programs, uncovering problems and opportunities, and informing them that a new unit of the Hanes Corporation was thinking about an entry into that market. No selling or soliciting of accounts was done at that time. Finally, focus groups were conducted with supermarket and drugstore shoppers to obtain their attitudes toward hosiery sold in food stores and drugstores.

A Market Without a Major Brand

The national profile study of the hosiery market showed that total retail hosiery sales in 1970 were expected to be $1.7 billion and 144 million dozen units. Food stores were expected to account for 18 percent of the units, and drugstores were expected to account for 10 percent of the units. Private-label and unbranded merchandise dominated the food and drug outlets. No hosiery brand had more than a 4 percent share, and pricing was the main form of competition. There was no price/value relationship in food and drug-store hosiery because the quality varied from package to package. Unlike almost every other line of merchandise sold in supermarkets, hosiery had no widely available, premium-priced brand that could serve as the reference point against which other products are compared.

Consumers Liked the Idea of a Major Food and Drug Brand

During the focus groups, many women said that their experience with super-market hosiery purchases had been that they'd had problems with fit or had not been able to get the color they wanted. Most said that they would like to have a supermarket hosiery brand that they could believe in, as they do with so many other things they buy in these stores. They would even like to hear advertising for a brand of hosiery that was available everywhere, that fit well, and that was premium quality but did not cost too much. They felt that no brand existed that filled that bill.

Thus, the research indicated that women wanted a supermarket brand that would eliminate the confusion and lack of confidence that they felt concerning the current wide variety of hosiery offerings in these outlets. They especially liked the convenience of being able to buy such a brand in super-markets.

The consumer research also identified fit as the most important need in the marketplace for pantyhose. Women wanted pantyhose that fit well. A good fit that would last for the life of the hosiery was the standard that most of the focus group respondents indicated for their hosiery. However annoying a run may be, hosiery that never looks or feels right was considered even more of a problem.

Distribution Would Require Extreme Retailer Convenience

The initial trade meetings were positive. The in-depth discussions with personnel from major supermarkets and drug chains indicated strong receptivity to the idea. They could see a need for a heavily advertised and promoted national brand of pantyhose that would be sold in supermarkets and drugstores. Retailers widely felt that a national brand would result in incremental sales for their stores by broadening the consumer market to include planned purchases as well as the impulse sales they were already getting. Most felt that it would be an increase in business that would be added to the already growing private-label sector.

However, these meetings also identified a major barrier to obtaining broad-scale distribution for L'eggs in supermarkets. Most of these merchandisers felt that their existing programs of selling private-label or unbranded hosiery were very costly as a result of overhead expenses such as inventory financing, fixtures, warehousing, distribution, out-of-stocks, and in-store housekeeping. If Hanes required them to incur these same costs in selling L'eggs, distribution would be very limited.

Another obstacle to successfully marketing a hosiery brand in supermarkets was service. These retailers were not looking forward to servicing a new brand on top of their own private-label or unbranded programs. One of the keys to obtaining broad-scale distribution, therefore, was to make it very easy for retailers to do business with Hanes. This indicated that what was needed was a full-service hosiery program that would require little or no risk or maintenance cost on the part of retailers, and that would therefore overcome the main obstacle to marketing branded hosiery profitably through these outlets.

The Research Resulted in a Series of Ambitious Objectives

Hanes management decided that there was an unusually good opportunity to create a dynamic, profitable, and timely new business for the company in the growing food and drug portion of the women's hosiery market. It also believed that there was an opportunity to establish a consumer brand franchise that would give this new business a position of permanency, sales dominance, and long-run profitability.

The overall strategy was to market this new brand as a packaged goods product, employing the same techniques that are typically used with other major branded items sold in supermarkets and drugstores. This was quite different from the strategy used for most other products in the textile industry at that time. The strategy included maintenance of true brand identity by delivering products of consistent quality. It also included heavy consumer advertising to communicate a single-minded story and the use of proven consumer promotion techniques.

A Harmonious Image Was Created Through the Name, Package, and Display

The new supermarket and drugstore hosiery venture was named L'eggs. One of the reasons that the name L'eggs was selected from a list of alternatives was that it worked well with a packaging concept that looked like an egg. The name also made interesting use of language by combining the word *egg* (which referred to the packaging) and the word *leg* (which was what the product was for). The package was to be preemptive to separate L'eggs from its low-quality competition.

The display, by its unique design, was to provide L'eggs with a distinctive and permanent presence at retail and to preclude intermingling L'eggs with other hosiery products. Both the package and the display were also designed with practical considerations in mind, such as nonpilferability and easy selection. The "egg" package and the distinctive L'eggs display were to communicate the brand's newness, quality, and permanence.

The L'eggs name/package/display combination made this new venture stand out in supermarkets and drugstores. In most cases, you could tell whether a store carried L'eggs even before you got out of the car. You could see the tall display from the parking lot, through the front window of the store. The display with the egg-shaped packages was featured in all the advertising and other consumer communications, so that after seeing the advertising, the consumer would have no problem finding the new product.

A Wrinkled and Strange-Looking Product

The original strategy was to market a compact line of women's one-size products in two styles (stockings and pantyhose). Hanes felt that this would avoid multiproduct confusion during the introduction of the program. There was to be consistent product quality, with all products delivering a single primary consumer benefit—good fit.

When they were originally introduced, L'eggs were offered in five colors: Suntan, Nude, Taupe, Coffee, and Off Black. These were considered the basic colors that were most in demand by supermarket and drugstore hosiery shoppers. The strategy was to keep the number of colors small, but to choose the most appealing shade from each of the most popular color families.

The term *Super Stretch* was coined to describe the L'eggs yarn because of the garment's ability to provide good fit retention at both the low and high ends of the height scale. These hosiery products would not bag or sag if worn properly. With this yarn, the L'eggs brand could meet the criteria of providing garments of consistent quality that delivered the promised benefit of good fit, as well as comfort and attractiveness.

Focus group research indicated that the wrinkled and strange look of the L'eggs garments when they were off the leg would not prove to be in any way an obstacle to consumer acceptance. Based on the focus group concept statements, consumers felt that the L'eggs brand would deliver its promised fit benefit and other promised attributes. The benefits included in the concept statement were fit, comfort, good sheerness or appearance on the leg, good colors, convenience, and durability. All of these were considered important by purchasers of mass-appeal, moderately priced hosiery.

Pricing Represented a Good Deal for Consumers and Retailers

Pricing was a very important part of the original marketing mix. The original price points represented a good deal for the consumer. These prices were in the average price range for supermarkets and drugstores, making L'eggs an excellent price/value product compared to the variable-quality hosiery products offered in these stores. Consignment terms were offered to retailers, and this was felt to be a critical factor in obtaining broad-scale distribution.

An Offer the Trade Couldn't Refuse

Service was identified as the main obstacle to the successful marketing of a hosiery brand in supermarkets. Most retailers were unwilling to service a new brand of hosiery. Therefore, Hanes designed the L'eggs distribution system so that there would be no risk and no investment for retailers. This eliminated the barriers identified during meetings with retailers and gave L'eggs maximum exposure to consumers.

A unique system of direct store delivery that was completely controlled by the L'eggs organization was developed. The inventory was totally on consignment. The display fixtures for the hosiery were provided by L'eggs, and L'eggs sales merchandisers serviced the display. This made it possible for L'eggs to tailor the inventory to individual stores' needs. The net result was pure profit for the retailers, without the costs of inventory, warehousing, display housekeeping, or out-of-stocks.

The store manager of an independent supermarket provided an interesting description of his first encounter with the L'eggs program during the time it was being introduced. He described standing in the front of his store on a sunny Tuesday morning, looking out the window into the parking lot. He noticed a new white van pull up, from which a L'eggs sales merchandiser jumped out. Wearing a smart L'eggs uniform, she burst into his store with a great big smile and a lot of enthusiasm. She explained to him that she had a tremendous offer to discuss with him and would like five minutes of his time.

When he said OK, the woman spread out a white scarf on the floor. It took up about two square feet of floor space. "Here is the deal," she said in an excited voice. "I would like you to give me this much space in your store. I will bring in an attractive L'eggs display full of hosiery. You will soon be seeing a lot of advertising for L'eggs on television. Over half of your customers will be given coupons for discounts on L'eggs. I will ask you to pay me nothing. After a week or so, I will come back and refill the display. You will pay me only for what you have sold. If at any time you decide you do not like the program, I will remove the display."

The store manager was impressed. This was an easy proposition to accept. He would be able to take on a major new brand of hosiery that would be supported by heavy advertising and promotion. He would not have to make any room on his shelves, because a freestanding display would be provided. Not only that, the whole thing would cost him nothing. He would pay only for what he had sold—after he had collected the money. He would not even have to restock the shelves, because the L'eggs sales merchandiser would do it for him. No wonder he thought this was an offer he could not refuse.

All Advertising Announced "Our L'eggs Fit Your Legs"

The primary objective of the initial L'eggs advertising was to convince women that L'eggs was the best-fitting hosiery they could buy. A single line was developed that summed up the entire L'eggs position. This line was intended to create permanent brand registration in the minds of consumers by inextricably tying the product and its name together. That line was: "Our L'eggs fit your legs." This statement was to play a prominent part in every piece of L'eggs copy.

This main copy line was clarified with the statement: "Our L'eggs hug you, they hold you, they never let you go." The advertising assured consumers that L'eggs would never bag at the knees or sag at the ankles. They were told that L'eggs would "Do whatever you do." This tight focus on the legs on the verbal level was enhanced and given further impetus by the visuals. In the commercials, attractive female limbs were the constant focal point of the product story. L'eggs and legs were always seen together.

During the introduction, the advertising also made a special point of informing women that L'eggs was a supermarket and drugstore product. Both the unique supermarket display and the unusual package were featured. TV commercials were set in supermarkets, and the display was clearly depicted in every piece of magazine and newspaper advertising.

The pool of introductory TV commercials included one commercial designed specifically to announce the arrival of L'eggs. The opening line,

"L'eggs are here," was created to give the consumer a feeling of newsworthy mass excitement. The video showed a host of women shoppers rushing to the L'eggs boutique as the L'eggs lyrics and score announced the new arrival in a cheerful, contemporary musical arrangement. A variety of women demonstrated the product and how L'eggs solved their particular individual problems.

Television Was the Primary Medium Used to Introduce L'eggs

To promote L'eggs during the introduction, a great deal of television advertising was done, along with some print advertisements to support the television ads. This advertising was front-end-loaded, with the largest portion of the advertising dollars being spent during the first few weeks of the introduction. Because the program was rolled out eleven different times in different regions, the heaviest advertising was done in only one region at a time.

The L'eggs media plans were designed to reach a large percentage of the target audience often enough to create a meaningful awareness of the L'eggs name, program, and benefits. In executing the strategy, television was selected as the basic medium because of its ability to reach a broad segment of the target audience. In addition, television provided the opportunity to demonstrate L'eggs's important product benefits visually.

Print was used both to increase reach and frequency and because of its visual properties. Daily newspapers were added during the introductory stages of the program to provide immediate impact and news value in an environment that was especially suited to supermarket and drugstore retail advertising.

Trial Was Stimulated by Coupons

The main thrust of the original consumer promotion was to achieve trial and retrial by women in the target audience as broadly and as deeply as possible at a reasonable cost per woman. This was primarily done through the use of high-value coupons.

The promotion plan consisted of sending high-value direct-mail store coupons to 50 percent of the target households four to six weeks after the start of the advertising. Somewhat lower-value coupons were mailed to these households approximately six months later for a sustaining promotion. The company's ownership of inventory, direct store delivery, and service precluded the need for trade promotion and "dealing."

L'eggs Made It Convenient for the Consumer to Find the Product

One of the things that Hanes determined during interviews with retail executives was that the best way to achieve broad-scale distribution on L'eggs would be to merchandise the product on a freestanding display. The result was a display unit that tied the entire merchandising program together. The original L'eggs display was a tall, round unit that took up about two square feet of floor space. It was designed in such a way that it would hold only the L'eggs egg-shaped packaging. It was so tall that it was typically visible from all over the store, regardless of where it was placed. It was so narrow that most retailers found it easy to make room for.

The L'eggs display was designed as the final link in the name/package/display entity, providing a distinctiveness and uniqueness that would immediately set L'eggs apart from the jungle of other hosiery products. The display was also designed to provide a proprietary home that could not be encroached upon by other brands. The objective was for L'eggs to be placed in key traffic locations where it could be instantly identified by the majority of customers who shopped in the store.

This display strategy was intended to provide L'eggs with a powerful advantage. Most brands in any category work diligently to achieve such an impact for brief periods of time, but they rarely succeed. The L'eggs goal was to achieve this high-impact, off-shelf presence on a permanent basis.

Publicity Was Used to Help Spread the Word

During the introduction of L'eggs, a traveling spokeswoman was used to discuss the L'eggs product and program with the media. The publicity program entailed personal appearances on television and radio plus selected interviews with key newspapers in each area. The introductory publicity program also included a contest for the most creative and/or humorous secondary use of the L'eggs egg, with the winners and winning ideas publicized in the local media.

Test Marketing Proved the Viability of the L'eggs Program

The L'eggs program was tested in four medium-sized U.S. cities. A high-level plan was tested in Milwaukee, Wisconsin, and in Sacramento, California. A low-level plan was tested in Kansas City, Missouri, and in Portland, Oregon. The four markets covered approximately 3.6 percent of all U.S. television households. These markets were selected to be representative of the total United States. They had sufficient sales to allow national projections. They had a typical media structure. They represented the national average in terms of receptivity to new product introductions. They also had an ethnic and economic balance. Finally, they were ideal from a distribution standpoint. These markets were controlled by relatively few retail chains, which lessened sell-in burdens.

L'eggs was test-marketed for seven months. In the test markets, the program was far more successful than originally anticipated with both the high-level and the low-level spending plans. The results, in terms of high trial, repeat sales rates, and overall consumer satisfaction, demonstrated that the opportunity had been accurately assessed. There was room for a carefully developed new hosiery program of this type. Test marketing began in January 1970, leading to a June decision on the first regional rollout, which took place in the fall.

No Significant Competition Was Expected

L'eggs made the assumption that no viable competitors would enter the market. If competition did appear in one or more of the rollout markets planned for L'eggs, the company had some flexibility to change the sequence of the rollout markets. This and other alternatives were to be considered only after careful evaluation of the competitive effort to assess its real potential impact on L'eggs.

In the test markets, L'eggs remained the only heavily advertised brand of hosiery with broad distribution in the food and drug outlets. The competition that did appear was in isolated markets only and generally was restricted to price cutting. In one market, one brand did a significant amount of newspaper advertising offering a twenty-five-cent coupon. In another market, a competitive brand slightly increased its television and newspaper advertising after L'eggs entered the market. None of this had any significant impact on the L'eggs brand during the test market period.

The L'eggs Investment Eventually Exceeded All of Its Financial Objectives

Because of capacity considerations and the unusual sales/distribution program, with its requirements for personnel and training, L'eggs had to expand region by region and required approximately three years to become fully national. The anticipated start-up costs and gradual buildup of distribution and consumer acceptance prevented L'eggs from achieving a profit during its expansion phase. However, the program became highly profitable in the fourth year. The actual financial results exceeded all anticipations, as L'eggs became the dominant brand of hosiery in the food and drug trade in every market it entered.

Thirty Years Later, the Market Has Changed

In 1969, when the original L'eggs marketing plan was being written, the market environment was ideal for the launching of a major new brand of pantyhose in supermarkets and drugstores. One of the biggest fashion trends of the times was the miniskirt, which made pantyhose almost a necessity. In addition, large numbers of women were entering the workforce for the first time, and hosiery was considered part of proper working attire in that era. Finally, there was no major brand of pantyhose in the food and drug channels at that time, leaving a perfect void for L'eggs to fill.

In 2003, L'eggs was the largest brand of pantyhose in the world, with over 50 percent market share. However, L'eggs was operating in a far different market environment in the twenty-first century. The incidence of pantyhose usage among women was over 90 percent in 1969, but it had dropped to only about 60 percent in 2003. That is a drop of about a third of the user base. The primary reason for this decline in the pantyhose market was a shift from formal to casual clothing (i.e., pants) in the workplace that began in about 1992.

In 2003, the younger generation had not grown up with pantyhose as part of their everyday work uniform. The baby boomers who had been part of the explosion of the pantyhose market in the early 1970s were now beginning to retire and leave the workforce. The younger women who were taking their place were not buying a lot of pantyhose. The casual lifestyles of the new millennium led to a trend to the use of slacks, which did not require traditional pantyhose, or bare legs.

A Good Beginning and a Willingness to Change Were the Keys to Longevity

L'eggs is one of the few "new products" that has lasted over thirty years, and there are several reasons for this longevity. One of the main reasons is that L'eggs did such an excellent job of marketing when it was launched. The brand equity that was created through excellent positioning and promotion has carried over all these years. Many women still associate L'eggs with the original egg-shaped packaging, which they identify with the time in their lives when they started wearing the product. For these women, there is an emotional connection with the time when they were coming of age, were flooding into the workforce, and had high hopes for the future.

The other reason for L'eggs's longevity is a determination on the part of L'eggs management to provide a constant solution to women's problems and to change as conditions change. Over the years, L'eggs has been willing to do what it had to do to continue to bring customers to the L'eggs display and to be a good business partner with its retailers. This vision has resulted in many changes in packaging, distribution, and, importantly, the development of new products.

Maintaining a good partnership with retailers has been a very important part of L'eggs's continuing success. The sales and distribution portion of the original L'eggs marketing plan, which included consignment and direct store delivery, was continued for twenty years. About ten years ago, however, the needs of retailers began to change. Retailers' physical distribution systems became highly sophisticated, and they no longer needed direct store delivery. Rather than insisting on continuing to do things the same way, L'eggs had the flexibility to modify the L'eggs distribution plan to conform to the needs of its retailers.

To meet consumers' needs, L'eggs eventually discontinued the plastic egg-shaped packaging. This was a change that required a lot of thought and emotion, but L'eggs management knew that it would be better for the environment. The symbol of the egg shape was maintained on most of the L'eggs packaging, but the package itself was changed to a more environment-friendly material. The consumer understood. There is still a lot of affection for the original egg-shaped packaging, however, and to many L'eggs will always be connected to the egg.

Category management and in-line displays have replaced the original freestanding L'eggs towers to meet the changing needs of retailers and the growth of the L'eggs brand. Over the past thirty years, the L'eggs brand has grown to include many different subbrands. The number of products has also increased substantially, and large in-line displays had to be developed to hold them. In addition, supermarkets, drugstores, and mass merchants required help in managing the large variety of hosiery business that L'eggs brought to their stores. L'eggs responded by developing a sophisticated category management system for these retailers.

New Products Became a Major Focus for L'eggs

In the 1990s, L'eggs realized that consumer needs were dramatically changing and that the key to maintaining L'eggs's leadership position would be product innovation. L'eggs management made a commitment to identifying the rapidly changing needs of its consumers, and to bringing new products to the market to meet these needs. The plan was to create a stream of new products to bring to retailers, and to constantly give consumers a new reason to visit the in-store display. Today innovation is driving the L'eggs business. L'eggs introduces several new products each year, and almost a fourth of L'eggs's sales are from new products.

System Established to Monitor Consumer Needs

A system has been put in place by L'eggs management to monitor the constantly changing needs of the American hosiery consumer. This system of qualitative and quantitative market research is used to keep track of attitudes toward existing L'eggs products and programs as well as to identify and test new products. L'eggs has become one of the most sophisticated textile manufacturers in its use of packaged goods research techniques.

A good example of how L'eggs uses market research to identify and satisfy consumer needs was the process that the company recently used to create anticellulite pantyhose. This is a product that visibly reduces the appearance of cellulite, something that most women find to be a concern. If they wear these unique pantyhose five days a week, eight hours a day, many users will notice results after just four weeks. Lasting effects require continued use of the product. The pantyhose contain microbeads that produce the results and remain effective through five washings. Even after the beads are no longer effective, however, the user still has a great pair of pantyhose.

The development of the anticellulite pantyhose product began with a series of brainstorming focus group sessions with consumers. A broad number of ideas emerged from these sessions. Respondents talked about aromatherapy capsules. They talked about perfumes. They suggested anti-varicose vein treatments. They even suggested pantyhose that would deliver a low dosage of drugs like aspirin or medications to help them stop smoking. One idea, however, reappeared in every session: anticellulite. This benefit was always number one, but respondents had a lot of trouble believing that a pantyhose could provide it.

During the next step, the L'eggs marketing department developed a series of concept statements about the anticellulite pantyhose idea to get the right language. Focus group respondents were so skeptical that L'eggs was concerned about being able to create a description that would get consumers over the hurdle of believability. A lot more focus groups were conducted with these concept statements to determine what should be put on the package to get consumers to fully understand the benefit. The winning description of anticellulite pantyhose emerged from these additional focus groups.

Microencapsulation technology was available to L'eggs from one of

L'eggs's sister companies. Using this technology, L'eggs created a prototype product with which to conduct two important tests. The first was a clinical trial, with clinical measurements, for twelve weeks to make sure that the anticellulite pantyhose actually worked. The second was in-home placements to measure consumer satisfaction after actually using the product. The prototype anticellulite pantyhose were placed in a total of 252 homes for three to four months. The results of both of these trials were very successful. Over 50 percent of the women who tried the product noticed a visible reduction in the appearance of cellulite. Based on these results, the new product was born.

The Vision Is to Continue to Be a Solution Brand

If there is one word that describes L'eggs's current vision, it is *innovation*. The current L'eggs organization is dedicated to keeping the brand fresh and vital to the interests of its consumers and retailers. Using the system it has established to monitor consumer needs, the company now introduces several new products each year. There are several subbrands under the L'eggs umbrella, and the brand managers for each of these brands are continuously working on the development of fun, affordable, contemporary new products that are very convenient.

All of the new L'eggs products are created to meet the timely needs of hosiery consumers. L'eggs Care® anticellulite pantyhose were created because more than 95 percent of the women surveyed said that they were interested in reducing cellulite. Toeless pantyhose were created because many women said that they wanted to improve the appearance of their legs, but they also wanted to leave their toes exposed. Women said that they wanted a very sheer support pantyhose. To meet this need, Sheer Vitality® was developed as a subbrand of Sheer Energy®. This new product took Sheer Energy to a new level by providing the sheerest Sheer Energy ever.

No-Hose pantyhose is another example of innovation. L'eggs Body Beautiful™ No-Hose™ was created to capitalize on an unmet consumer need. It has body-shaping and smoothing benefits that are delivered with such comfort that consumers can wear Body Beautiful all day, every day. A true evolution of hosiery, Body Beautiful captured the attention of younger ethnic women, bringing the L'eggs name to a new generation of consumers while giving current consumers another reason to love the L'eggs brand.

Convenience and Flexibility Are the Lessons to be Learned from L'eggs

Convenience is a key characteristic that often separates the new products that are winners from those that are not. Whether you are looking at it from a trade or a consumer standpoint, the new product or service must be easy to buy. There are so many options available today that people are just not willing to go to a great deal of trouble to do business with you. You must make it easy for them.

From a trade standpoint, you must remove as many barriers to the purchase as possible. L'eggs went to the ultimate extreme of consigning the product, delivering the product, and guaranteeing the sale. In your new product venture, make sure that you have done everything you can to make your offer one that your retailers cannot refuse.

From a consumer standpoint, make your new product or service very easy to find. You have to recognize that consumers will not look very hard to find you. L'eggs did this with unique packaging and in-store displays. Think about what you can do to help your customer find your product. Help your customer through the purchase process as much as you can. Think about what you might do to help your customer during the most critical phases of the purchase cycle.

Whatever your category, you also must not lose sight of your consumers and their changing needs. Lifestyles are changing, and the consumer is constantly evolving. You have to keep on doing what you do well, but you also have to be willing to change and fine-tune as you move forward. Don't be afraid to innovate and improve your product. L'eggs was one of the most successful new products introduced in the twentieth century. In the 1990s, however, the company recognized that the lifestyles of its consumers were dramatically changing with the movement toward casual dress. It is still number one because it was willing to be flexible and develop innovative new products.

Finally, L'eggs teaches us that if you are to be really successful, you should not constrain your thinking in any way. You should be willing to look at every piece of the business model. L'eggs was not just a new product story. It was a business story that went into every element of the marketing mix. Every piece of the business model was challenged, thrown out the window, and then recreated. This included what the product was like, how the product was packaged and presented, where the product was sold, how the product was positioned to the retailer, and even how the product was delivered.

> *Summary Marketing Plan for:*
> L'eggs Hosiery
> Sara Lee Hosiery[1]
> 1969

MARKETING PLAN SUMMARY

1. **BACKGROUND.** In the fall of 1969, the Hanes Corporation completed a historic marketing plan covering the selling of women's hosiery products in supermarkets and drugstores. The strategy was to make it easy for women to buy hosiery by selling this high-volume product in these conveniently located stores. There were no major brands of hosiery in the supermarket and drugstore channels at that time. The new brand was called L'eggs, and it became so successful that it has lasted more than thirty years and today is the largest-selling brand of pantyhose in the world.

2. **MARKET REVIEW.** A national profile study of the hosiery market showed that total retail sales in 1970 were expected to be $1.7 billion. Food stores were expected to account for 18 percent of the units, and drugstores were expected to account for 10 percent of the units. Private-label and unbranded merchandise dominated the food and drug outlets. No hosiery brand had more than a 4 percent share, and pricing was the main form of competition. There was no price/value relationship in food and drugstore hosiery because the quality varied from package to package. Unlike almost every other line of merchandise sold in supermarkets, hosiery had no widely available, premium-priced brand that could serve as the reference point against which other products could be compared.

3. **CONSUMER USAGE AND ATTITUDES.** In focus groups, many women said that their experience with supermarket hosiery purchases had been that they'd had problems with fit or had not been able to get the color they wanted. The research indicated that women wanted to have a supermarket brand that they could believe in and that would eliminate the confusion and lack of confidence that they felt concerning the current wide variety of hosiery offerings

---

[1] The brand name *L'eggs* is a trademark of Sara Lee Hosiery, and is used with permission.

in these outlets. The consumer research also identified fit as the most important need in the marketplace for pantyhose. Women wanted pantyhose that fit well.

4. **TRADE PRACTICES AND ATTITUDES.** In-depth discussions with personnel from major supermarket and drug chains indicated strong receptivity to the idea of a heavily advertised and promoted national brand of pantyhose that would be sold in supermarkets and drugstores. However, two obstacles were identified. Retailers felt that the existing programs of selling private-label or unbranded hosiery were very costly as a result of overhead expenses such as inventory financing, fixtures, warehousing, distribution, out-of-stocks, and in-store housekeeping. Another obstacle was service. Retailers were not looking forward to servicing a new brand on top of their own private-label or unbranded programs. One of the keys to obtaining broad-scale distribution, therefore, was to make it very easy for retailers to do business with Hanes.

5. **KEY STRATEGIC MARKETING OBJECTIVES.** The overall strategy was to market this new brand as a packaged goods product, employing the same techniques that are typically used with other major branded items sold in supermarkets and drugstores. The strategy included maintenance of true brand identity by delivering products of consistent quality. It also included heavy consumer advertising to communicate a single-minded story and the use of proven consumer promotion techniques.

6. **MARKETING PLAN ELEMENTS**

   A. *Brand name.* The new supermarket and drugstore hosiery venture was named L'eggs. One of the reasons that the name L'eggs was selected from a list of alternatives was that it worked well with a packaging concept that looked like an egg. The name also made interesting use of language by combining the word *egg* (which referred to the packaging) and the word *leg* (which was what the product was for).

   B. *Product line.* The original strategy was to market a compact line of women's one-size products in two styles (stockings and pantyhose). Hanes felt that this would avoid multiproduct confusion during the introduction of the program. There would be consistent product quality, with all products delivering a single primary consumer benefit—good fit.

   C. *Packaging.* The package, which was shaped like an egg, was to be preemptive to separate L'eggs from its low-quality competition.

D. *Pricing strategy.* Pricing was a very important part of the original marketing mix. The original price points represented a good deal for the consumer. These prices were in the average price range for supermarkets and drugstores, making L'eggs an excellent price/value product compared to the variable-quality hosiery products offered in these stores. Consignment terms were offered to retailers, and this was felt to be a critical factor in obtaining broad-scale distribution.

E. *Sales and distribution methods.* A unique system of direct store delivery that was completely controlled by the L'eggs organization was developed. The inventory was totally on consignment. The display fixtures for the hosiery were provided by L'eggs, and L'eggs sales merchandisers serviced the display. This made it possible for L'eggs to tailor the inventory to individual stores' needs. The net result was pure profit for retailers, without the costs of inventory, warehousing, display housekeeping, or out-of-stocks.

F. *Advertising copy strategy.* The primary objective of the initial L'eggs advertising was to convince women that L'eggs was the best-fitting hosiery they could buy. A single line was developed that summed up the entire L'eggs position. This line was intended to create permanent brand registration in the minds of consumers by inextricably tying the product and its name together. That line was: "Our L'eggs fit your legs." This statement played a prominent part in every piece of L'eggs copy. During the introduction, the advertising also made a special point of informing women that L'eggs was a supermarket and drugstore product.

G. *Advertising media strategy.* Television was the primary medium used to introduce L'eggs, along with some print advertisements to support the television ads. This advertising was front-end-loaded, with the largest portion of the advertising dollars being spent during the first few weeks of the introduction. Television was selected as the basic medium because of its ability to reach a broad segment of the target audience. In addition, television provided the opportunity to demonstrate L'eggs's important product benefits visually. Print was used both to increase reach and frequency and because of its visual properties.

H. *Sales promotion.* The main thrust of the original consumer promotion was to achieve trial and retrial by women in the target audience as broadly and as deeply as possible at a reasonable cost per woman. This was primarily done through the use of high-value coupons. The promotion plan consisted of sending high-value direct-mail store coupons to 50 percent of the target households four to six weeks after the start of the advertising.

I.   *Publicity.* Publicity was used to help spread the word. During the introduction of L'eggs, a traveling spokeswoman was used to discuss the L'eggs product and program with the media. The publicity program entailed personal appearances on television and radio plus selected interviews with key newspapers in each area. The introductory publicity program also included a contest for the most creative and/or humorous secondary use of the L'eggs egg, with the winners and winning ideas publicized in the local media.

J.   *In-store merchandising.* The display was a tall tower that would hold only the new L'eggs packages. Its unique design was intended to provide L'eggs with a distinctive and permanent presence at retail and to preclude intermingling L'eggs with other hosiery products. The "egg" package and the distinctive L'eggs display communicated the brand's newness, quality, and permanence.

K.   *Test marketing.* The L'eggs program was tested in four medium-sized U.S. cities. A high-level plan was tested in Milwaukee, Wisconsin, and in Sacramento, California. A low-level plan was tested in Kansas City, Missouri, and in Portland, Oregon. The four markets covered approximately 3.6 percent of all U.S. television households. L'eggs was test marketed for seven months.

7. **FINANCIAL PROJECTIONS.** Because of capacity considerations and the unusual sales/distribution program, with its requirements for personnel and training, L'eggs had to expand region by region, and required approximately three years to become fully national. The anticipated start-up costs and gradual buildup of distribution and consumer acceptance prevented L'eggs from achieving a profit during its expansion phase. However, the program became highly profitable in the fourth year. The actual financial results exceeded all anticipations, as L'eggs became the dominant brand of hosiery in the food and drug trade in every market it entered.

8. **CONTINGENCY PLANS.** L'eggs made the assumption that no viable competitors would enter the market. If competition did appear in one or more of the rollout markets planned for L'eggs, the company had some flexibility to change the sequence of the rollout markets. This and other alternatives were to be considered only after careful evaluation of the competitive effort to assess its real potential impact on L'eggs.

CHAPTER 5

Effectiveness Leads to Repeat Purchases

Example: Zicam Cold Remedy Nasal Gel

When they evaluate something new, potential customers are generally interested in how effectively the new product or service does its job. If they are not convinced that it will work, they will not buy it. If it is a new cleaning product, they must be reasonably sure that it will actually clean the surface it is supposed to clean. If it is a new lightbulb that is supposed to last longer, they must be fairly certain that it will last as long as it claims. You might ask people why they believe your new concept will do the job it is intended for and then listen carefully to find out whether they really feel that it will be effective.

In 1999 a new product was launched under the brand name Zicam that claimed that it could actually reduce the duration and severity of the common cold. For many years there has been a saying in the United States that if someone could find a cure for the common cold, he or she could make a lot of money. Well, it looks as if this might be true of Zicam. At the time of this writing, it has achieved distribution in approximately 90 percent of the nation's drugstores and 60 percent of its grocery stores, and it is being sold by all of the major mass merchants, including Target, Wal-Mart, and Kmart. Its sales have been increasing on average 48 percent a year, and that growth rate is continuing.

Clinical studies have shown that Zicam users can get over a common cold in just two days, compared to seven to fourteen days for the average person without it. The management of the company that launched Zicam believes that the basis of its success is this effectiveness of the product. Management believes that because this product really works, people keep buying it over and over again. It feels that many Zicam customers are so convinced that the product works that they not only use it themselves but tell others about it. This word of mouth helps to increase sales even further. Zicam is a perfect example of how effectiveness leads to repeat purchases.

The Birth of a Winning Idea to Reduce Cold Systems

Zicam began as an entrepreneurial venture by two individuals who believed that zinc could form the basis of a very effective cold remedy if it could somehow be applied directly to the nose. This belief was based on literature published in the mid-1990s on the effectiveness of zinc lozenges as a cold remedy. The entrepreneurs believed that while zinc was effective in a lozenge, it would be much more effective in the nose because the common cold is caused by a viral infection in the nose.

The first problem the Zicam venture faced was finding an effective way to apply zinc directly to the nose and keep it there long enough to be effective as a cold remedy. Most of the scientific literature at the time indicated that this would be difficult because of all the secretions in the nose. The nose is a self-cleaning organ, and it was felt that in about fifteen minutes anything that had been put in there would be lost.

The two entrepreneurs developed a gel in which zinc could be suspended and stabilized, coupled with a nasal applicator. This formed the basis of a prototype product that was tested on friends in a series of informal research projects. It seemed that the idea actually worked. This was then expanded into a larger base of initial clinical research, which also showed that applying zinc directly to the nose with a gel was an effective cold remedy. The initial research showed more than a 75 percent reduction in the duration and severity of a cold.

From Idea to Financially Viable Business Venture

At this point, the entrepreneurs realized that they had the basis of a great new product, but that they lacked the resources for obtaining a patent on the idea and for moving the venture through the production and distribution phases. They recognized that they needed help if their idea was ever to become a reality.

In 1999 they linked up with Gum Tech, a company that was in the business of manufacturing and selling functional gum products. For example, Gum Tech marketed a line of gum that contained a variety of vitamins. The company had gum to help people stop smoking, and it even had a zinc gum. Gum Tech also had two other important capabilities. The company held a lot of patents and knew how to obtain a patent for Zicam. It also was selling its gum products in retail stores and knew how to get retail distribution for Zicam. The entrepreneurs formed a joint venture with Gum Tech. The venture was called Gel Tech.

Gel Tech launched Zicam in 1999 by obtaining distribution in one large supermarket chain and one large drugstore chain. There was no marketing plan, no advertising, and no promotion. The company simply had a product that worked, and it used its retail connections and guaranteed sale terms to obtain shelf placement. However, while Zicam had achieved distribution, it was going nowhere. Sales off the shelves were very slow, and the chains were about to discontinue distribution and send the product back.

Gel Tech management realized that consumers were not going to buy Zicam unless it was publicized. One of the principals of the company, therefore, informed the media of the results of the clinical research that showed about a 75 percent reduction in the severity of a cold. *USA Today* picked up the news release and made it a front-page story. Because of the *USA Today* article, store sales of Zicam took off and new retailers started calling up asking for the product. Distribution quickly went from only two retail chains to national distribution.

Funding the Venture for Growth

At this point the Zicam venture needed money, and a lot of it, to finance the growth stimulated by the *USA Today* article. Gum Tech provided some of the financing for growth, and some initial financing was provided by venture capital. The real solution to the funding problem, however, came in the fall of 2001, when Gum Tech sold all its gum-making assets to the Wm. Wrigley

Jr. Company and then bought out the original entrepreneurs. At this point, Gel Tech became Zicam, LLC, a wholly owned subsidiary of Matrixx Initiatives, Inc. (formerly Gum Tech), and the company's entire focus was placed on making Zicam a success.

Proving that Zicam Really Works

In order to legally claim on the packaging and in advertising that Zicam can lessen the duration and severity of the common cold, Gel Tech paid for an independent formal clinical trial of the product. The purpose of the research was to prove that the direct application of the ionic zinc nasal gel within twenty-four hours of the onset of common cold symptoms significantly shortens the duration of those symptoms. This was actually the third clinical trial of Zicam, but it was the first one that enabled the company to make claims for the product on packaging and in advertising.

Subjects were recruited at four sites in the Los Angeles area. The study included 213 subjects, who were randomly assigned to receive either the zinc nasal gel or a placebo. Only subjects who had had cold symptoms for twenty-four hours or less were enrolled in the study. Subjects were required to have had at least three of the following symptoms: cough, headache, hoarseness, muscle ache, nasal drainage, nasal congestion, scratchy throat, sore throat, or sneezing. The results were amazing. The duration of each patient's cold was defined as the number of days from entry into the study to the complete resolution of symptoms. The zinc nasal gel had a significant effect in shortening the duration of the symptoms. The mean resolution time was 2.3 days for the patients who received zinc and 9.0 days for the controls. There were no significant side effects, other than a few subjects reporting a slight tingling or burning sensation.

Formalizing the Marketing Plan Elements

Like many entrepreneurs, the developers of Zicam launched the product without the benefit of a formal marketing plan. The product was developed, some distribution was obtained through good salesmanship and aggressive trade terms, and then it was hoped that the consumer would buy the product.

Luckily, a press release caught the attention of *USA Today*, resulting in enough publicity to generate consumer and broad-scale trade interest. To efficiently manage the growth that followed, however, Zicam had to be implemented on a larger scale with a combination of integrated marketing plan elements.

Expanding the Product Line

The initial Zicam product launched in 1999 was a nasal spray that actually reduced cold symptoms very quickly and shortened the length of the cold. There was a big difference between Zicam and other nasal sprays. The others simply made you feel better while you had the cold. With Zicam, you were over the cold in two days, whereas with traditional remedies, you had to use them for as long as you had the cold, which was typically seven to fourteen days. The Zicam gel matrix was patented, and the patent was good until 2018.

In 2000 the Zicam product line was expanded with a unique formulation allergy product, and in 2002 the company engaged in a major new product effort. A total of five new products were launched in 2002. Adult- and child-sized premoistened swabs were added, where you swab the nose and throw the swab away. These swabs were for people who found a nasal spray somewhat frightening. Two nasal decongestant products were also added in 2002, along with a nasal moisturizer.

The Creation of Appropriate Product and Brand Names

The entire Matrixx Initiatives, Inc., product line uses the Zicam brand name. Company management believed that Zicam was a good name because it was unusual, and therefore memorable. The name actually came from the technical features of the product. "Z" is the chemical designation for zinc, and "icam" was included because the product is effective in blocking the icam receptors in the body. These are terms that are recognized only by medically trained people and were not intended to be known by the consumer.

As line extensions were added under the Zicam brand name, names were created that simply described the functions of the product. The allergy relief products were called Allergy Relief, and the cold remedies were called Cold Remedy. The swabs were simply labeled Cold Remedy Swab and Cold Remedy Kids Size Swab. The nasal decongestants were labeled Extreme Congestion Relief and Sinus Relief. The nasal moisturizer was simply called what it was—Nasal Moisturizer. The idea was to use the Zicam brand for all the products, then clearly tell the consumer the purpose of each specific product.

Creating Packaging That Communicated the Benefit

The design of the Zicam packaging was a very important part of the overall marketing mix. It was critical to communicate to consumers that this was a product that actually shortened the cold. One way this was done was by placing the statement "actually shortens the cold" in a prominent location on the label. As the product line was expanded, the label was modified with a color-coded banner that distinguished the different types of products. The cold remedies all had an orange banner, the allergy products had a blue banner, and the decongestants had a blue-green banner.

The bottle itself was also an important part of the packaging design. For cost reasons, the company decided to go with an existing bottle rather than designing one from scratch. All of the alternatives available from outside suppliers were reviewed. Zicam does not go into the nose as a mist because it is a gel. Therefore, the company had to find a special pump designed for a gel. It also had to find something unique, since Zicam was very different from other cold remedies because of its ability to shorten a cold. The result was the selection of a very upscale bottle that functioned well and sent the right message to the consumer.

Sending a Message with Pricing

When Zicam was introduced, its price was $10.99, whereas the price of the average cold remedy was $5.29. Thus, Zicam cost almost twice as much as the average cold remedy. This price was mainly based on the company's financial requirements. It was not based on consumer research to determine how much the consumer would be willing to pay. The company simply added to its production costs the margin needed to cover all of the marketing costs and trade margins. The product also carried an unconditional guarantee. The customer could send back the bottle with a receipt and Matrixx would send back whatever the customer had paid for Zicam.

The premium price of Zicam had several ramifications. First, it sent a signal to consumers that this was not an ordinary cold remedy. It had to be something special to justify the price. Second, it prevented the brand from gaining distribution in some of the smaller convenience stores. Third, it could be cost-justified against the competition if the consumer took the time to do the financial analysis. For example, a competitive zinc lozenge sold for about half the price, but it was good for only one cold. Zicam was good for two colds, and some people had actually been able to stretch it to three or four colds.

Creating an Effective Sales and Distribution Strategy

The objective was to obtain distribution for Zicam in all the major retailers that carried cold remedies. This was to be done by using a network of brokers in each local market. This strategy was very effective for the brand once the publicity began. As stated previously, at the time of this writing, Zicam was in all the major mass merchandisers, such as Wal-Mart, Kmart, and Target. It also had 90 percent distribution in drugstores. Food store distribution was about 60 percent and growing.

Maintaining Awareness with Advertising

Publicity was effective in achieving initial awareness of Zicam. The company realized, however, that it would have to conduct an advertising campaign in order to maintain this awareness. The decision was made to use primarily television advertising for the cold remedies because of the ability to make visual demonstrations through this medium. The media plan included one thirty-second television commercial run on morning network stations and two sixty-second direct-response commercials on cable television. A print campaign was used for the allergy and decongestant products.

The media strategy for the cold remedies was to start advertising in mid-October and finish in mid-March. This would result in these products being advertised only during the cold season. The print campaign for the allergy products and congestion relief products started in April. The two sixty-second television commercials would include all of the copy from the thirty-second commercial plus an additional thirty seconds on swabs in one case and on Extreme Congestion Relief in the other.

Direct-response television advertising was used for the sixty-second commercials on cable television in order to get a rate break. The cable television industry is set up in such a way that the price of a sixty-second direct-response commercial is approximately the same as that of a thirty-second non-direct-response commercial. Direct response was used, therefore, because the additional media exposure for swabs and Extreme Congestion Relief could be obtained at no significant additional cost. In the direct-response commercials, consumers were given the Zicam.com web address and were told that they could order Zicam over the Internet from either drugstore.com or walgreens.com.

The Zicam advertising campaign was extremely successful. The company received weekly sales data from Wal-Mart, and it could actually tell on what day the advertising was running because sales increased substantially on that day. In other words, the dollars spent on advertising actually paid off over the course of a season. Matrixx management felt that it was getting a real return on its investment in advertising, and it tried to put every dollar it could into media expenditures.

Future advertising plans for the Zicam brand include trade advertising for the first time. Matrixx management plans to go to trade shows and advertise in trade journals. It is also going to try to get some articles published in trade journals. The goal of this trade marketing effort is to firm up trade support and to enable pharmacists to discuss Zicam intelligently with their customers. If people ask their pharmacist about Zicam, the company wants the pharmacist to know enough about the product to explain it to them.

The Advertising Message Was Aimed Directly at the Consumer

The purpose of the Zicam advertising was to drive awareness and trial at the consumer level. It was not aimed at the trade. Matrixx management believed that the advertising would bring in new customers and that these customers would become loyal users who would spread the word, creating more new users. Management felt that this demand from the consumer level would also maintain and expand retail distribution. At the time of this writing, Zicam had a lot of room to grow from an awareness standpoint. It started the year with an awareness level of only about 25 percent.

The primary television advertising copy strategy for the cold remedy was "Zicam gets rid of your cold three times faster." This was the only message in the thirty-second television commercials. At the time of this writing, the company could not claim that Zicam would prevent a cold. The sixty-second television commercials also introduced the swabs and Extreme Congestion Relief. The print campaign focused on introducing the allergy and decongestant products.

Sales Promotion Used for Targeted Opportunities

Sales promotion was not used during the introductory launch of Zicam, and price discounting to stimulate sales is still not a primary tool. The company really wants to sell this unique product at full price. However, a one-dollar coupon was included in a Sunday freestanding insert for the first time in November 2002. The main objective of the coupon was to build awareness of the brand, not to give a price break. The promotion worked well; it cleaned out the shelves in many stores, resulting in numerous out-of-stock situations. Sales promotions like this are planned for targeted opportunities when they are felt to be appropriate.

As Many Off-Shelf Displays as Possible

Off-shelf displays were an integral part of the marketing plan for Zicam. Matrixx offered the trade a wide variety of Zicam displays, including gravity feed units, large wing displays, floor-mounted displays, and an eight-unit counter display.

The company tried to get as many off-shelf displays as possible up during the cold season. Thus far the company has had mixed success in getting retailers to use displays. Some chains would use a fair number of displays, while others would not use any. Some of the smaller stores always bought the counter displays, which hold only eight units, because with their low volume they could not justify purchasing normal cases that hold seventy-two units.

A Very Small Staff of People

Zicam began with only two highly motivated entrepreneurs who brought the venture from a raw idea to an actual product to being folded into an ongoing organization. At the time of this writing, the original product is in national distribution, and the company has launched six additional products (five in just the last year). All of this was done with a very small staff. At this point the company employs only fourteen people. New people are being brought on board as the company grows. The goal is to keep the company lean and to add staff only where absolutely necessary.

Adding Market Research to Manage and Expand the Brand

Although Zicam was developed and launched without the benefit of a formal market research effort, market research is now being used to manage and expand the brand. In the past year the company has done three rounds of formal focus groups to measure consumer attitudes and test new ideas. It has also used a tracking study before and after the cold season to measure consumer awareness and usage of Zicam cold remedies. It wants to quantify how advertising and word of mouth have expanded Zicam's consumer base.

The management of Matrixx Initiatives believes that the company can grow by expanding consumer awareness and usage of its existing products and by introducing new products. The company has introduced five new products in the past year, and it is planning more new product introductions. To reduce the risk of these new product introductions, the company is using several concept testing methods. It is plugging in descriptions of new concepts to a service called BASES® to obtain scores on how well these ideas are likely to perform in the marketplace. It is also using another service called NFO to test new products in order to get measurements of the probability of success before the product is launched.

Protection from Competition

The management of Matrixx Initiatives is aware of the current competition for Zicam and the possibility of future competition. The main competition at this point is from zinc lozenges. There are several brands of zinc lozenges currently on the market, as well as a growing number of private-label brands. Matrixx's competitive strategy against these zinc lozenges is to promote the greater benefits of Zicam relative to those of the lozenges. The company has clinical proof of the effectiveness of nasal applications of zinc, and it believes that this is much more effective than oral application with a lozenge.

The company is also aware of the possibility that the competition will develop a competitive nasal application of zinc. Matrixx has a patent on the Zicam gel matrix that is good until 2018. Management believes that this patent will protect the company from the competitive development of another product that is as effective as Zicam. There may be other traditional sprays developed that use zinc in the formulation. However, the company believes that traditional sprays will not be effective because they will not stay in the nose for a sufficient time period. The competitive strategy to combat another zinc spray will be created once management sees the nature of the competitive product.

A Firm Commitment to Growth

Zicam has been very successful up to this point. It has gone from simply an idea to a nationally distributed brand that is known by over 25 percent of American households. It has also been able to maintain an annual growth rate of more than 45 percent. From a qualitative standpoint, the company has received a lot of very positive feedback from its customers. Its market research has uncovered numerous positive consumer comments, such as, "I love this product, and I've told everybody at work about it."

Despite the success of Zicam thus far, Matrixx management feels that the company has a long way to go. At the beginning of this cold season, Zicam had a 25 percent consumer awareness, which leaves 75 percent of households that must be made aware of the product. Management knows that there is a lot of room to grow, and it is willing to keep pouring on the marketing effort in order to achieve this growth. The entire company is firmly committed to investing all of its resources in the company's continued growth.

The Lessons to Be Learned from Zicam

There are two important lessons to be learned from Zicam. The first is that effectiveness leads to repeat purchases. Zicam customers believe that the product really works, and therefore they keep buying it over and over again. Many of these customers are so convinced that Zicam works that they not only use it themselves but tell others about it. Clinical studies have shown that these customers have a good reason for their confidence. This research shows that Zicam users can actually get over a common cold in just two days, compared to seven to fourteen days for the average person without it.

Another important lesson to be learned from the Zicam story is the importance of marketing. The saying "build a better mousetrap and people will beat a path to your door" obviously did not apply to this product. The company's initial placement into distribution of this new product that represented a very effective new way to reduce the severity and duration of the common cold almost failed because there was no marketing. There are undoubtedly many very effective and well-designed new products that don't go anywhere because they are not properly marketed. Effectiveness alone is not enough.

It wasn't until Zicam was publicized in *USA Today* that the product started moving off the shelves. Further sales results clearly demonstrated that sales grew dramatically as a result of additional advertising. New product introductions based on solid market research findings further stimulated the growth of the brand. You can have an effective product, but you must also invest the money and make the marketing effort to make it known.

Summary Marketing Plan for:
Zicam Cold Remedy Nasal Gel
Matrixx Initiatives, Inc.[1]
1999

MARKETING PLAN SUMMARY

1. **BACKGROUND.** In 1999 a new product was launched under the brand name Zicam that claimed that it could actually reduce the duration and severity of the common cold. At the time of this writing, Zicam has achieved distribution in approximately 90 percent of the nation's drugstores and 60 percent of the grocery stores, and it is being sold by all of the major mass merchants, including Target, Wal-Mart, and Kmart. Its sales have been increasing on average 48 percent a year, and that growth rate is continuing. Clinical studies have shown that Zicam users can get over a common cold in just two days, compared to seven to fourteen days for the average person without it.

2. **CONSUMER CLINICAL TRIALS.** Subjects were recruited at four sites in the Los Angeles area. The study included 213 subjects, who were randomly assigned to receive either the zinc nasal gel (Zicam is based on zinc) or a placebo. Only subjects who had had cold symptoms for twenty-four hours or less were enrolled in the study. The results were amazing. The duration of each patient's cold was defined as the number of days from entry into the study to the complete resolution of symptoms. The zinc nasal gel had a significant effect in shortening the duration of the symptoms. The mean resolution time was 2.3 days for the patients who received zinc and 9.0 days for the controls. There were no significant side effects, other than a few subjects reporting a slight tingling or burning sensation.

3. **MARKETING PLAN ELEMENTS**

   A. *Brand name.* The entire Matrixx Initiatives, Inc., product line uses the Zicam brand name. Company management believed that Zicam was a good name because it was unusual,

---

[1] Zicam is a registered trademark of Matrixx Initiatives, Inc., and is used with permission.

and therefore memorable. The name actually came from the technical features of the product. "Z" is the chemical designation for zinc, and "icam" was included because the product is effective in blocking the icam receptors in the body. As line extensions were added under the Zicam brand name, names were created that simply described the functions of the product. For example, the allergy relief products were called Allergy Relief, and the cold remedy products were called Cold Remedy. The idea was to use the Zicam brand for all the products, then clearly tell the consumer the purpose of each specific product.

B. *Product line.* The initial Zicam product launched in 1999 was a nasal spray that actually reduced cold symptoms very quickly and shortened the length of the cold. The Zicam gel matrix was patented, and the patent was good until 2018. In 2000 the Zicam product line was expanded with a unique formulation allergy product, and in 2002 the company engaged in a major new product effort. A total of five new products were launched in 2002.

C. *Packaging.* The design of the Zicam packaging was a very important part of the overall marketing mix. It was critical to communicate to consumers that this was a product that actually shortened the cold. One way this was done was by placing the statement "actually shortens the cold" in a prominent location on the label. The bottle itself was also an important part of the packaging design. For cost reasons, the company decided to go with an existing bottle rather than designing one from scratch. It had to find a special pump designed for a gel. It also selected a very upscale bottle that functioned well and sent the right message to the consumer.

D. *Pricing strategy.* When Zicam was introduced, its price was $10.99, whereas the price of the average cold remedy was $5.29. Thus, Zicam cost almost twice as much as the average cold remedy. This price was mainly based on the company's financial requirements. The company simply added to its production costs the margin needed to cover all of the marketing costs and trade margins. The product also carried an unconditional guarantee. The premium price of Zicam sent a signal to consumers that this was not an ordinary cold remedy. It could also be cost-justified against the competition if the consumer took the time to do the financial analysis. For example, a competitive zinc lozenge sold for about half the price, but it was good for only one cold. Zicam was good for two colds, and some people had actually been able to stretch it to three or four colds.

E. *Sales and distribution methods.* The objective was to obtain distribution for Zicam in all the major retailers that carried cold remedies. This was to be done by using a network of brokers in each local market. This strategy was very effective for the brand once the publicity began. At the time of this writing, Zicam was in all of the major mass merchandisers, such as Wal-Mart, Kmart and Target. It also had 90 percent distribution in drugstores. Food store distribution was about 60 percent and growing.

F. *Advertising copy strategy.* The primary television advertising copy strategy for the cold remedy was "Zicam gets rid of your cold three times faster." This was the only message in the thirty-second television commercials. At the time of this writing, the company could not claim that Zicam would prevent a cold. The sixty-second television commercials also introduced the swabs and Extreme Congestion Relief. The print campaign focused on introducing the allergy and decongestant products.

G. *Advertising media strategy.* The decision was made to use primarily television advertising for the cold remedies because of the ability to make visual demonstrations through this medium. The media plan included one thirty-second television commercial run on morning network stations and two sixty-second direct-response commercials on cable television. A print campaign was used for the allergy and decongestant products. The media strategy for the cold remedies was to start advertising in mid-October and finish in mid-March. This would result in these products being advertised only during the cold season.

H. *Sales promotion.* Sales promotion was not used during the introductory launch of Zicam, and price discounting to stimulate sales is still not a primary tool. The company really wants to sell this unique product at full price. However, a one-dollar coupon was included in a Sunday freestanding insert for the first time in November 2002. The main objective of the coupon was to build awareness of the brand, not to give a price break.

I. *Publicity.* The media were informed of the results of the clinical research, which showed about a 75 percent reduction in the severity of a cold. *USA Today* picked up the company's news release and made it a front-page story. Because of the *USA Today* article, store sales of Zicam took off and new retailers started calling up asking for the product. Distribution quickly went from only two retail chains to national distribution.

J. *In-store merchandising.* Off-shelf displays were an integral part of the marketing plan for Zicam. Matrixx offered the trade a wide variety of Zicam displays, including gravity feed units, large wing displays, floor-mounted displays, and an eight-unit counter display. The company tried to get as many off-shelf displays as possible up during the cold season.

4. **FINANCIAL PROJECTIONS.** Zicam has been very successful up to this point. It has gone from simply an idea to a nationally distributed brand that is known by over 25 percent of American households. It has also been able to maintain an annual growth rate of more than 45 percent. At the beginning of this cold season, Zicam had a 25 percent consumer awareness, which leaves 75 percent of households that must be made aware of the product. There is a lot of room to grow, and Zicam is willing to keep pouring on the marketing effort in order to achieve this growth.

5. **CONTINGENCY PLANS.** The management of Matrixx Initiatives is aware of the current competition for Zicam and the possibility of future competition. The main competition at this point is from zinc lozenges. There are several brands of zinc lozenges currently on the market, as well as a growing number of private-label brands. Matrixx's competitive strategy against these zinc lozenges is to promote the greater benefits of Zicam relative to those of the lozenges. The company has clinical proof of the effectiveness of nasal applications of zinc, and it believes that this is much more effective than oral application with a lozenge. The company is also aware of the possibility that the competition will develop a competitive nasal application of zinc. Matrixx has a patent on the Zicam gel matrix that is good until 2018. Management believes that this patent will protect the company from the competitive development of another product that is as effective as Zicam.

CHAPTER 6

Preemptive Ventures Are Often Winners

Example: Treo™ Mobile Phone, Web/E-Mail Device, and Organizer

New business ventures that are preemptive generally have a greater chance of success than those that are not. Many successful new business ventures have been true breakthroughs that jumped years ahead of their competition. If your new product is viewed as "the only alternative," you will significantly increase the odds of your success.

The Treo from Handspring, Inc., was one of the first devices to integrate a mobile phone, Palm OS® organizer, and wireless data applications in one compact, full-color communicator. Handspring® was founded by some of the same people who founded Palm and invented the Palm Pilot.

The company began by producing a product called Visor, which was an organizer that had an expansion slot called Springboard that allowed the user to add a number of different functions to the unit, including wireless capability. The Visor was a little less expensive than Palm's products at the time, and it came in a number of different colors, which made it stand out. In addition to selling directly over the Internet, Handspring achieved national distribution for Visor in the major office supply, computer, and electronics stores. Visor quickly became a significant alternative to the Palm Pilot.

One of the original visions of the founders of Handspring was to add wireless capability to an organizer. This came from spending a lot of time with individual users of organizers. These one-on-one observations and discussions with Visor customers and users of competitive products were typically not done in formal settings. They took place in locations where organizers and other portable devices are often used, such as restaurants, while traveling, and even while sitting in traffic in their cars.

An example of these interviews is one that took place in a business meeting with a user of multiple devices. This person was carrying three different devices: a mobile phone on her belt, a Palm V organizer in her purse, and a Blackberry wireless device in her pocket. She also had a variety of different power cables and cradles for these different devices in her briefcase. During the lunch, as she was juggling all these devices, she said, "Why do I have all these things? I want to have just one thing." It was this user observation, and others like it, that ultimately led to the creation of the Treo.

Based on this understanding of unfulfilled customer needs, Handspring began to experiment with wireless devices. Handspring's first wireless product, called the Visor Phone, was a Springboard module that added phone capability to a Visor. The Visor Phone enabled Handspring to learn a lot about building wireless products and a lot about working with wireless carriers. From its interviews with and observations of users, however, the company knew that there was much more to do. There was an obvious need for effective Web access. Handspring could also see that the phone networks were becoming good enough on the data side for a high-quality merged device.

Market Research Narrowed the Vision

Handspring used a combination of market research vehicles to narrow its vision of what an effective mobile communicator should be like. Some of this research involved traditional focus groups, and other research involved talking to a lot of customers face to face, on the phone, and through e-mail over the Internet. Some consumer input came from unsolicited customer feedback over the Handspring web site. This input taught Handspring a lot about what people wanted in a mobile communication device. It also identified what they did not like about the Visor Phone and other early competitive devices, such as the Palm VII.

Based on consumers' likes, dislikes, and stated desires, Handspring constructed a nonworking model of a potential new wireless product that was far more advanced than the Visor Phone, or anything else in the marketplace at that time. The device was a mobile phone, a Web device, an e-mail device, and an organizer. Models are necessary for focus groups because people have trouble conceptualizing the idea if they cannot actually see it. Although this was not a working model, potential users could hold it in their hand and see what it would look like. Computer screens were created to show the software concepts.

Once Handspring had this prototype, it went to formal focus groups to finalize everything. A variety of different types of respondents were recruited for these focus groups, including Palm OS users and non-Palm OS users. The timing of the focus groups was staggered so that changes could be made from one set of groups to another. The focus groups were held in various cities in the United States and in Europe. Europe was included because this was planned as an international venture, and Handspring wanted to understand the needs of consumers on both sides of the Atlantic Ocean.

Based on consumer input concerning the prototype, an actual product was built to an engineering quality level. It did not really use the final hardware or software, and it did crash from time to time. However, it gave the respondent a pretty good idea of what the new device would actually be like. More focus groups were conducted to obtain reactions to this refined prototype. Handspring wanted to see how people would actually use the product. It wanted to see how they would dial the phone, how long it would take them to learn to use the device, how long it would take them to look up a phone number, and where they had to struggle. A whole series of questions about the perceived benefits and negatives were also asked. Respondents were also exposed to a variety of different positioning statements.

The Opportunity Became Obvious

The market research, together with scores of unsolicited comments from people asking about a combined device, clearly indicated that there was an opportunity for a multifunction communication device. Many of the users of existing mobile phones, mobile Internet devices, and organizers expressed an unfulfilled need for such a device. Many of those who were shown the prototype combined device expressed a strong purchase intent. It was obvious that a percentage of people wanted to add a mobile phone to their organizer, or to add an organizer to their mobile phone. Many more wanted to add e-mail capability. Handspring firmly believed that it had identified a new niche.

Handspring reasoned that there were two large consumer segments in which this opportunity existed. The first was the fifteen to twenty million users of Palm organizers. Based on its research, Handspring believed that a percentage of these people would want to replace their organizer with a device that included a mobile phone. The second was the huge number of high-end mobile phone users. The research indicated that a percentage of these people currently felt a need for an organizer, but did not want to carry another device. Handspring believed that a merged device would appeal to many of these people. Given the size of these two segments, Handspring believed that there was a sizable opportunity.

The Objective Was to Create a New Category of Products

Handspring's objective was to create a device that would be the only thing a user would have to carry. This one device would be an excellent mobile phone, a great organizer, and a very effective Internet device. There were other combined products on the market, but none of them did everything well. There were mobile phones with large screens that could handle data, but they were not also organizers. The Blackberry 6720 was an Internet device that had phone capability, but it was not a great phone. Many users found that they also had to carry a separate mobile phone.

The objective was that when customers bought this new device, they would get rid of their present organizer and get rid of their present mobile phone. There would simply be no reason for them to have another phone or organizer, or an Internet device such as the Blackberry. By doing customer surveys after the product was introduced, Handspring found that it had achieved this objective. Over 90 percent of the people who bought a Treo stopped using one or more of their other communication devices.

The New Product Was Called Treo

The name Treo came from the idea that the product replaced three things: the phone, the organizer, and the wireless e-mail or Internet device. Research showed that most people liked the name because it was short and easy to remember. Handspring liked the name because it communicated the three different uses of the device. The company even went a step further and created model numbers that were all divisible by three: the Treo 90, Treo 180, Treo 270, and Treo 300.

Naming the Treo was not an easy task. Many alternative names were created, and Handspring had to get everybody inside the company to agree on which name to use. This turned out to be harder than originally thought, and Handspring quickly discovered that naming is very controversial. To further complicate the problem, after everyone had finally agreed on certain names, those names had to be submitted to a legal search to see if they were clear—and many were not. Even Treo was not totally free of conflict. A Scandinavian pharmaceutical company had a trademark on the name Treo, which meant something in that language. Handspring decided to take the risk and attempt to register the name anyway. Fortunately, it worked out.

Treo Became the Overall Handspring Product Line

The first Treo was a black-and-white version that was designated the Treo 180. It had a sleek design and was much smaller and lighter than the Visor Phone, Handspring's initial experiment with combining a mobile phone and an organizer. There was nothing quite like it on the market at the time. The Treo 180 effectively integrated a mobile phone, a Palm OS organizer, and wireless data applications in one compact communicator. The Treo 180 came in two versions, one with a keyboard and the other with Graffiti handwriting recognition.

One of the lessons we can learn from the development of the Treo is the importance of situational awareness. You cannot rely strictly on one type of data, such as focus group results or survey data. In making important decisions, it is important to compare input from one source with other input and with your own judgment.

There is a story that is often told in some segments of the marketing community that illustrates that what people say in focus groups and what they do are not always the same. Focus group respondents were asked if they preferred black or yellow items. The majority of the respondents in these groups concluded that the yellow items were much better than the plain boring black ones, indicating that yellow was the color that was most wanted. As the respondents were leaving at the end of the focus group, however, they were given the opportunity to take either a black or a yellow item home with them. Almost all of the respondents took a black item. This same phenomenon occurred with the Treo 180.

Focus groups were conducted in Europe to determine whether the new mobile communicator should have a keyboard or simply a screen with the Graffiti feature, which enables the user to write right on the screen. Many of the European respondents indicated that they had to have the Graffiti version because they were used to using this feature on their current organizers. Handspring concluded that it would have to launch the new product in both versions. As it turned out, when the product was launched, most Europeans bought the keyboard version. Handspring's interpretation of the focus groups was incorrect. The lesson it learned was that you cannot always rely on the comments made in focus groups.

The Treo line today has four different versions, all with a keyboard. Handspring's experience with the Treo 180 proved to the company that a separate Graffiti version was unnecessary. The black-and-white Treo 180 is still available. The Treo 270 is a full-color GSM communicator that enables the user to see text and graphics in vivid color. The Treo 300 is a color version designed specifically for the Sprint PCS network. Finally, there is a Treo 90, which has the same kind of design as the other versions but is purely an organizer. As of this writing, the overall Handspring product line is completely Treo. The only Visor products available from Handspring today are refurbished units.

Product Design Was Critical to Treo's Success

Handspring knew that the design of the Treo was very important in differentiating it from all the other mobile communication devices on the market.

Before coming up with the final design, the company developed a lot of different models. They differed in terms of form factors, orientations, input methods, ways of handling the ten-key keypad for the phone, and many other factors. Handspring would start working with one design, discover problems, and then move on to another.

At the beginning of the design effort, Handspring focused on the mechanics and usability of the device. This included things like making the hinge in the lid work and seeing what the unit did when you closed the lid and opened the lid. A lot of time was spent on these mechanical issues. Once the engineers had figured out the basic mechanics of the device, they worked on its appearance. This included things like the shapes, curves, and colors of different parts of the unit. It also included the textures to be used. This design effort was carried out by internal people and by outside designers hired by Handspring.

The addition of the keyboard was a key differentiator for the Treo. The keyboard made it easy for the user to find contacts, dial the phone, type messages, and enter data quickly and easily. The backlit keyboard also let the user do everything in low light conditions. Consumer research made Handspring realize that the keyboard was just as important for the phone as it was for the organizer and Web functions. Consumers also felt that it was better than Graffiti for adding things like calendar events.

All Treo Products Were Sold Through Wireless Phone Carriers

Handspring started out selling the Treo through its existing Visor distribution channels. This proved difficult for two major reasons. First, there was some customer confusion because customers did not really know where to find the Treo. People don't always think about buying a mobile phone at Circuit City or Office Max.

The other problem was that the retailers could not get used to this business model. Handspring actually had to charge the retailers more than the cost to the end user so that the retailers could discount it with their carrier subsidy. If Handspring had not done this, retailers would have had the same margin on the Visor and the Treo, but when they sold a Treo, they would also have received a subsidy from the carriers. They would have wound up making twice as much money on the Treo as on the Visor.

Because of the consumer confusion and the pricing problems, Handspring decided to sell Treo directly to the wireless phone carriers. The carriers then sold the Treo through their own stores as well as through many of the same retailers that sold the Visor. This solved both of the distribution problems. Consumers were used to shopping for mobile phones in mobile phone stores. When they bought the Treo through a traditional retailer, the subsidy from the carriers would flow through in a normal manner. With the new distribution model, Handspring sold all Treo products directly to wireless phone carriers.

A Build-to-Order Production Strategy

Because of the different Treo customer base, after some learning the hard way, Handspring found it necessary to make a major change in its production strategy. The original Visor product line was sold to customers from Handspring's web site. This was measurable and consistent, making it very predictable. Then Handspring started selling to retailers who sold the Visor to consumers. This turned out to be much less predictable. Handspring would build the Visor product line to a sales forecast that sometimes turned out to be quite different from the actual sales.

Because of several inaccurate sales forecasts, Handspring wound up building inventory on some of the wrong products. This turned out to be a costly mistake, teaching Handspring that building inventory on a product that very few people buy can be very expensive. To lower this inventory risk on the Treo, the company moved to a build-to-order mode. This was feasible because most Treo customers were wireless phone carriers that bought products in bulk with a contractual commitment that stated exactly how many units they were going to buy. This move reduced Handspring's inventory risk significantly.

The Treo Has a Very Complex Pricing Strategy

Handspring's pricing strategy for the Treo is to sell the devices to the wireless phone carriers at a wholesale price that will cover all of the company's costs and generate a sufficient profit. The carriers set the retail prices, which consist of a base price coupled with subsidies for users who sign up for the carrier's service. In many cases, the carriers will use discounts to further reduce the prices and entice new customers to sign up with them. Retailers may also offer discounts on the Treo. In this case, the customer may get a discount from a retailer or a wireless carrier's store plus a subsidy for signing up for wireless service. A customer may also buy direct from Handspring's web site and then get a subsidy from a carrier for signing up for service.

This combination of selling direct from a web site, through carriers' stores, and through traditional retailers can be quite complicated. When this is coupled with a variety of subsidies, the price a customer pays for a Treo can vary considerably depending on how the device is purchased. The carrier provides a subsidy to people who get that carrier a subscriber. If that is the retailer, the retailer gets the subsidy. If a customer buys a Treo from Handspring's web site, then Handspring gets the subsidy. If a user who is already a customer of the carrier buys the product, in most cases that customer doesn't get a subsidy. Because of this, in today's market a customer may pay anywhere from $499 to $299 for a Treo.

Packaging Is Used to Help Stimulate Consumer Interest

One of the ways in which Handspring tried to communicate the Treo sales message to consumers in the retail model was through packaging. The packaging for all Treo products showed pictures of the product and examples of the screens (in color for the full-color models). The packaging also explained each of the features of the Treo device, along with product information and a list of the equipment that came with the purchase. The packaging used by the wireless phone carriers is customized to their specifications. When Handspring went to the sell-through-the-carrier model, the carriers controlled the look and feel of the packaging. Handspring also produced brochures and other collateral material that it offers to retailers and used at trade shows.

Advertising Is Mostly Done by the Carriers

Handspring's primary advertising strategy is to help the wireless phone carriers communicate the benefits of the Treo to their customers. The bulk of the advertising is actually done by the carriers. The Treo is a unique product, and the carriers often include it in their advertising to motivate consumers to sign up for their wireless phone service. In some cases Handspring runs additional advertising in newspapers and on radio to get people into stores to see a demonstration of the Treo. Handspring believes that once people try the Treo and start using the keyboard, they will want to take it home with them.

Handspring believes that consumers are motivated to sign up for a new wireless service by seeing something tangible that is unique. The Treo is just such a unique tangible device. Handspring therefore prepares mock-up advertisements and point-of-purchase material to give the carriers examples of how they might communicate the benefits to customers of using a Treo with their particular wireless service. Naturally the final advertising strategy is created by the carriers because they are the ones running the advertising.

A recent Sprint advertising campaign provides a good example of Treo advertising. Sprint spent a lot of money advertising the Treo and one of its key services, the PCS Business Connection, which is an e-mail solution. The Treo model advertised was optimized for that service. Sprint placed ads in *Time, Newsweek, Business Week,* and the *Wall Street Journal.* These ads told people about Sprint's Business Connection services and showed a Treo as an example of an ideal product for this service.

Direct Sales Over the Internet Is a Key Marketing Strategy

Direct marketing is a key part of Handspring's marketing strategy. This is one of Handspring's most profitable distribution channels because the company does not have to give margins to retailers and receives a subsidy from the carriers for signing up new users. Much of Handspring's direct marketing takes place over the Internet. Handspring spends a lot of time and energy making its web site easy to use. It collects names through registration and sends people information on Treo. Another use of the web site is to educate sales reps about the product.

Handspring also uses other Internet marketing tools beyond its web site. The Treo newsletter is a very successful tool. Handspring tries to make these newsletters really valuable so that people will read them instead of deleting them. It does this by adding tips and tricks as well as alerting customers to new and interesting applications that can run on the Treo. Handspring creates the Treo newsletter internally. It also does classic banner and search engine advertising. Handspring has found that advertising on sites that people visit when they are thinking about buying a mobile communication device is far more effective than advertising on popular sites. It has found that putting a banner on CNN or Yahoo! is less effective than putting a banner on something like PDA reviews or wireless reviews.

Publicity Is a Big Part of Consumer Communication

Although the bulk of the Treo advertising is controlled by the wireless phone carriers, Handspring has a lot of control over the public relations aspects of communication for the Treo. Handspring believes that this is the most leveraged form of marketing that it has. Publicity was an important part of the initial Treo product launch, and it continues to be a significant part of ongoing communications.

The public relations objective is to get the media to talk about, write about, and review the Treo as often as possible. Handspring often sends the media Treo units so that they can write independent reviews. The company has been very effective in getting to key writers and motivating them to review the device. Part of the reason for this success has been the unique nature of the Treo. That is one of the advantages of a preemptive product.

The Treo Has Rapidly Become a Category Icon

Although Handspring had been working on the general concept of an effective integrated communication device since the inception of the company, the actual development of the Treo was accomplished in a fairly short period of time. The actual Treo concept, with the flip lid, window, and keyboard, was conceived in June of 2000, and the product hit the market in a limited initial launch in December of 2001. Shipping in quantity in the United States started in February of 2002.

The Treo has become an icon in the category of merged communication devices. There is now a large group of core users who just love the product, and the word is spreading to new users every day. A few competitors are now adding keyboards to their devices, and some are attempting to emulate the Treo. As of this writing, however, the Treo stands as a true category leader.

Key Lessons to Be Learned from the Treo

A key marketing lesson to be learned from the Treo is that you must recognize who your real customer is. Prior to launching the Treo, Handspring focused mainly on the end user as its real customer. This worked out fine with the Visor because this was a traditional product sold through traditional retailers. With the Treo, however, the customer focus had to shift. Because the Treo was a mobile phone and a wireless Internet device, the wireless phone carriers were a very important element in the chain because their subsidies played such an important role in the pricing of the Treo. They were also very important to the end user because the Treo was of little use unless it was connected to a carrier.

Shortly after launching the Treo, Handspring realized that it had to walk a fine line between satisfying the needs of the carriers and satisfying the needs of the end users. In many cases, it is the carrier that really decides to buy the product. Handspring quickly recognized that if it didn't satisfy the carrier's needs, even if those needs were opposed to the end users' needs, there would not be much of a market for the Treo. The carrier is the one who must certify the product, put it into distribution, and sell it to its customers.

Today Handspring is totally focused on satisfying the needs of the carriers. It has account teams that are assigned to different carriers. These teams totally understand how the carriers do their pricing, how they sell their services, and how they think. When they give the carriers advice on how to market the Treo, they give this advice in the carriers' context, and the advice is focused on how the carriers can accomplish their mission. Handspring now firmly believes that you must know who your customer is and understand your customer's needs.

The other lesson to be learned from the Treo is that if you can create a preemptive product, you will improve your chances of success. The mobile phone carriers were interested in the Treo because it was a unique solution to their customers' problems. For the same reason, the media were willing to publicize the Treo as something that was new and newsworthy. If you can create the "only alternative" for your customers, you will significantly increase the odds of your success.

Summary Marketing Plan for:
Treo™ Mobile Phone, Web/E-Mail Device,
and Organizer
Handspring, Inc.[1]
2001

MARKETING PLAN SUMMARY

1. **BACKGROUND.** One of the original visions of the founders of Handspring, Inc., was to add wireless capability to an organizer. This came from spending a lot of time with individual users of organizers. The result was the Treo, which was one of the first devices to integrate a mobile phone, Palm OS organizer, and wireless data applications in one compact, full-color communicator. Handspring was founded by some of the same people who founded Palm and invented the Palm Pilot.

2. **MARKET REVIEW.** There were two large consumer segments that represented an opportunity for Treo. The first was the fifteen to twenty million users of Palm organizers. Based on its research, Handspring believed that a percentage of these people would want to replace their organizer with a device that included a mobile phone. The second was the huge number of high-end mobile phone users. The research indicated that a percentage of these people currently felt a need for an organizer, but did not want to carry another device. Handspring believed that a merged device would appeal to many of these people. Given the size of these two segments, Handspring believed that there was a sizable opportunity.

3. **CONSUMER USAGE AND ATTITUDES.** Handspring used a combination of market research vehicles, including traditional focus groups and informal research that involved talking to a lot of customers face to face, on the phone, and through e-mail over the Internet. This market research, together with scores of unsolicited comments from people asking about a combined device, clearly indicated that there was an opportunity for a multifunction communication device. Many of the users of existing mobile phones, mobile Internet devices, and organizers expressed an unfulfilled need for such a device. Many of those who were shown a prototype combined device expressed a strong purchase intent. It was obvious that

---

[1] The brand name Treo is a trademark of Handspring, Inc., and is used with permission.

a percentage of people wanted to add a mobile phone to their organizer, or to add an organizer to their mobile phone. Many more wanted to add e-mail capability.

4. **KEY STRATEGIC MARKETING OBJECTIVES.** Handspring's objective was to create a device that would be the only thing a user would have to carry. This one device would be an excellent mobile phone, a great organizer, and a very effective Internet device. There were other combined products on the market, but none of them did everything well. The objective was that when customers bought this new device, they would get rid of their present organizer and get rid of their present mobile phone.

5. **MARKETING PLAN ELEMENTS**

   A. *Brand name.* The new product was called Treo. The name Treo came from the idea that the product replaced three things: the phone, the organizer, and the wireless e-mail or Internet device. Research showed that most people liked the name because it was short and easy to remember. Handspring liked the name because it communicated the three different uses of the device. The company even went a step further and created model numbers that were all divisible by three: the Treo 90, Treo 180, Treo 270, and Treo 300.

   B. *Product line.* The Treo line today has four different versions, all with a keyboard. One is the black-and-white Treo 180. The Treo 270 is a full-color GSM communicator that enables the user to see text and graphics in vivid color. The Treo 300 is a color version designed specifically for the Sprint PCS network. Finally, there is a Treo 90, which has the same kind of design as the other versions but is purely an organizer. As of this writing, the overall Handspring product line is completely Treo.

   C. *Product design.* Product design was critical to Treo's success. Handspring knew that the design of the Treo was very important in differentiating it from all of the other mobile communication devices on the market. The addition of the keyboard was a key differentiator for the Treo. The keyboard made it easy for the user to find contacts, dial the phone, type messages and enter data quickly and easily. The backlit keyboard also let the user do everything in low light conditions.

   D. *Packaging.* One of the ways in which Handspring tried to communicate the Treo sales message to consumers in the retail model was through packaging. The packaging for all Treo products showed pictures of the product and examples of the screens (in color for the full-color models). The packaging also explained each of the features of the Treo device, along with product information and a list of the equipment that comes with the purchase. The packaging used by the wireless phone carriers is customized to their specifications.

E. *Pricing strategy.* Handspring's pricing strategy for the Treo is to sell the devices to the wireless phone carriers at a wholesale price that will cover all of the company's costs and generate a sufficient profit. The carriers set the retail prices, which consist of a base price coupled with subsidies for users who sign up for the carrier's service. In many cases, the carriers will use discounts to further reduce prices and entice new customers to sign up with them. Retailers may also offer discounts on the Treo. In this case, the customer may get a discount from a retailer or a wireless carrier's store plus a subsidy for signing up for wireless service. A customer may also buy direct from Handspring's web site and then get a subsidy from a carrier for signing up for service. In today's market a customer may pay anywhere from $499 to $299 for a Treo.

F. *Sales and distribution methods.* Handspring decided to sell the Treo directly to the wireless phone carriers. The carriers then sold the Treo through their own stores as well as through other retailers. Direct marketing is also a key part of Handspring's marketing strategy. This is one of Handspring's most profitable distribution channels because the company does not have to give margins to retailers and receives a subsidy from carriers for signing up new users. Much of Handspring's direct marketing takes place over the Internet. Handspring spends a lot of time and energy making its web site easy to use.

G. *Advertising strategy.* Handspring's primary advertising strategy is to help the wireless phone carriers communicate the benefits of the Treo to their customers. The bulk of the advertising is actually done by the carriers. The Treo is a unique product, and the carriers often include it in their advertising to motivate consumers to sign up for their wireless phone service. In some cases Handspring runs additional advertising in newspapers and on radio to get people into stores to see a demonstration of the Treo.

H. *Internet marketing.* In addition to its web site, Handspring also uses Internet marketing. The Treo newsletter is a very successful tool. Handspring tries to make these newsletters really valuable so that people will read them instead of deleting them. It does this by adding tips and tricks as well as alerting customers to new and interesting applications that can run on the Treo. Handspring creates the Treo newsletter internally. It also does classic banner and search engine advertising.

I. *Sales promotion.* Handspring produces brochures and other collateral material that it offers to retailers and uses at trade shows.

J. *Publicity.* Publicity was an important part of the initial Treo product launch, and it continues to be a significant part of ongoing communications. The public relations objective is to get the media to talk about, write about, and review the Treo as often as possible. Handspring often sends the media Treo units so that they can write independent reviews. The company has been very effective in getting to key writers and motivating them to review the device.

K. *Test marketing.* Handspring began to experiment with wireless devices with its first wireless product, called the Visor Phone. The Visor Phone enabled Handspring to learn a lot about building wireless products and a lot about working with wireless carriers. From its interviews with and observations of users, however, the company knew that there was much more to do. There was an obvious need for effective Web access. Handspring could also see that the phone networks were becoming good enough on the data side for a high-quality merged device. All of this led to the development of the Treo.

PART 2

SAMPLE MARKETING PLANS

The objective of Part 2 of this book is to provide you with a series of sample marketing plans that you can use as guides in the development of your own marketing plan.

Disclaimer: The specific information in the sample marketing plans in Part 2 of this book was compiled for intended use as examples only. Although each of these marketing plans is based on actual products from real companies, the specific information in these plans is hypothetical and is not intended to compete with or divulge proprietary ideas, company structure, or the financial status of any company. The names, numbers, and some of the facts in these marketing plans have been changed because of the confidential nature of the information. The information is intended to be used as a guide only.

CHAPTER 7

Secondary Research to Develop Market Reviews

Example: Satellite Brand Alkaline Batteries

One of the best starting points in developing a marketing plan is a formal market review. The purpose of the market review is to clearly present all of the available data that are relevant to the marketing of the products or services to be included in the marketing plan. In some cases this involves looking at the company's present business, while in other cases the market review is directed toward a new market that the company is planning to enter. The market review typically looks at the growth and nature of the market for the product category involved. If the company is currently participating in that category, the market review should identify the company's past and projected participation.

The main reason for doing a market review is to provide good visibility on the overall marketing situation before attempting to do something new. It just makes sense to know basic details such as how big the market is, the market's history and trends, and competitive activity before sitting down to draft a comprehensive marketing plan. Most market reviews also include things like the number of appropriate retail outlets by trade class and geographic region, product movement through the various retail channels, shares of market by manufacturer, price points by manufacturer and trade class, and industry advertising expenditures by manufacturer and medium.

This book outlines a number of different ways to complete a market review. One of the best ways to start is by reviewing data that already exist. This includes data written up in secondary sources such as magazines, trade publications, government publications, catalogues and directories, annual reports of principal competitors, and newsletters; information available on the Internet; and information in company files. It is amazing what you can find by simply looking around you. This information will generally provide you with a framework for the market and how it breaks down by major market segments.

Many people further round out this search of secondary information with data-gathering field trips. These may include both telephone and personal interviews with government agencies, trade associations, and the authors of some of the articles about the industry. It is not a bad idea to do some quality store checks for the purpose of writing down prices, shelf facings, and other things you might see that can help you to verify some of the information you have read about. Doing a market review is a lot like being a detective, except that instead of searching for a criminal, you are looking for information.

The market review in the following marketing plan example for Satellite Alkaline Batteries is a good example of how this is done. Although the specific data in this market review have been altered because of the confidential nature of the information, the plan is based on an actual marketing plan that was approved and implemented by a major manufacturer. This market review should give you a good idea of how a market review should be structured and the information that should be included. As you accumulate information for your market review, be sure to include as many tables and other specifics as you can.

The Satellite Alkaline Batteries market review was primarily completed using secondary sources and information that was available to the company in its private files. These data included Department of Commerce year-end summaries, data on actual company shipments, information from trade publications, information that the company had purchased from A.C. Nielsen Company (a market research organization), competitive price schedules, and some basic projections made by company marketing personnel.

The Satellite Alkaline Batteries marketing plan is also a good example of how to put together a total marketing plan. In addition to a market review, it includes sections on consumer usage and attitudes, trade practices and attitudes, planning assumptions, key strategic marketing objectives, and all of the strategic programs. The marketing plan also includes financial projections and an interesting section on contingencies, just in case something goes wrong.

Marketing Plan for:
Satellite Brand Alkaline Batteries
Consumer Product Division
Hsinchu Electric Company, Ltd.[1]
April 14, 1997

INTRODUCTION

The purpose of this report is to develop a four-year marketing plan for a major new Hsinchu Electric Company venture in the consumer segment of the alkaline battery market. This report is divided into the following sections:

1. **BACKGROUND.** This section reviews the background of this project and outlines the steps that led to the development of this marketing plan.

2. **MARKET REVIEW.** This section reviews the growth and nature of the alkaline battery market, and identifies Hsinchu's past and projected participation in that market.

3. **CONSUMER USAGE AND ATTITUDES.** This section outlines present consumer practices, desires, and expectations regarding alkaline batteries.

4. **TRADE PRACTICES AND ATTITUDES.** This section reviews the retail food trade's current involvement in the alkaline battery market, its attitudes toward the product category, and its specific reactions to the venture outlined in this marketing plan.

[1] **Disclaimer:** The specific information in this sample marketing plan was compiled for intended use as an example only. Although this marketing plan is based on actual products from a real company, the specific information in the plan is hypothetical and is not intended to compete with or to divulge proprietary ideas, company structure, or the financial status of any company. The names, numbers, and some of the facts in this marketing plan have been changed because of the confidential nature of the information. The information is intended to be used as a guide only.

5. **PLANNING ASSUMPTIONS.** These are key conclusions based on the facts presented in the previous sections.

6. **KEY STRATEGIC MARKETING OBJECTIVES.** This section provides the specific objectives of this venture over the next five years.

7. **STRATEGIC PROGRAMS.** This section presents very specific and implementable plans that the Consumer Product Division intends to use to accomplish the objectives of the venture.

8. **FINANCIAL PROJECTIONS.** This section provides detailed calculations of the costs, volume, and payout of the venture from initial rollout to national expansion.

9. **CONTINGENCIES.** This section presents plans for retaliation against possible competitive action directed at either this venture or the regular Hsinchu line of consumer batteries.

The scope of this report is primarily directed at developing plans to launch a totally incremental venture in alkaline batteries for the consumer market through the grocery channel of distribution. These plans are designed to function as an incremental marketing effort, and are intended to be compatible with present activities involving the regular product line in the grocery trade as well as other channels of distribution.

The information required to develop this marketing plan was gathered in five stages. Each stage was designed to provide a systematic understanding of the current activities in the consumer alkaline battery market and how a major new Hsinchu venture might fit within the framework of that market. The following specific steps were taken:

1. **MARKET RESEARCH.** Eight consumer focus groups were conducted in representative markets throughout the United States (Los Angeles, Minneapolis, Atlanta, and Philadelphia). In addition to this qualitative research, a quantitative survey of consumers was conducted in various markets in an effort to test various advertising alternatives.

2. **NAME/PACKAGE/DISPLAY.** Based on an analysis of the results of the consumer market research, a design consultant was retained to develop a totally unique name, package, and display for this venture. The name developed for the venture was Satellite. On completion

of the design of the name, package, and display, these were exposed to consumers in additional focus groups and were determined to be highly acceptable and motivating.

3. **ADVERTISING CAMPAIGN DEVELOPMENT.** An advertising agency was retained to assist in the development of an advertising campaign. In addition, a promotion plan for the venture was developed by this advertising agency and an outside marketing consultant. Details of the promotion plan are included in the Strategic Programs section of this report.

4. **TRADE PROBES.** Detailed interviews were conducted with key executives at the headquarters of nineteen major food store organizations in ten representative geographic areas throughout the United States. The purpose of these interviews was to determine the viability of the Satellite venture.

5. **MARKETING PLAN DEVELOPMENT.** Upon completion of the previous steps, a complete national marketing plan was developed for the venture. This plan included all of the objectives, strategies, and tactical plans for the total venture. The balance of this document deals with the specifics of this plan.

BACKGROUND

The Hsinchu Electric Company is a large manufacturer of general-purpose batteries and specialty batteries. The company is headquartered in Chongquin, China, and has offices in five other countries, including the U.S. headquarters in Atlanta, Georgia. Hsinchu is one of the largest marketers of alkaline batteries to the U.S. consumer market, and currently commands approximately a 16 percent share of this market.

In 1994, extensive consumer and trade research was conducted by Hsinchu, leading to the conclusion that there was an opportunity for a new brand of alkaline batteries in supermarkets in the United States. This led to the formation of an internal task force to examine this opportunity. The net result was the creation of Project Alpha. The objective of Project Alpha was to capture and maintain a major incremental share of market in the U.S. food environment. This was to be done by launching a major advertising and promotion program for a compact line of long-lasting, general-purpose batteries. The brand was to be sold into distribution as an additional brand for the retail outlet.

Project Alpha was launched in three test markets in 1995. The first market was in New Jersey, and no advertising was used. The second market was in Buffalo, with introductory advertising only. The third market was in Houston, with a full, sustained advertising program.

Project Alpha was successful in demonstrating Hsinchu's ability to obtain incremental distribution with this new line of batteries. Three accounts, with a total of twenty-seven stores, were obtained in New Jersey. Four accounts, with a total of nineteen stores, were obtained in Buffalo. Two accounts, with a total of fifty-two stores, were obtained in Houston. This demonstrated the ability of a unique program to penetrate accounts that were otherwise closed to Hsinchu. The remainder of this document deals with future plans for this venture, and the steps that are recommended to expand this venture nationally over the next five years.

MARKET REVIEW

1. *The total market for general-purpose batteries in 1996 was $521 million in net factory dollar sales, and 1,574 million in unit sales.* Hsinchu achieved a market share of 19.5 percent of industry dollars and 20.3 percent of units in 1996. This equated to net factory dollar sales of $101 million and unit sales of 320 million for Hsinchu.

2. *The total industry historical unit growth has averaged about 3 to 4 percent per year.* Future unit growth is projected to be only 2 percent per year, or approximately equal to population growth. Industry dollar sales have been growing at an average of 9.2 percent from 1991 through 1996, reflecting the impact of inflation. Dollar growth is forecasted to continue at approximately a 7 percent level through 2001.

3. *Hsinchu's growth over the past six years has slightly lagged that of the total industry.* The company's 1996 unit sales were 8 percent below those that the company moved in 1991, versus a slight increase for the total industry. Similarly, Hsinchu's dollar sales increased from 1991 to 1996 at an average of 6.6 percent, compared to 9.2 percent for the total industry. The company is forecasting unit growth through 2001 in the area of 3 to 4 percent per year, and dollar increases in the range of 8 to 9 percent per year. These estimates do not include the potential impact of the Project Alpha program.

4. *The total consumer market for alkaline batteries in 1996 was $259 million, or 49.7 percent of the total alkaline battery market.* Total consumer market dollar growth from 1991 to

1996 averaged 10 percent per year; however, 1996 showed a 20 percent increase. Growth in total industry units lagged dollar growth, with an average growth rate of 7.6 percent per year; however, 1996 growth was 17 percent. Total consumer market units are projected to grow at a rate of 3 percent through 2001, with dollar increases at the rate of 6 to 7 percent.

5. *Hsinchu's consumer alkaline battery sales for 1996 were $41 million and 152 million units.* This translated to a dollar share of 15.8 percent and a unit share of 15.9 percent. These shares had dropped slightly from 1991, when Hsinchu had a dollar share of 17 percent and a unit share of 16.3 percent.

6. *Hsinchu's dollar growth in the alkaline battery consumer market has averaged 8 percent per year since 1991.* Like the industry, Hsinchu enjoyed a significantly higher than average growth rate in 1996 (17 percent). In terms of unit growth, Hsinchu has averaged 7 percent per year since 1991, with a 1996 growth of 17 percent.

7. *Hsinchu is projecting a growth rate in dollars and units through 2001 of approximately 5 percent per year.* These projections are based upon marketing activities currently planned for the regular product line and do not reflect the impact of the Project Alpha program.

8. *Food stores are the dominant consumer channel for alkaline batteries, accounting for 54 percent of total consumer market sales.* Food stores are followed, in rank order, by mass merchandisers, with 17.9 percent; hardware/auto stores, with 15.4 percent; and drugstores, with 7.5 percent. These four channels of distribution account for 94.8 percent of total retail alkaline battery sales.

9. *Food stores also represent the largest single distribution outlet for Hsinchu consumer sales, accounting for 46.6 percent of the company's total retail alkaline battery sales.* Hsinchu has a 13.9 percent share of sales through food stores; however, this is significantly lower than its 16.1 percent share for all retail channels of distribution. Hsinchu also has a marginally lower than average share through hardware/auto stores, while its mass merchandiser share (21.4 percent) and drugstore share (21.7 percent) show that it is outperforming the industry through these two distribution channels.

10. *The grocery market for alkaline batteries in 1996 represented $140 million in net dollar sales, or 27 percent of total alkaline battery sales, and 54 percent of total consumer sales.*

The growth of the grocery market has been, and is anticipated to be, approximately the same as that of the total consumer market. Total grocery dollar growth over the past five years has averaged 9.8 percent. On a unit basis, the total grocery industry has shown a 5 percent growth over the past five years. The industry's units through 2001 are anticipated to grow at approximately a 3 percent rate, with dollar growth of 4 to 7 percent per year.

11. *Hsinchu has lagged the total industry in growth through grocery stores in terms of both dollars and units.* On a dollar basis, Hsinchu has shown a 6.8 percent growth rate over the past five years, or about 70 percent of the industry growth rate. In terms of units, Hsinchu has shown a 3.8 percent growth rate versus the industry's 5 percent. In 1996 Hsinchu did not enjoy the significant increase in alkaline battery grocery dollar sales seen by the industry.

12. *The Hsinchu grocery share for 1996 was 13.9 percent for both dollars and units.* This represents a decrease from the company's 15.9 percent share of dollars and 14.7 percent share of units in 1991. Hsinchu is forecasting a unit growth through the grocery segment of approximately 6 to 7 percent per year through 2001 and dollar growth of 6 to 10 percent per year.

13. *On a geographic basis, the grocery market for alkaline batteries is largest in the Eastern Zone and smallest in the Western Zone.* Approximately 42 percent of total grocery sales dollar volume is in the Eastern Zone, 38.6 percent in the Central Zone, and 19.7 percent in the Western Zone. Hsinchu's sales and resulting shares are stronger than the industry average in the Eastern Zone, and weaker than the industry average in both the Central and Western Zones. Specifically, on a share basis, Hsinchu shows an 18.6 percent share in the Eastern Zone, an 11.5 percent share in the Central Zone, and an 8.6 percent share in the Western Zone.

14. *In terms of grocery store types and sizes, Hsinchu's volume is skewed more heavily toward chain groceries than that of the total industry, and Hsinchu shows a significant deficiency in terms of its business through the largest independent outlets.* Specifically, chain groceries account for 74.6 percent of Hsinchu's total grocery store dollar volume versus 64.8 percent of the volume for the total category. As a result, chain groceries are 15 percent more important to Hsinchu than to the total market.

The large independent stores account for only 11 percent of Hsinchu's grocery store volume versus 22.4 percent for the total industry. As a result, Hsinchu's business development through these accounts is less than half that of the total industry.

15. *Nielsen data show that Hsinchu's retail grocery inventories are the highest of the three primary manufacturers, and that as a result, the retail turns on Hsinchu merchandise are lower than those for either competitor.* The average grocery account's supply of Hsinchu alkaline batteries is 2.58 months versus 2.17 for the total market. Similarly, Hsinchu shows 4.65 retail turns on its inventory per year versus 5.53 for the total industry.

16. *On the basis of consumer unit consumption (actual grocery store units purchased), the alkaline battery grocery market is relatively stable, with a low point in July/August of 85 percent of an average month and a high in the November through February period of 111 percent of an average month.* Hsinchu follows the total market seasonality almost exactly, while its two major competitors show marginally less seasonality than the total market.

17. *AA batteries are the dominant battery type sold through food stores, accounting for over 65 percent of both unit and dollar volume for 1996.* This AA dominance has remained relatively constant since 1994. AAA batteries remain the second largest category, accounting for 23.4 percent of units and 19.4 percent of dollars in 1996. The remaining battery types accounted for 11.2 percent of units and 14.8 percent of dollars in 1996.

18. *Grocery AA battery consumption is highest on the West Coast and lowest in the metro Chicago area.* The area with the highest AA battery consumption is the Pacific area, with an index value of 113 versus the total United States. The area with the second highest consumption is metro Los Angeles, with an index of 111. The remaining areas are relatively close to the U.S. average of 100 with the exception of metro Chicago, which shows an index value of only 42 versus the total United States.

19. *Nielsen data indicate that actual grocery selling prices are below suggested list prices and that Hsinchu tends to get discounted significantly more than the competition.* The grocery trade seems to be discounting competitive AA batteries by approximately 10 percent and discounting Hsinchu batteries by upwards of 20 percent.

20. *Total industry consumer advertising expenditures have averaged about $2 million per year from 1992 through 1996.* The significant exception to this average was in 1995, when total industry expenditures dropped to under $1 million for the year. As would be expected, the company with the dominant market share also emerges as the dominant advertising spender, accounting for 55 percent of total industry advertising expenditures from 1992 to

1996. Hsinchu's advertising expenditures have accounted for 20 percent of total industry spending from 1992 to 1996 and totaled $1.9 million.

CONSUMER USAGE AND ATTITUDES

1. *The retail alkaline battery category is heavily female-oriented, with women accounting for 70 percent of total alkaline batteries purchased.* Research indicates that the heaviest users of alkaline batteries are females, twenty-five to forty-five years old, living in households where there are children in the family.

2. *The retail alkaline battery category is characterized by a relatively low purchase frequency.* Typically a household will make an alkaline battery purchase between four and five times per year. Each of these purchases usually involves five to six individual batteries. At the time of purchase, the consumer will purchase more than a single battery type. Purchases are almost universally made (87 percent of the time) to replenish the average household inventory of six batteries.

3. *Most alkaline battery purchases are made in supermarkets.* The respondents in the focus group sessions verified Hsinchu's information on distribution, indicating that supermarkets are by far the largest single outlet for alkaline batteries.

4. *Alkaline batteries emerge as an extremely low-interest category to their prime consumers.* For example, virtually all of the consumers interviewed during the focus group sessions indicated that alkaline batteries were of minor importance, that this was a category that they didn't know much about and were not very interested in spending a great deal of time thinking about. In sum, the alkaline battery category is viewed largely as a commodity category.

5. *Consumer comments indicated that alkaline battery purchases were often based largely on impulse.* This impulse can stem from being confronted with a battery display in the supermarket and realizing that the in-home inventory is in need of some replenishment.

6. *Correct battery type emerged as the primary purchase criterion.* Interestingly, price was rarely a critical factor. Consumers did indicate that the presence of a sale on batteries could

motivate an impulse purchase, but they were basically unaware of the normal pricing or the actual price they paid for the product.

7. *The overall alkaline battery category appears to suffer from significant consumer confusion.* In addition to being a category of very low interest, batteries tend to be very confusing to the average consumer. Consumers have a great deal of trouble understanding the difference between the different types of batteries available on any given merchandiser. Similarly, consumers are unsure of the advantages or disadvantages of the various battery brands. There appears to be very little understanding of the difference between one brand and another.

8. *There is no strong brand preference in the alkaline battery category.* Awareness of the various brands available is almost identical to their individual share of distribution. Although people are generally aware of the brand that they regularly purchase, they do not make any effort to seek out this brand when repurchasing. This stems from the fact that consumers perceive no difference between the major brands.

9. *Manufacturers' marketing programs have not been effective in motivating consumers.* Only 17 percent of the 1,000 people interviewed during a 1992 consumer survey could remember seeing any recent battery advertising. Additionally, consumers were unable to state the advertising claims of one brand relative to another.

10. *The focus groups indicated that consumers find one primary area of complaint within the current alkaline battery category.* The major complaint about alkaline batteries cited by consumers was that they go dead too fast. A battery's going dead is generally a frustrating and irritating experience for a consumer.

11. *Consumers clearly indicated that a long-life alkaline battery would be the most significant single improvement that a manufacturer could offer within the category.* Quantitative research indicated that over 83 percent of consumers felt that long life would be the only benefit of any importance in terms of a battery product improvement. Similarly, the consensus from the focus group research was that increased battery life was the most meaningful benefit that could be developed. The significant information regarding a long-life battery that emerged from the focus group discussions can be summarized as follows:

A. *Consumers indicated a willingness to pay a premium price for a truly long-lasting battery.* Very few of the people interviewed during the group sessions objected to paying a higher price for a longer-lasting battery. At least half of the people interviewed would actually prefer to pay a premium price for a long-lasting battery than a low price for "cheap batteries" that would require frequent changing.

B. *While endorsing the concept of a long-lasting battery, consumers indicated that the combination of the extra life and the incremental price should result in a meaningful dollar saving.* The concept presented during the focus groups was a battery that was 2¹/₂ times longer lasting for only 36 percent more in price. Most consumers found this satisfactory because it would be economically advantageous to them.

C. *While they were receptive to the concept of a long-life battery, consumers questioned the credibility of a manufacturer's claim of long life.* A part of this skepticism stemmed from the fact that consumers found it difficult to believe that a manufacturer would actually produce a long-life product that would provide significant in-use savings. The following comments were offered regarding the credibility issues:

1. *Consumers wanted to be told why a battery lasts longer.* In this regard, most of the focus group participants responded favorably when they were given specific reasons why a battery would last longer.

2. *Consumers felt that a long-life battery should come with some sort of a manufacturer's guarantee.* The feeling was that if a manufacturer were willing to guarantee the performance of its products, this would add considerable credibility to the claim.

D. *Consumers indicated that they would evaluate the effectiveness of a long-lasting battery on the basis of how often they were required to change this new battery compared with standard batteries.* Most people recognized that this would be a very difficult evaluation. Most consumers really do not have any idea of how long their current batteries last. Therefore, they recognize that it will be very difficult for them to evaluate an improved battery. Nevertheless, most people felt that if, in their subjective opinion, the new battery did not last longer than their old battery, they would not repeat the purchase.

TRADE PRACTICES AND ATTITUDES

The following findings stemmed from an extensive series of trade interviews conducted on behalf of the Project Alpha program. The purpose of the trade interviews was to elicit overall attitudes toward the alkaline battery category and specific reactions to the Project Alpha program concept. A total of nineteen major food store organizations in ten geographic areas were contacted and given a preliminary presentation on the Project Alpha program.

1. *The overall trade reaction to Project Alpha was positive.* Retailers generally recognize that alkaline batteries are now sold basically as a commodity. It was generally felt that the Project Alpha marketing programs could be successful in capturing a major share of the market for a long-life alkaline battery. Most retailers were willing to participate in a test of such a venture, and if the test were successful, they would be willing to take on such a program in permanent distribution.

2. *The primary strengths perceived by the trade regarding the Project Alpha program were the strengths of the marketing communications programs, and the ease for them of taking on such a program in distribution.* The trade generally believed that Project Alpha would provide the consumer with a meaningful benefit, and that this benefit would be well communicated through advertising/promotion and a totally unique name/package/display. Additionally, the trade felt that it would not be difficult to take on such a program because it would be provided to retailers in addition to their current brands of batteries. Finally, the trade liked the small number of stock-keeping units (only five battery types) because this would minimize space requirements, both at the warehouse and at the retail outlet.

3. *The trade clearly indicated that the key to obtaining broad-scale distribution for the Project Alpha program was a high sustained level of advertising and promotion spending.* The trade was not willing to take on a new brand of long-life batteries unless this brand were heavily pulled through the distribution channel by a strong marketing communications program. It was indicated that in order to sell such a brand, it would be necessary for a manufacturer to incur high levels of advertising spending on a continuous basis, similar to those for other successful packaged goods.

4. *The supermarket trade was unanimously impressed with Project Alpha's name/package/ display.* Supermarkets felt that the new brand name and package were very consumer oriented and totally unique, and that they would help add credibility to a claim of long life. The trade liked the compact and flexible nature of the Project Alpha merchandiser, and felt that it was designed to accommodate various-sized stores.

5. *The trade felt that the two-year guarantee would add considerable credibility to the product, and would be easy for retailers to handle.* The trade generally recognized that a major task of the marketing plan for a long-life battery would be to overcome consumer skepticism. The guarantee was felt to greatly assist in this effort. Additionally, because this guarantee did not require store redemption, it would be very easy to gain trade cooperation. Finally, most of the trade felt that the amount of redemption by consumers would be minimal.

6. *The trade generally felt that Hsinchu should increase the suggested retail list price of Project Alpha batteries.* Because of the longer life of the Project Alpha batteries, the trade wanted the spread between the prices of standard batteries and the long-life product to be as great as possible. Most people felt that they would do very little discounting from this high price, as they would expect to make Project Alpha their high-profit contributor. In sum, it was felt that Hsinchu should test alternative price levels to determine how high the price could go before volume dropped substantially.

7. *Most of the supermarket executives interviewed during this study indicated that they would be willing to accept a 50 percent margin on the Project Alpha venture.* These people recognized that a heavily advertised brand could not support a higher margin. The acceptance of a 50 percent margin obviously depended on the movement of Project Alpha product and an overall improvement in the trade's dollar profits. The notable exception to this was wholesalers, who wanted a higher margin than chains because of the extra service that they provide their accounts.

8. *In sum, many trade executives indicated that they would be forced to take on distribution of the Project Alpha program because of the heavy advertising expense.* It was indicated that if Project Alpha were to become heavily demanded by their customers, they would be forced to take on the program, just as they are forced to take on many new packaged goods products. The executives indicated that they were in the business of satisfying their customers' needs, and that they could not afford to not carry a product that was demanded by a large number of their customers. The following additional comments were offered regarding the distribution opportunities on Project Alpha:

   A. *Improved profits are the key requirement.* It was clearly indicated that the key requirement for obtaining distribution for Project Alpha would be that the trade's overall profitability on batteries be improved. The actual movement requirements would be the same as those on their current battery programs. The trade felt, however, that Project

Alpha should offer an improved profit from that movement because Project Alpha's longer life would ultimately result in a reduction in repeat sales.

B. *Project Alpha would achieve broad distribution.* It was generally felt that because of the heavy advertising of Project Alpha, it would be difficult for Hsinchu to limit the overall amount of distribution. In sum, all stores would probably put pressure on Hsinchu to allow them to carry the new brand.

C. *Taking on Project Alpha would be an operating decision.* In most supermarket organizations, the decision to take on Project Alpha could be made by an operating executive. The trade indicated that the decision to shift brands of batteries is currently a major decision requiring top management approval. Because Project Alpha is a totally new product, the decision to take on the new product would not have to be made at such a high level. In most cases a merchandising vice president could authorize distribution.

D. *A major presentation would be required.* Most of the people interviewed during this study felt that Hsinchu should introduce the new Project Alpha brand in a very major way through the use of a formal presentation. The trade would expect to see a well-thought-out presentation provided by senior Hsinchu management personnel. The company should not simply have the product introduced in a casual manner by the normal sales force.

9. *The trade generally felt that the competition would react conservatively to the Project Alpha entry.* It was felt that the primary reaction would be for the competition to attempt to talk the trade out of taking on the Project Alpha brand. Competitors would attempt to convince the trade that selling a long-life battery in the large quantities envisioned for Project Alpha would reduce the market. The second competitive action thought likely by the trade would be a price cut by the competition. It was felt to be possible, but unlikely, that the competition would put together a similar program and produce another new brand of long-life batteries. Importantly, a number of trade executives felt that if Project Alpha were successful, the competition might be checkmated.

PLANNING ASSUMPTIONS

1. *In the current business environment, growth opportunities for manufacturers of alkaline batteries are severely limited.* Because of this, Hsinchu will probably continue to experience

difficulties in substantially increasing its market penetration by continuing to use "traditional" battery marketing techniques. Traditional marketing techniques could, in fact, result in further losses of market share. The following specific factors are currently inhibiting growth opportunities:

A. *Limited market growth.* The growth of the alkaline battery market is relatively flat, with units increasing only at approximately the rate of population growth. Most of the dollar growth of the market has stemmed from price increases.

B. *Successful dominant brand.* One brand is a dominant and growing factor in the overall market. Given the strength of this brand, it would appear to be difficult to make competitive inroads into its existing volume. In the face of the strength of this competitor, Hsinchu has shown volume and share weaknesses over the past few years that would appear to be difficult to reverse using traditional battery marketing methods.

2. *Consumer research indicates that long-lasting batteries provide a consumer benefit suitable for the establishment of a viable brand franchise that would result in broad distribution and significant volume.* Market research has shown that 83 percent of consumers would like to have a truly long-lasting battery.

3. *The fact that long-lasting batteries have previously been produced and offered to the public does not diminish the opportunity for this consumer benefit to generate a viable branded new product entry.* The reason for this is that the long-life concept has never been properly promoted in order to build consumer believability and therefore demand for the concept.

4. *A complete and powerful "branded goods" marketing approach will be required to successfully exploit the opportunity inherent in the long-life concept.* The primary elements that would be required as part of a "branded goods" approach for alkaline batteries can be briefly described as follows:

A. *Meaningful and unique consumer benefit.* It would be necessary to go to market with a battery that has a life significantly longer than that of the average product now on the market. Additionally, any marketing advantages (e.g., an understandable guarantee) that might enhance the consumer value of the product should be included.

B. *Distinctive brand name.* In developing a consumer franchise for this product, it is important that it be distinguished in the consumer's mind as something new, apart, and totally different from the balance of the Hsinchu battery product line. The name Satellite Batteries should provide this distinction.

C. *Unique package and display.* To further strengthen Satellite Batteries' unique and independent positioning, they should be sold in a unique and attractive package. Additionally, they should initially be sold from a freestanding merchandiser. An in-line merchandiser should be provided to stores that require one.

D. *Extensive advertising and promotion.* The application of a "branded goods" approach demands that Satellite Batteries receive significant support, both during the introduction and on a continuing level.

5. *A strong branded approach to Satellite Batteries will result in significant broad-scale distribution for the brand.* The trade interviews have clearly indicated that if consumer demand for Satellite Batteries is as strong as envisioned, most retailers will take on the brand in distribution. We estimate distribution in approximately 30,000 retail grocery outlets.

6. *Hsinchu needs to develop a national network of food brokers supervised by Hsinchu field sales personnel, separate and apart from the division's basic sales force.* As outlined in the Strategic Programs section of this marketing plan, a national network of food brokers can be developed to provide excellent in-store service. In addition, a separate Hsinchu organization to supervise these brokers can provide excellent control of the venture.

7. *The entire selling and servicing function for the Satellite Batteries program should be handled by a separate Hsinchu organization together with the food brokers, not by the current sales force.* The need for a separate field organization to supervise the activities of the Satellite Batteries food brokers and to assist and oversee the sales function can be summarized as follows:

A. *Lack of current capacity.* Broker supervision is a full-time job requiring fifteen additional field personnel, which the division currently does not have in place.

B. *Unique skills required.* The function of broker supervision, motivation, evaluation, selection, and/or termination requires specific skills and experience separate and apart from those already existing within the bulk of the division's field sales force.

C. *Totally separate brand.* Satellite Batteries will be sold as a separate, and in many instances a competitive, entry relative to the regular Hsinchu line. The presence of a totally independent sales supervision network for Satellite Batteries will ensure that neither this new entry nor the basic line will be compromised at the field level in its efforts to achieve its full marketing objectives.

D. *Totally different marketing approach.* The significant differences between the marketing approach of Satellite Batteries and that of the regular Hsinchu line, as well as the overall potential volume and profit impact, dictate the need for a separate and specialized field organization to sell, support, and supervise the brand's field efforts.

8. *The Satellite Batteries brand has the potential to provide Hsinchu with total retail sales of $94 million and factory sales of $47 million by 2001.* This would represent the largest single battery program in Hsinchu history and would establish Hsinchu as the marketing leader of the industry.

9. *The risk to Hsinchu from developing and launching the Satellite Battery venture can be substantially reduced by continuing the current program of step-by-step consumer and trade research efforts.* Steps taken to date, such as extensive consumer focus group research, trade probe activity, consumer package research, and copy development consumer research, have all been undertaken to ensure that there are no significant gaps in the marketing planning effort and that the program moves forward with the best series of program elements available. The subsequent steps outlined in the Strategic Programs section of this document should continue to minimize the risks of the venture.

10. *In addition to the volume and profit contributions previously discussed, the successful introduction of the Satellite Batteries program will provide a series of secondary benefits to both the battery division and the overall Hsinchu Electric Company.* Specifically, the following benefits are envisioned:

A. *Definite growth plan.* The successful launch of the Satellite Batteries venture will provide the division with a definite plan of action for achieving substantial growth over the next five years. In gradually expanding the plan from research through test to national rollouts, the division will be forced to focus on a definite growth plan.

B. *An incremental effort.* The development of this brand can be accomplished in addition to the current marketing efforts. It is not be necessary to sacrifice marketing planning on the regular consumer battery line in order to launch the Satellite Batteries brand. Both programs can be developed in tandem, leading to a strong, two-pronged attack on the marketplace.

C. *Higher profitability.* Because the Satellite Batteries brand will be a premium line, overall division profitability will be substantially increased. Satellite Batteries will add incremental volume at a higher profit contribution than the current product line.

D. *Improved trade reputation.* By effectively launching a hard-hitting consumer program, Hsinchu will substantially increase its reputation in the food trade. It is believed that such a success will result in Hsinchu's being viewed by the trade as a leader in consumer marketing. This reputation will be extremely valuable in expanding the current regular product line, as well as in other ventures by this division and other Hsinchu divisions.

E. *Improved corporate image.* Because this will be a highly visible venture with the general public, it is believed that such an effort will be extremely valuable for Hsinchu corporatewide. Because of the high levels of spending on advertising and promotion, a secondary benefit of this venture could be favorable publicity for the corporation.

KEY STRATEGIC MARKETING OBJECTIVES

The key objective of Satellite Batteries over the next five years is to develop a highly profitable, major new brand of alkaline batteries that will be sold to the consumer market through the grocery channel of distribution. The specifics of this objective are as follows:

1. **PREMIUM PRODUCT.** The objective is to provide the consumer and the trade with a truly superior product that has a meaningful consumer benefit. It is intended that this product provide the consumer with an excellent price/value relationship, and the trade with an opportunity to significantly increase its profits.

2. **NAME/PACKAGE/DISPLAY.** The intention is to communicate the uniqueness of the Satellite Batteries brand through a totally revolutionary name, package, and display.

3. **BRAND FRANCHISE.** The objective is to create a brand franchise of loyal customers equating to 11 percent of the total consumer alkaline battery market units. The plan is to do this through a high-level sustained advertising and promotion program.

4. **DISTRIBUTION OBJECTIVES.** The objective is to obtain distribution of the Satellite Batteries brand in 30,000 food stores by the time the brand reaches full national distribution.

5. **VOLUME OBJECTIVES.** The objective of the Satellite Batteries brand on achieving national distribution is $47 million in factory sales. Hsinchu hopes to do this strictly through the food channels of distribution, and it hopes to use Satellite Batteries as a vehicle to expand the supermarket category by drawing volume from other traditional outlets (drugstores, mass merchandisers, and so on).

6. **FINANCIAL OBJECTIVES.** The objective is to achieve an after-tax return on net sales of 14.0 percent. Additionally, the expectation is that the Satellite Batteries brand will show a return on investment that meets or exceeds that of the balance of the division.

7. **SALES AND DISTRIBUTION SYSTEM.** The objective is to launch the Satellite Batteries brand through a series of food brokers, coupled with a separate Hsinchu organization specifically set up to supervise these brokers.

8. **RISK OBJECTIVES.** The objective is to minimize the risk and investment required in the Satellite Batteries venture by carefully testing the program and through gradual expansion plans.

9. **TIMETABLE OBJECTIVES.** The objective is to complete the necessary activities in time for a 4/1/98 introduction in the first rollout area.

STRATEGIC PROGRAMS

1. **OVERALL OBJECTIVES.** The key objective of the Satellite Batteries program is to develop maximum profitable battery volume for Hsinchu via:

    A. Establishing a solid position within the current supermarket alkaline battery category.

    B. Expanding the supermarket category by drawing battery volume from other traditional outlets (drugstores, mass merchandisers, department stores, and so on).

These objectives will be accomplished by:

    A. The introduction of a new branded alkaline battery product, Satellite Batteries, that is unconditionally guaranteed to provide the consumer two years of service.

    B.   Providing strong advertising and promotion support, on a sustained basis, designed to generate consumer awareness of and demand for the Satellite Batteries brand.

    C.   Limiting the distribution of Satellite Batteries to grocery outlets in order that this trade class may enjoy the full benefit of the consumer demand generated for the Satellite Batteries brand.

2. **PRODUCT.** The key elements of the Satellite Batteries product line can be summarized as follows:

    A.   The product will be offered only in AA, AAA, C, D, and 9-volt sizes, which account for 77.9 percent of total alkaline battery volume.

    B.   The product will carry an unconditional guarantee of a two-year use life.

3. **PRODUCT NAME.** The product will be marketed under the brand name Satellite Batteries. The strategic reasons for the selection of this name are as follows:

    A.   The name is memorable.

    B.   The name is preemptive and proprietary in that it can be trademarked for exclusive Hsinchu utilization in the battery category.

    C.   The name has the ability to lend itself to advertising and promotional activities on behalf of the brand.

    D.   The name in and of itself connotes the long-life aspects of the product.

    E.   The name has the ability to provoke consumer interest in the product.

    F.   The name has a timeless quality.

4. **PACKAGE.** The Satellite Batteries package has been designed to provide the following strategic advantages:

    A.   It offers a unique and readily identifiable new shape in battery packaging.

    B.   It provides the consumer the opportunity to see and recognize the unique printing design on the Satellite Batteries product.

    C.   It provides satisfactory protection for the product.

    D.   It clearly and quickly communicates the product name, logo, and product specifications.

    E.   It reinforces the communications aspects of the Satellite Batteries program by stressing the two-year use life of the product and by stating the full product guarantee.

F. As a result of its unique shape, the package precludes intermingling of the Satellite Batteries brand with other battery brands and packages in the store.

G. The package is aesthetically attractive and offers a fresh, clean, and appealing appearance in its own in-store display with the minimum of housekeeping effort.

H. It lends itself to automatic packaging.

I. It is affordable (2.05 cents per unit).

5. **DISPLAY.** The Satellite Batteries display offers the following strategic advantages:

A. The display has dramatic visual impact, either when used singly in a small store situation or when used in multiples in larger stores.

B. The display has been designed to be flexible in order to accommodate various store sizes and store locations. For smaller stores or low-profile stores, the top two trays of the overall display can be eliminated, thus reducing its overall size and product capacity.

C. The display uses a minimal amount of square footage of floor space within a store. When used as a single unit, the display requires little more than one square foot of actual store space.

D. The display is usable either in a freestanding configuration or as an end-aisle display by itself or in multiples, or it can be converted to in-line utilization.

E. The display accommodates up to eight dozen packages.

F. The display provides an excellent showcase for the Satellite Batteries package and product.

G. The display facilitates quick and easy selection of the product by the consumer and similarly requires a minimum amount of restocking time.

H. The display is constructed to accommodate only the Satellite Batteries packages in order to prevent other manufacturers' brands and products from utilizing the proprietary Satellite Batteries in-store location.

I. The display is solidly constructed and is projected to provide an in-store use life of between three and five years.

J. The display is within the previously forecasted price range for the Satellite Batteries program and, in rollout quantities, can be produced at a cost of $55 to $60 per individual unit.

6. **PRICING AND MARGINS**

    A. *Retail pricing and consumer economics.* It is planned that the Satellite Batteries brand will carry a premium price for all sizes. This retail pricing, nevertheless, will result in a significant consumer savings in terms of costs per hour of use life for Satellite Batteries versus the competition.

    B. *Trade terms and economics.* Trade terms for Satellite Batteries will be established at a 50 percent margin (percentage off retail), with the product sold on an outright guaranteed sale basis and extended terms of 2 percent on the fifteenth of the second month or net at the end of the second month. Trade interviews have indicated a willingness on the part of food retailers to accept the Satellite Batteries program at the 50 percent margin.

    C. *Manufacturer' s margin.* Satellite Batteries will carry a gross margin to Hsinchu of 50 percent of its recommended list price to the trade. While this is considerably above the normal 41 percent manufacturer's margin on retail alkaline battery products, it must be remembered that Hsinchu will be investing significant marketing dollars in this program and that the additional margin does not necessarily fall to the bottom line. The overall financial results of the program are presented later in this document.

7. **DISTRIBUTION/VOLUME/SHARE OBJECTIVES**

    A. *Distribution objectives.* Satellite Batteries' objective is to achieve distribution in 30,400 stores accounting for 52.5 percent of total grocery store all-commodity volume. The plan anticipates a range of distribution by store size, with 75 percent of the largest stores stocking Satellite Batteries, trending down to only 5 percent of the smaller stores stocking the brand. Further, the plan has not assumed any distribution in convenience stores.

    B. *Volume objectives.* Based upon the total store distribution, the Satellite Batteries brand is expected to generate annual going-year sales of $94 million per year in retail sales and $47 million per year in factory sales.

    C. *Share objectives.* Satellite Batteries' volume objectives translate to an 11 percent unit share and a 17.4 percent factory dollar share of the total consumer alkaline battery market and a 20.6 percent unit share and a 33.6 percent factory dollar share of total grocery alkaline battery sales. The brand's dollar shares are significantly higher than its unit shares as a result of the premium pricing of the product.

8. **DISPLAY REQUIREMENTS.** Based on the expected distribution store count and estimates of the number of displays used per store, it is projected that there will be a requirement for 53,300 displays by the time the brand has completed its full national rollout. This is because it is expected that the vast majority of the large accounts will utilize multiple display units.

9. **SALES PLAN**

   A. *Sales objectives.* The principal sales objectives of the Satellite Batteries program can be summarized as follows:

      1. To obtain and maintain Satellite Batteries' distribution and volume objectives.

      2. To implement approved brand sales-oriented plans and promotions both at headquarters and at retail store levels.

      3. To provide retail store coverage in order to:

         a. Minimize brand out-of-stocks.

         b. Solicit turnover orders.

         c. Sell trade and consumer promotion offers at the retail level.

         d. Obtain retail-level display and merchandising support for the brand.

         e. Maintain a high level of housekeeping for the Satellite Batteries display area.

      4. To serve as a source of management information regarding the Satellite Batteries sales and volume situation and competitive market information.

   B. *Sales strategies.* The specific strategies that will be employed in order to achieve the overall Satellite Batteries sales objectives are as follows:

      1. *Sales organization.* For the reasons stated in the Planning Assumptions section, Satellite Batteries will use a sales organization that is wholly separate and apart from the division's existing sales force. The Satellite Batteries organization will involve a national network of food brokers supervised by an organization of Hsinchu field personnel.

      2. *Sales organization functions.* The principal functions of the various levels of the Satellite Batteries sales organization are as follows:

         a. *Brokers.* The individual food broker organizations bear primary responsibility for introductory and ongoing selling activities at the headquarters and retail levels.

   b. *District managers.* Each district manager bears the responsibility for the overall performance and accomplishments of approximately four food broker organizations. In this respect, the district manager is responsible for providing ongoing supervision, evaluation, and motivation of the individual brokers. The district manager will be expected to work at the retail level both with broker personnel and on his or her own to determine the effectiveness of each broker's efforts. The district manager will also assist the brokers in making headquarters calls and sales. If necessitated by poor broker performance, the district manager will have the responsibility for recommending the termination of an individual broker and for the screening process involved in determining that broker's replacement.

   c. *Zone managers.* Each of the three zone managers is responsible for an average of five district managers and twenty food broker organizations. The zone manager is responsible to the company for achieving overall Satellite Batteries distribution and volume objectives in his or her geographic territory. The zone manager also bears the responsibility for recommending to company management the addition or deletion of Satellite Batteries promotions or marketing plans in order to maximize the brand's volume and profit in his or her geographic area.

   d. *Sales and marketing manager.* This individual bears primary and overall responsibility for both the development and the implementation of Satellite Batteries' annual marketing and sales activities. He or she is responsible to company management for the construction of the brand's annual marketing plan, volume forecast, and profit forecast. Additionally, he or she has line responsibility to the Satellite Batteries sales organization to ensure that the objectives and results of the approved marketing and sales plans are achieved.

3. *Sales support information.* In order to provide optimum supervision of the activities of the food broker network, the plan is to use an outside organization to provide an ongoing "mystery shopper" function that will report regularly on such areas as distribution, out-of-stocks, retail pricing, and merchandising support for both Satellite Batteries and competitive brands. This service will provide information on a broad sampling of the largest stores on a biweekly basis and monthly detail on smaller accounts.

The reports from this service will be issued on a broker-by-broker basis so that the brokers' supervisors can utilize them most productively with their individual broker principals. Additionally, the same data will be provided for each of the three geographic zones of the country so that both zone managers and divisional management will have a timely and usable overview of the Satellite Batteries field situation.

C. *Sales costs.* Based on the organizational structure described, Satellite Batteries' going-year sales costs are projected at $5.1 million. It should be noted that these costs assume brokerage commission charges of 6 percent and further allow for the implementation of the sales support information system (mystery shoppers). If, in actual implementation, either of these assumptions proves to be overly conservative, the overall sales expenses might be significantly reduced.

10. **COPY.** The objective of Satellite Batteries' advertising is to build consumer awareness of and demand for the brand through the registration of the following points:

A. The brand name.

B. The two-year in-use life span of the product.

C. The fact that the product is unconditionally guaranteed to provide its two-year life span.

D. The unique package shape and design.

E. The Satellite Batteries display.

F. The fact that Satellite Batteries are available through supermarkets.

11. **MEDIA**

A. *Media objectives.* Satellite Batteries' year one media objectives are as follows:

1. To build high awareness and trial of Satellite Batteries by introducing the brand with media expenditures significantly above the total industry's sustaining levels.

2. To maximize message delivery to the target audience—women age twenty-five to fifty-four in households with three or more members, with consideration given to the working woman segment.

3. To achieve a minimum reach and frequency of 90/4.0 during the introductory period and 60/4.0 for the sustaining period.

4. To advertise in each new market for a minimum of thirty weeks during the introductory year.

    5. To utilize a media mix that will most effectively and efficiently reach the target audience.

B. *Media strategies.* The Satellite Batteries media objectives will be accomplished by:

    1. The use of television advertising as the primary and most effective method of communicating the Satellite Batteries copy points.

    2. The use of magazines as a supplementary medium in order to:

      a. Increase pressure on the light television viewing consumers.

      b. Take advantage of print's unique copy potential.

      c. Serve as a coupon-carrying vehicle.

    3. The selection of television programming to provide maximum impressions to the target audience.

    4. The use of flighting: a heavy-weight introductory period of thirteen weeks, followed by sustaining flights of four to five weeks of advertising each.

    5. Adjusting the spending plan seasonally as the brand rolls out in order to optimize the media impact during the heavy battery consumption periods.

    6. The use of thirty-second TV announcements and four-color print pages.

12. SALES PROMOTION

A. *Sales promotion objectives.* Satellite Batteries' introductory-year sales promotion objectives are as follows:

    1. To assist the sales force in obtaining distribution for Satellite Batteries in its targeted food outlets.

    2. To create awareness, trial, and repeat purchase among the broadest possible base of target consumers.

B. *Trade strategies and plans.* The trade strategies that will be employed to meet the promotion objective are as follows:

    1. Provide the broker organizations and the Satellite Batteries field force with sales presentation and/or meeting materials to accommodate an orderly and effective sell-in of the brand.

    2. Offer an introductory trade allowance on initial inventory quantities of Satellite Batteries.

3. Provide an advertising allowance once Satellite Batteries has established itself as a viable business within the food store environment.

4. Stress the strengths of the overall consumer marketing effort and the trial-oriented promotion efforts in particular.

C. *Consumer strategies and plans.* The consumer events that will be utilized in order to create awareness, trial, and repeat purchase are as follows:

1. Offer via the brand's magazine advertising an introductory "Get One Free" print coupon with a face value equal to the full retail price of a single Satellite Battery.

2. Provide a "bounceback" coupon packed in the initial quantities of Satellite Batteries to encourage retrial.

3. Offer a self-liquidating "Satellite Batteries–related" premium item as a method of extending trial to those consumers who are motivated more by an impulse offer at a display than by a cash coupon offer.

4. Provide a second media coupon late in year one in order to extend trial and generate retrial.

D. *Promotion spending.* Over half (57 percent) of the brand's total promotion spending will be directed toward consumer-oriented offers. Trade spending will account for 31 percent of total promotion, and the remaining 12 percent will be accounted for by display material and sales aids.

E. *Year two and going-year promotion spending.* After the brand's introductory year, Satellite Batteries will continue to focus its promotion spending on the consumer by using promotion offers designed to stimulate continued trial and retrial of the brand. These offers (i.e., media coupons) will be tailored back from the year one effort to accommodate the brand's available promotion budget.

13. **EXPANSION PLANS.** *Satellite Batteries will move toward national distribution along a careful path of regional rollouts.* Satellite Batteries will undertake a regional rollout starting in April 1998 that will see the brand achieve full national distribution in January 2000. The first rollout area will be the West Coast, currently the weakest area for the overall Hsinchu business. This will be followed sequentially by expansions into the Midwest, the East Coast, and, lastly, the balance of the United States. Table 7-1 summarizes the rollout schedule.

14. **TIMETABLE.** Table 7-2 details a number of the principal steps that must be taken to enable the brand to achieve its planned April 1, 1998, introduction into the first rollout.

TABLE 7-1. Satellite Batteries National Rollout Schedule

Beginning Date	Rollout	% Incremental Households	Cumulative % of Households
4/1/98	First rollout	10.81%	11.49%
1/1/99	Second rollout	25.04%	36.53%
7/1/99	Third rollout	29.86%	66.39%
1/1/00	Fourth rollout	33.61%	100.00%

TABLE 7-2. Tentative Timetable

Finalize marketing plan	4/11/97
Marketing plan presentation	4/14/97
Commit $1.0 million for display tooling	5/19/97
Marketing plan approval	5/28/97
Commit $4.0 million for display mold	6/2/97
Assign project director	9/6/97
Approval of display units	9/9/97
Authorize automated packaging equipment	9/23/97
Order initial product and package production	9/23/97
Commence TV and print advertising production	9/30/97
Authorize media buys	9/30/97
Start of display production	10/21/97
Start of program sell-in in initial cities	10/30/97
Commercial production completed	12/11/98
Ship initial product	2/18/98
Ship initial displays	2/18/98
Initial displays arrive	3/25/98
Balance of displays in initial cities	4/1/98
Start of retail placement	4/1/98
Start of advertising	4/1/98

FINANCIAL PROJECTIONS

1. **FINANCIAL OVERVIEW.** Assuming that the Satellite Batteries program achieves its anticipated sales, and that the venture is expanded according to the planned rollout schedule, Satellite Batteries will generate net sales of $46,092,000 in 2001. In order to accomplish this, advertising and sales promotion expenditures for 2001 would be $6,750,000. This would result in an income, after tax, of $6,450,000. Assuming that the venture continues to meet sales projections, Satellite Batteries will show an after-tax loss of $150,000 in 1998, and then proceed to generate a significant profit in each of the following years.

It should be noted that the build toward the 2001 after-tax return rate of 14 percent is a result of the introductory investment expenditures as the brand expands regionally. In point of fact, the Satellite Batteries brand is projected to achieve this 14 percent return in its second year in any given area. For example, were the program to be terminated after its initial West Coast expansion, the company should be able to realize the 14 percent after-tax return from the West Coast area as of April 1, 1999—a year following the West Coast rollout date.

Table 7-3 provides a financial overview of the Satellite Batteries venture as it is rolled out nationally.

2. **FINANCIAL DETAILS.** A detailed income statement for the Satellite Batteries brand from 1998 through 2001 is shown in Table 7-4.

3. **FINANCIAL ASSUMPTIONS.** The principal assumptions used in the construction of Satellite Batteries' four-year income statement are as follows:

   A. *Fixed dollars.* The four-year income statement makes no provision for increases in costs or selling price. The assumption is that cost increases will be offset by increasing the list price of a Satellite Batteries unit.

   B. *Unit sales.* Unit sales are based on the rollout schedule detailed in the Strategic Programs section of this document.

   C. *Sales billed.* Sales billed are assumed to be 50 percent of the suggested retail price of the Satellite Batteries product.

   D. *Cash rebate.* This is assumed to be 2 percent of sales billed in all years.

   E. *Packaging costs.* The packaging cost is broken down into two components: the wrapper and the shipper. For 1998, the wrapper costs for the first 73,000 batteries is assumed

TABLE 7-3. Satellite Batteries Financial Overview (Dollars in 000s)

	Net Sales	Adv. & S.P. Cost**	I.A.T.***	%
1998	$ 3,322	$ 825	$150*	45%*
1999	20,119	4,504	810	4.0%
2000	43,908	7,447	5,038	11.5%
2001	46,092	6,750	6,450	14.0%

*Loss.   **Strategic Programs.   ***Income after tax.

TABLE 7-4. Satellite Batteries Forecasted Four-Year Income Statement (in Thousands)

	1998	1999	2000	2001
Sales billed	$3,390	20,530	44,804	47,033
Cash rebate	68	411	896	941
Net sales	3,322	20,119	43,908	46,092
Direct Product Cost				
Factory cost	979	4,384	9,568	10,044
Package cost	233	1,276	2,785	2,924
Cash discount	68	411	896	941
Transportation	118	672	1,450	1,521
Product warranty	11	68	148	155
Broker compensation	203	1,232	2,688	2,822
Direct Marketing Expenses				
Advertising	599	3,418	5,790	5,250
Sales promotion	225	1,086	1,657	1,500
Display	345	1,798	1,394	635
Display freight	34	174	137	63
Display conversion cost	—	11	60	117
Sales organization	124	719	1,250	1,250
Mystery shoppers	83	514	999	1,000
Store setup	100	528	469	315
Market research	60	48	79	60
Project development	60	—	—	—
Other indirect costs	367	2,222	4,849	5,091
Total cost	3,609	18,561	34,219	33,688
Income before tax	(287)	1,558	9,689	12,404
Income after tax	(150)	810	5,038	6,450

to be 4.8 cents per battery. The next 2.4 million batteries carry a wrapper cost of 2.49 cents per battery, or $59,800. The balance of the wrappers purchased for that year are assumed to cost 2.2 cents per battery, or $122,200. Shipper costs for 1998 are at a cost per battery of 0.00592 cents. Wrapper costs for 1999–2001 are assumed to be at the lowest possible wrapper costs of 2.05 cents per battery, with the shipper cost at that point in time continuing at 0.00205 cents per battery.

F.   *Cash discounts.* Cash discounts are consistently assumed to be 2 percent of sales billed.

G. *Transportation cost.* For all rollouts, an average cost of 0.01361 cents per battery has been used.

H. *Product warranty costs.* These costs are based on the assumption that the return rate against the warranty will be one battery returned for every 1,000 batteries sold. The cost per return has been given as $1.40 per battery on costs supplied by a qualified redemption house.

I. *Broker compensation.* This item has been assumed to be a consistent 6 percent of sales billed in all years.

J. *Advertising expenses.* These expenses have been allocated in accordance with the media plan as outlined in the Strategic Programs section of this report. The 1998 advertising expenditures include production costs of commercials over and above the out-of-pocket measured media expenses.

K. *Sales promotion.* These costs have been assumed to be in accordance with the sales promotion plan as outlined in the Strategic Programs section of this report.

L. *Display cost.* The displays are assumed to have a unit cost of $60.50, which also includes the amortization of mold charges to produce this item.

M. *Display freight.* The display freight charges use an average cost per unit based on estimates provided by the display manufacturer.

N. *Sales organization.* The sales costs assume the implementation of the sales organization and broker expenses as illustrated in the Strategic Programs section of this report.

O. *Mystery shoppers.* This item assumes that mystery shoppers call on 120 of each food broker's 500 average stores every two weeks. This results in a total of 186,900 store checks in a full year. The total number of store checks equates to an annualized cost of $1 million per year.

P. *Store setup costs.* This item assumes a charge per store for initial setup of the display. It is further assumed that this service will be performed by an outside service organization, and that the total time per store, including drive time, will be two hours.

Q. *Market research.* These costs include anticipated ongoing needs for usage and attitude research in rollout areas.

R. *Project development.* This item represents outside professional fees and expenses.

S. *Other indirect costs.* This line item includes such elements as the following:

1. Holiday and vacation expenses

2. Depreciation expenses

3. Service expenses for the shipping and traffic department

4. Distribution warehouse expenses

5. Plant engineering expenses

6. Insurance and taxes for manufacturing and warehousing facilities

7. All administrative and general expenses

8. Manufacturing development expenses

9. Corporate interest expense

10. Corporate managed charges

11. Group and company managed charges

12. Corporate research and development charges

13. Built-in factory variances

CONTINGENCIES

It is believed that there is likely to be strong competitive retaliation against the Satellite Batteries venture. Because of the magnitude of the program, it is felt to be unlikely that major competitors will simply do nothing while this venture is eroding their market share. Because of the strong probability of competitive action, the following assumptions and reactions have been prepared:

1. **LOWER PRICE.** If the competition were to substantially reduce prices in reaction to Satellite Batteries, the plan would be to counter these price reductions by temporary promotions. These could be either on the Satellite Batteries brand or on the regular product line. It is believed that temporary promotions in specific markets would effectively counteract price reductions without permanently reducing the profitability of either Hsinchu product line. These temporary promotions could take the form of trade allowances (retailer puts product on sale) or couponing (e.g., on-pack discount).

2. **INCREASED ADVERTISING.** Because of the very high spending levels on advertising for Satellite Batteries, the competition may very likely increase its spending levels. Because it is believed that Satellite Batteries' spending levels are already set at an optimum level, the plan would be to simply review the nature of competitive advertising, continue Satellite Batteries' advertising, and modify our program only if absolutely necessary. The specific reaction would

obviously depend on the message that competitors are trying to achieve. For example, if competitors are promoting the wrong consumer benefit, it would certainly not be necessary for Satellite Batteries to increase its advertising expenditures.

3. **LONGER–LIFE PRODUCT.** The competition may decide to produce a battery that lasts even longer than the Satellite Batteries product. It is believed to be unlikely that the largest competitor would do this, as it would simply be reducing the total market and would affect its sales more than Hsinchu's. On the other hand, a number of smaller manufacturers may decide to take this action. If this longer-lasting product appears to be successful, the plan would be to react by simply improving the Satellite Batteries product.

4. **ANOTHER MAJOR BRAND WITH A FREESTANDING DISPLAY.** The competition may decide to launch a venture similar to Satellite Batteries. Satellite Batteries would plan to counteract this by stepping up promotion activities (coupon drops), stepping up the advertising spending level, and perhaps even launching a competitive advertising program.

There is a possibility that a new brand would be introduced during the rollout period of Satellite Batteries, with the new entry attempting to gain an initial foothold in non-Satellite Batteries areas. In such an event, the plan would be to alter the rollout schedule and meet or beat the new brand into key market areas.

5. **INCREASED HEADQUARTERS CALLS.** A likely competitive reaction would be for other manufacturers to substantially increase their communications with retail headquarters' personnel. The plan would be to counteract this by increasing Satellite Batteries headquarters' servicing to an even greater degree.

CHAPTER 8

Using Telephone Surveys in Completing Market Reviews

Example: The Executive Conference Phone

It is not unusual to find that there is not enough information on your market available just from secondary sources. Normally these directories, magazines, trade publications, government reports, and other such sources provide a good starting point. Sometimes, however, they are just not enough. You wind up with a ton of information, but there is still a huge hole in the information. This is the time for primary research.

One good way to develop new information on a market is through a telephone survey. By contacting a few hundred people over the telephone, you can often get a pretty good idea of the missing part of the puzzle. Typically this is done by contracting with a market research organization that is capable of developing and implementing a custom survey. Such an organization will generally be able to work with you to prepare a questionnaire, identify the proper sample of respondents, administer the survey, and then tabulate the results. Many times it can also help you analyze the results.

The following marketing plan for the Executive Conference Phone is a good example of a market review that was done by combining data from secondary sources with a telephone survey. Although the specific information in this marketing plan has been altered because of its confidential nature, the plan will show you how a market review based on primary and secondary research can be structured. Although this plan is hypothetical, it is based on an actual marketing plan that was prepared by an actual company in a related business.

The Executive Conference Phone market review began with information from trade directories and Census data on population and business. It then included information from a telephone survey that was conducted with business equipment dealers in seventeen cities around the United States. Estimates were then compiled based on a combination of secondary data and the results of the survey. These projections, along with information from the consumer and trade interviews, enabled the company to prepare the planning assumptions and marketing objectives on which this marketing plan is based.

The Executive Conference Phone marketing plan is for telephone conferencing devices to be sold in a variety of different retail stores that carry telephone equipment. The consumers of this equipment include businesses and individuals who operate businesses out of their homes. This comprehensive plan includes a market review on the telephone conferencing device market, a review of consumer usage and attitudes, a review of trade practices and attitudes in appropriate channels of distribution, planning assumptions, marketing objectives, and each of the key marketing plan elements. It also includes detailed financial projections and a detailed set of contingency plans.

Marketing Plan for:
The Executive Conference Phone
Quinn Technologies Corporation[1]
October 1, 1999

INTRODUCTION

The purpose of this document is to develop a comprehensive marketing plan for a new conference phone system. This report is divided into the following sections:

1. **BACKGROUND.** This section reviews the background of this project and outlines the research efforts that led to the development of this marketing plan.

2. **MARKET REVIEW.** This section reviews the growth and nature of the market for conference phone devices. A detailed profile is provided on a national, regional (New York, New Jersey, Connecticut, Delaware, and Pennsylvania), and New Jersey only basis.

3. **CONSUMER USAGE AND ATTITUDES.** This section outlines present consumer practices, desires, and expectations regarding telephone conferencing devices.

4. **TRADE PRACTICES AND ATTITUDES.** This section reviews the retail trade's current involvement with telephone conferencing devices and its attitudes toward the product category.

5. **PLANNING ASSUMPTIONS.** This section presents the key conclusions based upon the facts presented in the previous sections, and the assumptions used in the development of specific plans and strategies.

[1] **Disclaimer:** The specific information in this sample marketing plan was compiled for intended use as an example only. Although this marketing plan is based on actual products from a real company, the specific information in the plan is hypothetical and is not intended to compete with or to divulge proprietary ideas, company structure, or the financial status of any company. The names, numbers, and some of the facts in this marketing plan have been changed because of the confidential nature of the information. The information is intended to be used as a guide only.

6. **KEY STRATEGIC MARKETING OBJECTIVES.** This section provides the specific objectives for this venture over the next five years.

7. **MARKETING PLAN ELEMENTS.** This section presents the specifics of the various plans developed to achieve the key strategic marketing objectives of this venture.

8. **FINANCIAL PROJECTIONS.** This section provides detailed calculations of the costs, volume, and payout of the venture from test market to national expansion. Pro forma profit-and-loss statements are provided on a national, regional, and New Jersey basis.

9. **CONTINGENCIES.** This section presents plans for retaliation against competitive actions affecting this venture.

The scope of this report is directed primarily at developing plans to launch a totally incremental venture on telephone conferencing devices. The information required to develop this marketing plan was gathered in eight stages. Each stage was designed to provide a systematic understanding of the current activities in the market for telephone conferencing devices, and to show how a new venture might fit within the framework of that market. The following specific steps were taken:

1. **INFORMATION GATHERING.** A careful review of technical material and previously available consumer research reports was conducted. A clipping service was retained to obtain copies of advertisements placed by manufacturers and retailers in selected key cities within the five-state eastern region.

2. **FIELD TRIPS.** Store checks and in-store interviews were conducted. A total of 101 stores in Connecticut, New York, and New Jersey within various trade classes were visited. In order to gain geographical perspective, an additional thirty stores in Los Angeles and elsewhere in California were personally visited.

3. **TELEPHONE SURVEYS.** In order to broaden the base of the store checks conducted during this study, additional surveys were conducted. Telephone interviews were conducted with a total of 130 retail outlets within the five-state region.

4. **MARKET PROFILE.** Based upon an analysis of the information gathered from the 261 stores surveyed and the secondary source data, a statistical profile of the U.S. market for telephone

conferencing devices was developed. This model was designed to provide a complete picture of the total market as well as of all the logical segmentations. This information is provided in the Market Review section of this report.

5. **CONSUMER RESEARCH.** Eight focus group sessions with eight to ten participants each were conducted by an independent moderator. The purpose of this research was to develop an understanding of consumers' present practices and attitudes as well as their reactions to concepts developed for various product offerings.

   To broaden the base of these focus groups, telephone surveys were conducted with 125 consumers in order to obtain specific data regarding attitudes and buying habits. The findings of both the focus group research and the consumer surveys are provided in the Consumer Usage and Attitudes section of this report.

6. **INDUSTRY/TRADE CONTACTS.** Interviews were conducted with manufacturers and distributors of telephone conferencing devices. From these sources, information on manufacturers' attitudes, trade margins, and pricing practices was developed on an industrywide basis.

7. **PLANNING ASSUMPTIONS.** Based on an analysis of the market profile, consumer research, manufacturer and trade practices, and trends in the industry, specific assumptions were made concerning whether the company should enter the telephone conferencing device market and what it would have to do to capitalize on any opportunities present in that market.

8. **MARKETING PLAN DEVELOPMENT.** Upon completion of the previous steps, a complete national and regional marketing plan was developed for the venture. This plan includes all the objectives, marketing elements, tactical plans, and financial projections needed for a consumer-oriented marketing venture.

BACKGROUND

In August 1999, a research study was completed that examined alternatives for providing improved customer satisfaction with telephone conferencing/speakerphone devices. The study examined ways to enlarge the appeal of these devices to small businesses and residential consumers. One of the main conclusions reached in this study was that the market potential for sophisticated devices was quite promising

In this study, the concept for a new product (to be called the Executive Conference Phone) achieved a clear preference over products currently on the market among both business and residence customers. The primary reason for this preference, according to the study, was very high voice quality.

In September 1999, Quinn Technologies Corporation decided to investigate the feasibility of launching a major telephone conferencing device program. The Executive Conference Phone was selected as the initial product to be used in this program. Preliminary plans called for a significant level of advertising expenditures. Since these expenditures would be made in a product category in which the company would face established competition, it was decided that it would be prudent for the company to thoroughly research the opportunity and to create a formal marketing plan for the venture. The balance of this document deals with the specifics of the research findings and the overall marketing plan.

MARKET REVIEW

1. *The primary retail channels of distribution for telephone conferencing devices are discount stores, department stores, electronic supply dealers, business equipment outlets, and record shops.* Among these five retail trade classes, there are 28,164 potential outlets available to sell telephone conferencing devices. Table 8-1 provides a breakdown of the number of retail outlets in each of these five retail trade classes by geographic region in the United States.

2. *In the five-state marketing region of New Jersey, New York, Pennsylvania, Connecticut, and Delaware, there are 6,075 potential outlets for selling telephone conferencing devices in the five retail trade classes, with 1,086 of these potential outlets being located in New Jersey.* Table 8-2 provides a breakdown by retail trade class of the number of outlets in both the five-state region and New Jersey.

3. *Electronic supply dealers tend to stock telephone conferencing devices to a significantly greater degree than do the other retail trade classes.* Approximately 83 percent of electronic supply dealers, 42 percent of record shops, and 30 percent of department stores stock

TABLE 8-1. Number of Selected Retail Outlets in 1999 by Type and Geographic Region

Region	Discount Stores	Dept. Stores	Electronic Supply Dealers (Retail)	Record Shops	Business Equipment Outlets	Total Outlets
Northeast	1,486	1,536	1,285	1,005	2,179	7,491
North Central	1,845	2,113	1,517	945	983	7,403
South	2,047	2,073	2,083	1,191	959	8,353
West	999	1,040	1,222	693	964	4,918
Total U.S.	6,377	6,762	6,107	3,834	5,085	28,165

Source: Estimates based on data from 1999 directories, Census data on population and business, and a sampling of business equipment dealers in seventeen cities.

TABLE 8-2. Number of Retail Outlets by Trade Class (1999)
New Jersey and Five-State Region

	Total Number of Stores	
	N.J.	Five-State Region
Discount	191	1,089
Department	224	1,249
Electronic supply	177	1,010
Record shops	360	1,871
Business equipment	134	856
Total	1,086	6,075

Note: Five-state region includes New Jersey, New York, Connecticut, Delaware, and Pennsylvania.
Source: Estimates based on data from 1999 directories, Census data on population and business, and a sampling of business equipment dealers in seventeen cities.

telephone conferencing devices. Only 15 percent of business equipment outlets and 14 percent of discount stores stock this product category.

4. *There is a wide variation among the retail trade classes in terms of their annual average movement per store stocking and their average retail price per unit.* As shown in Table 8-3, average annual movement per store stocking ranges from a high of 40 units in department stores down to a low of 7 units in business equipment stores. Similarly, the average retail price ranges from $62 per unit in discount stores up to $196 in business equipment stores.

5. *The retail trade sells a total of 299,000 telephone conferencing devices on a national basis.* The majority of the unit movement, 52 percent, is accounted for by electronic supply stores,

TABLE 8-3. Average Unit Movement and Price for Each Retail Outlet
Stocking Telephone Conferencing Devices (1999)

Retail Trade Class	Average Annual Unit Movement per Store Stocking	Average Retail Price
Discount stores	36	$ 62
Department stores	40	195
Electronic supply dealers	31	105
Record stores	24	164
Business equipment stores	7	196

Source: Estimates based upon store checks and telephone surveys within the five-state region.

with an additional 27 percent coming from department stores. Thus, these two retail trade classes account for 79 percent of the total national unit volume of telephone conferencing devices.

6. *Retail channels of distribution generate $39.5 million in retail dollar sales from the sale of telephone conferencing devices.* At an average 39 percent trade margin, this represents $23.9 million in factory dollar sales. On a New Jersey and five-state basis, respectively, retail dollar sales are $1.36 million and $7.6 million. Table 8-4 provides a breakdown of retail dollar sales by retail trade class for New Jersey, the five-state region, and the total United States.

7. *Significant unit and dollar volumes are generated through channels of distribution other than retail outlets.* These channels include mail order, catalog sales, factory direct sales, and

TABLE 8-4. 1999 Dollar Sales Through Retail Channels of Distribution, Telephone Conferencing Devices
(In Thousands)

Outlet Category	Retail Dollar Sales Retail Trade Five-State		
	N.J.	Region	U.S.
Discount	$ 62	$ 341	$ 1,984
Department	527	2,925	15,795
Electronic supply	473	2,730	16,485
Record shops	82	500	2,296
Business equipment	216	1,068	2,940
Total retail trade outlets	$1,360	$7,564	$39,500

Source: Estimates based upon store checks, telephone surveys, and traditional retail practices in different channels of distribution.

other telephone companies. In total, these other channels account for an additional 23,600 units, $9.5 million in retail sales, and $8.3 million in factory sales. Table 8-5 provides a breakdown of unit sales, retail sales, and factory sales by each of these other distribution channels.

8. *Through all channels of distribution, the total 1999 market for telephone conferencing devices amounted to 322,600 units and $49.0 million in retail sales.* As summarized in Table 8-6, retail distribution channels accounted for an estimated 93 percent of units and 81 percent of retail dollars. The difference between the retail levels of dominance for units and dollars results from the fact that higher-priced and more sophisticated units travel through the nonretail distribution channel, while virtually all of the low-priced equipment in the market is sold through traditional retail outlets.

9. *The total market for telephone conferencing devices is projected to grow to 429,400 units and $68.9 million in retail dollar sales by 2002.* The projections for 2000 through 2002

TABLE 8-5. 1999 Unit and Dollar Sales Through Distribution Channels Other Than Retail Trade Outlets Total United States (In Thousands)

Distribution Channel	Unit Movement	$ Sales Retail	Margin %	$ Sales Factory
Mail order	2.4	$ 400	40%	$ 240
Catalog sales (department, electronic supply)	7.0	975	40%	585
Factory direct	4.0	2,000	0%	2,000
Other phone companies	10.2	6,170	13%	5,368
Total	23.6	$9,545		$8,193

Source: Estimates based upon normal industry relationships between distribution channels and discussions with industry research personnel.

TABLE 8-6. 1999 Summary of Total Industry in Units and Dollar Sales

	Unit Sales		
	Units (000)	% of Units (000)	Retail $
Retail outlet distribution channels	300.0	93%	$39,500
Other distribution channels	22.6	7%	9,545
Total	322.6	100%	$49,045

Source: Estimates based on data from directories, Census data on population and business, and a sampling of equipment dealers in seventeen cities.

represent a relatively conservative growth rate of 12 percent per year in dollar volume and 10 percent per year in unit volume. Table 8-7 outlines the history and forecasted growth of the telephone conferencing market by each of the three geographic breakdowns from 1997 to 2002.

10. *In 1999 the telephone conferencing device market was relatively concentrated, with Acme, Phone Shack, and Able Industries accounting for 76 percent of unit sales and 71 percent of factory dollar sales.* Phone Shack was estimated to have the highest unit share, with 35 percent; however, its share of factory dollars was estimated to be only 17 percent as a result of the low-priced nature of the Phone Shack product. Table 8-8 provides a breakdown of market shares in units and dollars for the major manufacturers of telephone conferencing devices.

11. *On a price point basis, units selling for $200 and under accounted for 90 percent of total unit sales and 78 percent of retail dollar sales in 1999.* Units priced at $100 or under accounted for an estimated 46 percent of unit sales and 26 percent of retail dollar sales. Units falling into the price range of $101 to $200 accounted for 44 percent of unit sales and 52 percent of total retail dollar sales. Table 8-9 provides a breakdown of unit and dollar sales by major breaks in price points.

TABLE 8-7. Telephone Conferencing Devices
Total United States Market History and Forecast (1997–2002)
(Thousands of Dollars and Units)

	1997	1998	1999	2000	2001	2002
Retail $ Sales						
New Jersey	1,313	1,464	1,687	1,889	2,116	2,370
Five-state region	7,313	8,154	9,393	10,520	11,782	13,196
United States	38,183	42,574	49,045	54,930	61,522	68,905
U.S. growth/year	11.5%	15.2%	12%	12%	12%	—
Unit Sales						
New Jersey	8.2	9.1	10.5	11.6	12.8	14.1
Five-state region	46.3	51.6	59.3	65.2	71.7	78.9
United States	251.6	280.5	322.6	354.9	390.4	429.4
U.S. growth/year	11.5%	15.0	10.0	10.0	10.0	—

Source: For the years 1997–1999, estimates are based upon store checks, telephone surveys, and trade interviews. For the years 2000–2002, a conservative growth rate of 12 percent per year in dollar volume and 10 percent per year in unit volume is estimated, reflecting a trend toward more sophisticated units for home use.

TABLE 8-8. Market Share by Manufacturer (1999)
Total United States

| | | | Dollar Sales | | | |
| | Unit Sales | | Retail | | Factory | |
Manufacturer	(000)	%	$MM	%	$MM	%
Phone Shack	113	35%	$ 9.0	18%	$ 5.4	17%
Acme	108	33	17.5	36	10.5	33
Able Industries	25	8	8.9	18	6.9	21
Centrex	25	8	5.0	10	3.0	9
Hatachi	15	5	2.5	5	1.5	5
Griffin	10	3	1.7	4	1.0	3
Moble	4	1	2.0	4	2.0	6
All Others	23	7	2.4	5	1.9	6
Total	323	100%	$49.0	100%	$32.2	100%

Source: Estimates based upon store checks, telephone surveys, trade publications, and the use of Dun & Bradstreet reports.

TABLE 8-9. 1999 Summary of Unit and Retail Dollar Sales Through Retail Channels of Distribution by Price Point

| | Unit Sales | | Total Retail Trade Retail Dollar Sales | |
| | # | % | | |
Unit Sales	(000)	(000)	$	%
$0–$100	137.8	46%	10,124	26%
$101–$200	130.3	44	20,693	52
$201–$300	29.7	10	8,215	21
$301 and up	1.2	0	468	1
Total	299.0	100%	39,500	100%

Source: Estimates based on store checks and a telephone survey with retailers.

12. *The pure business segment accounted for 52 percent of 1999 unit volume and, more importantly, 67 percent of the industry's total factory dollar sales.* The residence business category (business in the home) accounted for 43 percent of unit volume and 29 percent of factory dollar sales. Pure residential purchase, for personal use only, accounted for 5 percent of unit volume and 4 percent of factory dollar sales. Table 8-10 provides a purchase summary by market segment.

13. *Total manufacturer advertising for telephone conferencing devices has ranged from a low of $158,000 in 1998 to a high of $1.1 million in 1996, with little consistency in expenditure*

TABLE 8-10. Breakdown of 1999 Business and Residence Purchases in Units and Factory Dollars
(In Thousands)

	Unit Sales		Factory $ Sales	
Market Segment	#	%	#	%
Business	166.6	52%	$21,675	67%
Residence business	137.6	43	9,294	29
Residence personal	18.8	5	1,267	4
Total	323.0	100%	$32,236	100%

Source: Estimates based upon store checks, telephone surveys, and industry interviews.

level by manufacturer. The highest year for both Acme and the industry was 1996, in which
Acme spent 75 percent of total advertising dollars. The lowest year was 1998, in which
advertising amounted to only $158,000, with Acme spending only $37,000, or 23 percent
of the total. Table 8-11 provides a breakdown of advertising expenditures by manufacturer.

14. *Though media usage varied significantly from year to year, total TV expenditures for 1996
    through 1999 amounted to $1.1 million and represented the largest single media segment,
    with 39 percent of total industry spending.* The second largest category was consumer
    magazines, with total 1996 to 1999 expenditures of $782,000, or 28 percent of total industry
    spending. Radio was the only other significant medium, with $634,000 in total spending
    from 1996 to 1999, representing 23 percent of total manufacturer media outlays. Table 8-
    12 provides a breakdown of advertising expenditures by medium.

TABLE 8-11. Industry Advertising by Manufacturer (1996–1999)
(In Thousands)

	1996		1997		1998		1999		Total 1996–1999	
	$	%	$	%	$	%	$	%	$	%
Acme	$804	75%	$681	73%	$37	23%	$285	49%	$1,807	66%
Phone Shack	69	6	34	4	94	60	107	18	304	11
Able Industries	24	2	14	1	26	16	118	20	182	7
Centrex	92	9	77	8	—	—	79	13	248	9
Hatachi	29	3	7	1	1	1	—	—	37	1
Griffin	53	5	122	13	—	—	—	—	175	6
Total	$1,071	100%	$935	100%	$158	100%	$589	100%	$2,753	100%

Source: Radio expenditure reports, media records, newspapers, business publications, magazine services.
Note: Does not include retailer cooperative advertising or catalog space and charges.

TABLE 8-12. Industry Advertising by Medium, 1996–1999 (In Thousands)

	1996		1997		1998		1999		Total 1996–1999	
	$	%	$	%	$	%	$	%	$	%
Consumer magazines	295.6	28	219.7	23	22.9	15	$243.5	41	$781.7	28
Business publications	65.3	6	25.4	3	12.6	8	21.5	4	124.8	5
Newspapers	52.9	5	3.8	—	28.8	18	37.1	6	122.6	5
Radio	296.6	28	137.9	15	90.4	57	111.5	19	636.4	23
TV	360.3	33	547.4	59	3.0	2	176.4	30	1,087.1	39
Total	$1,070.7	100%	$934.2	100%	$157.7	100%	$590.0	100%	$2,752.6	100%

Source: Radio expenditure reports, media records, newspapers, business publications, magazine services.

CONSUMER USAGE AND ATTITUDES

1. *The current and potential users of telephone conferencing devices can be divided into three categories.* Based upon place and nature of use, these categories break down as follows:

   A. *Businesses that operate out of nonresidence locations.* This usage is primarily during business hours.

   B. *Residence usage for business-related purposes.* This type of usage is typically for a sales or management type of occupation. Although the majority of use in this segment is business, some personal usage does occur.

   C. *Residence use for solely personal reasons.* The motivations here normally center on the need to communicate with social contacts.

2. *Current owners of high-quality telephone speakerphone systems consider these systems to be superior to the alternative of simply using the speakerphone on their business telephone.* High-quality telephone speakerphone systems are considered to be expensive, but far superior to the normal speakerphone on a telephone.

3. *Almost 90 percent of all owners use their devices daily.* They tend to use the devices between 7:00 A.M. and 7:00 P.M.

4. *The fundamental justification for buying and using an expensive telephone conferencing device is that it will pay for itself within a short period of time by allowing high-quality meetings without travel.* Another advantage is eliminating the possibility of irritating exist-

ing customers and causing potential customers to go elsewhere because of poor-quality teleconferencing.

5. *The average period to make a decision to purchase a telephone conferencing device is two months.* These devices are rarely purchased on impulse. The time frame of consideration was only a matter of days in some cases, but the decision frequently took as long as a year.

6. *The actual decision to buy takes place when the need to have quality teleconferencing meetings becomes of paramount importance.* Poor-quality calls may have resulted in either lost business or irritated customers and friends. This problem then motivates potential buyers to overcome their guilt feelings over the high cost of the machine.

7. *Once the decision to buy is made, only a minimal amount of comparison shopping is done.* Generally the features desired are fairly well defined in the potential buyer's mind. The actual selection may be reduced to one or two manufacturers and two or fewer models. In addition, most people who are potential buyers of telephone conferencing devices have a general awareness of how much such a device should cost. In general, it is felt that low-quality units are available for under $100, with "decent" units costing from $150 to $200.

8. *Males make the majority of purchases, and they do so in retail stores at which they currently shop.* Regardless of who uses the device, the actual purchase is usually made by the man. Since the purchase usually involves a significant amount of money, familiar stores are used. In the event that a problem occurs and a return or exchange is necessary, the consumer feels that it will be easier to have things settled to his satisfaction at a store where he normally shops.

9. *Purchase is the predominant form of acquisition.* It is generally considered much more economical to buy than to rent or lease. Consumers feel that the only time that rental or leasing is appropriate is for the higher-priced units (those costing about $1,500).

10. *Consumers are unable to identify a dominant brand of telephone conferencing devices.* When asked, consumers mentioned the names of several manufacturers, some of which don't even make telephone conferencing devices.

11. *Consumers feel that the minimum warranty period on a telephone conferencing device should be six months.* Manufacturers' warranties vary considerably in length of coverage.

Consumers believe that ninety days or less is too short, six months should be the minimum, and a year is the maximum expected.

12. *Generally, current owners and potential buyers had very definite ideas about what features they desire in a telephone conferencing device.* Consumer desires can be broken down into two areas: "major" features that influence the purchase decision, and "minor" features that are not critical but are nice to have as long as the price is not increased. Major features include an A/C plug and good voice quality. Minor features include adjustable volume settings and a choice of colors.

13. *Consumers have definite opinions on what features they don't like in a telephone conferencing device.* Battery operation and poor voice quality are seen as negatives. In many cases, it is current owners who are particularly vocal about the negative features and their dissatisfaction with their own devices.

14. *The Executive Conference Phone concept was generally well liked by consumers.* The consumers interviewed gave the unit high marks on appearance, voice quality, features, and apparent sturdiness. The unit was viewed by consumers as having a high price/value relationship, given the price and the features offered. One of the criticisms of the product was that it appeared cumbersome.

TRADE PRACTICES AND ATTITUDES

The retail sector of the telephone conferencing device market is clearly the dominant market segment. Therefore, it was necessary to gain a full understanding of retailer attitudes toward this product category in order to evaluate what opportunities might exist and what competitive actions against a new venture would be either likely or possible. The following findings are the result of an intense retail survey to determine the practices and attitudes of the retail sector.

1. *The established demand for and high profitability of telephone conferencing devices results in a generally positive retailer attitude.* The product category has an established demand that requires little or no effort to stimulate on the part of the retailer. Each sale yields a high profit compared to other retail merchandise because of the following factors:

A. *It is a high-ticket item.* The average retail price in department and business equipment stores is $195, which is significantly higher than the average sale in those stores. This relationship holds in the other channels also. For example, a discount store with an average retail price of $62 still finds this significantly above its average purchase transaction.

B. *It is easy to demonstrate.* With only a small amount of training, the average store clerk can learn how to operate and explain the features of telephone conferencing devices.

C. *It has a small SKU count.* The number of stock-keeping units (SKUs) is usually limited to two items. The small size of the units requires little backroom inventory space.

2. *A large negative in the minds of retailers is the problem of pilferage.* Because of the high value of these devices, most of them are displayed underneath expensive glass displays for security reasons. It is necessary to have a sales clerk unlock the display and take out the unit in order to give a demonstration.

3. *Generally retailers carry two brands of telephone conferencing devices to offer the broadest selection to their customers.* The major exception to this is Phone Shack, which, for the most part, promotes its own private label. The breadth of selection is largest in department stores. In other channels, the selection is usually limited to a few fast-moving models.

4. *Retailer dissatisfaction with either a brand or the product category is usually the result of defective merchandise.* Faulty merchandise is usually returned to the store during the first thirty to ninety days. In order to prevent customer unhappiness with the store, the retailer is forced to either exchange one unit for another or refund the customer's money. When this happens often with either a particular brand or the whole product category, the desirability of selling telephone conferencing devices is greatly diminished.

5. *Delivering a high-quality, up-to-date product on time is more important than price or margins.* A high-quality vendor is very important, since the margins provided by various manufacturers are almost all about the same. The average margin is 39 percent off list, with the range being from about 35 to 45 percent. For competitive reasons, most product offerings are also priced near the same price points.

6. *Except for being in a manned location, telephone conferencing devices have no established home in the retail outlet.* The location in the store varies among outlets in the same chain

and among different retail distribution channels. In discount stores and department stores, these devices are located with either electronics equipment, office supplies, or cameras. In electronic supply stores and record stores, they are usually located near a manned counter and under glass. In business equipment stores, they are usually not prominently displayed and must be asked for by the customer.

7. *Display practices are normally to have two models on display, with the balance of the inventory in the backroom.* Not all the units available are put into the display case, since the only difference between the various models offered by a particular manufacturer is the features provided. During the sales demonstration, the salesperson explains the features available on the various models from that manufacturer.

8. *Retail displays make minimal use of point-of-purchase material.* It was the exception when point-of-purchase material was available without asking. The normal procedure is for the potential customer to be given a brochure only after the demonstration, and even then the sales clerk usually has to be asked for it.

9. *Monthly replenishment of store inventory results in frequent out-of-stock situations.* Most stores are shipped a monthly allotment of telephone conferencing devices through the chain warehouse. Often, these allotments do not reflect customer preference or sales history. Consequently, it is not uncommon for lower-priced units to be quickly sold out, leaving the retailer with only the higher-priced units in stock.

10. *The function of in-store personnel is that of a basic order taker.* The sales clerk normally does not actively solicit the sale. When asked about the product, the sales clerk will explain the product features and pull stock from the back room. In-store personnel are not well trained. In all outlets except the electronic supply stores, sales personnel had very limited product knowledge. In electronic supply stores, salespeople not only knew the product thoroughly, but also were aware of why one model was to be preferred over another and why one brand was seemingly better than another.

11. *Telephone conferencing devices as a product category are generally sold at suggested list price by retailers.* The major exception is discount stores, which specialize in either the lower-quality brands or discontinued merchandise. In all other retail channels, when sales

or promotions do occur, they usually provide only a small dollar saving (like $10 or $20), not a major price reduction.

12. *Most retailers deal directly with the manufacturer.* The larger discount and department store chains utilize their centralized buying power to deal with the manufacturer, and then use their chain warehouses to distribute the product to the individual stores. Electronic supply dealers like Phone Shack contract directly with foreign manufacturers for their private-label units. Nonchain retailers use distributors, while some other retailers actually become distributors in order to gain an increased profit margin.

PLANNING ASSUMPTIONS

1. *The market for telephone conferencing devices is worthwhile and growing.* The projected 12 percent annual growth rate will expand the market from the 1999 level of 323,000 units and $49 million in retail dollar sales to 429,000 units and $68.9 million in retail dollar sales by 2002.

2. *There is a strong consumer preference for outright purchase rather than rental.* This definite preference held by the majority of consumers is the result of the following factors:

    A. *The majority of units are inexpensive.* The relatively low cost (under $200) of the majority of units offered for sale makes the dollar outlay required for purchase well within the reach of the average consumer.

    B. *Leasing is viewed as being for high-priced units.* The leasing of a telephone conferencing device is felt to be appropriate only for very sophisticated equipment priced at over $500. Recognizing that their needs were fairly simple, the vast majority of consumers rejected the idea of a lease or rental arrangement as an unacceptable alternative because they associate it with high cost.

3. *A full product line is required in order for the company to take full advantage of the incremental business opportunity offered by telephone conferencing devices.* A complete product line will offer the potential for penetrating all market segments. By having a variety of conferencing devices priced competitively, Quinn Technologies should be able to generate sufficient volume to cover all program costs and provide a reasonable profit.

4. *In order for Quinn Technologies to successfully launch a program to sell telephone conferencing devices, a complete marketing plan is required.* Because of the competitive nature of the market, a comprehensive plan with the following primary elements should be developed:

A. *Achieve consumer awareness.* It will be necessary to develop consumer awareness of the fact that Quinn Technologies has its own brand of telephone conferencing devices, that these devices are competitively priced, and that they are available on an outright sale basis. In addition, consumers must be aware that all a person has to do is go to a local retailer to obtain a conferencing device.

B. *Price the product competitively.* The pricing structure will have to be competitive with that of the current product offerings.

C. *Utilize existing organization.* The program will have to be designed so that it can be launched within the framework of the existing organization.

D. *Limit risk.* The risk to Quinn Technologies from developing and launching a venture on telephone conferencing devices will be substantially reduced by a step-by-step consumer research and marketing effort. The use of a test market prior to national expansion provides a logical checkpoint. Various forms of research (focus groups, surveys, and copy testing) will ensure that the final program contains the best-developed series of program elements available.

KEY STRATEGIC MARKETING OBJECTIVES

1. *To create and maintain, over the next five years, a highly profitable consumer franchise and to establish Quinn Technologies as a major source of telephone conferencing devices.* This objective centers on the goal of obtaining a significant share of the market for telephone conferencing devices by developing a definite consumer preference for the product offerings of Quinn Technologies.

2. *To expand the total market for telephone conferencing devices dramatically through a low-key, yet aggressive, marketing effort.* The first part of this objective is to increase the acceptability of using telephone conferencing devices by conducting a semi-institutional advertising program. The second part of the objective is to obtain a major market share of these "converts" as buyers of Quinn's unique brand of telephone conferencing devices.

3. *To target the thrust of the marketing effort toward the business and residence business market segments.* This objective defines those consumers toward whom the elements of the marketing plan will be oriented.

4. *To provide the consumer with a product that has an excellent price/value relationship.* This objective will fulfill consumer expectations regarding the high quality of equipment that is available from Quinn Technologies, and for a competitive price.

5. *To appeal to the broadest range of consumers by offering a broad product line for maximum reach.* A total of four models will be offered so that the needs of all market segments will be addressed from both a feature and a price standpoint.

6. *To offer the products to the consumer on a direct-sale basis only.* The aim of this objective is to maximize the market potential by responding to the consumer's preference for purchase and to minimize the overhead costs associated with leasing or rental so that the product will be competitive.

7. *To price the products at a slight premium.* It is anticipated that once a unit is engineered to be competitively priced, a small premium ($5 to $20 per unit) will be added to reflect the quality image of products from Quinn Technologies.

8. *To obtain a 20 percent market share of unit and retail dollar sales.* This objective seeks to achieve a realistic sales level in order to justify a national program.

9. *To generate sales of 104,000 units and $19 million in retail dollar sales in 2002.* This objective assumes a 1/1/01 introduction of a national program, and seeks to obtain sales through market penetration and market expansion resulting from Quinn Technologies' entry into the market.

10. *To produce an average income before tax rate equal to a minimum of 10 percent of net sales.* This objective is aimed at setting a minimum cutoff point in the evaluation of profitability.

11. *To minimize the financial risk by using a test market approach prior to national expansion.* Four test market cities will be used to test various elements of the marketing plan. Marketing

plan elements and financial projections will be revised and presented to Quinn Technologies management prior to national expansion.

12. *To begin test marketing on 7/1/00, and to go national by 1/1/01.* Although this timetable will require an all-out management commitment, it seems to be a worthwhile target on which to plan.

MARKETING PLAN ELEMENTS

1. *A product line consisting of four models will be developed in order to obtain the broadest consumer appeal.* These units will be an economy unit; a basic unit, which will be the standard unit of the product line; a deluxe unit; and a deluxe unit with remote access. Specifically, these units will have the following features:

   A. *Economy unit.* This conferencing device is designed to match the limited feature needs of a significant part of the market, with a price that is affordable by most potential users. Intended to be a competitive product pricewise, this unit is battery-operated. Since many users and potential users indicated that battery operation was a negative, an A/C adapter will be available as an option.

   B. *Basic unit.* This model is to serve as the fundamental unit in the product line in that its technological design will be the basis for the other two models. This conferencing device has all the features of competitive units at similar prices. This unit provides A/C plug-in.

   C. *Deluxe unit.* This unit includes the feature of voice activation. The other features of the deluxe unit are identical to those of the basic unit.

   D. *Deluxe unit with remote access.* The remote access feature provides the user with the ability to adjust the telephone conferencing device from anywhere in the room. The other features of this model are identical to those of the deluxe unit.

2. *The design of the product line will be contemporary and distinctive.* The units will have an appearance that will allow instant consumer identification of what the unit is and that it is from Quinn Technologies. Specifically, the product line will adhere to the following design objectives:

A. *Reflect the actual value of the product.* The device's appearance at all price points will be that of a premium product that obviously has been manufactured so that it will last a long time.

B. *Reflect Quinn Technologies' quality image.* The quality image of the units will be consistent with that of other Quinn Technologies offerings in order to fulfill consumer expectations and therefore maintain Quinn Technologies' image.

C. *Design upgraded by price point.* Although all units will be designed around a common theme, and will therefore have a similar appearance, as the price of the models increases, so should the overall appearance of the unit. For example, the deluxe unit might be in a wood-grained enclosure with black trim, while the economy unit might be available in plain white.

3. *The actual production of the entire product line will be done by an outside supplier.* Quinn Technologies will develop and provide the specifications and engineering input for the product line. Current manufacturers of telephone conferencing devices will then be contacted to determine their willingness and ability to supply Quinn Technologies' product needs on a private-label basis. The units will then be purchased by Quinn Technologies, which will serve as the distribution system for the national program.

4. *The product line will be offered at four price points.* The sales prices of the four models are provided in Table 8-13.

5. *For the most part, the telephone conferencing devices will be intended for self-installation by the consumer.* Each device will have a connector that will fit into either of the two types of telephone jack receptacles. When no telephone jack exists, the telephone company will have to make a separate house call to install one at the normal telephone jack installation charge.

TABLE 8-13. Product Pricing

Model	Price
Economy unit	$ 99
Basic unit	$180
Deluxe unit	$210
Deluxe unit with remote	$315

6. *If a unit is defective, it will be replaced with either a new or a reconditioned unit.* During the warranty period (six months), the conferencing device will be replaced free. After the warranty period, the consumer may have a defective unit replaced for a small cost. This additional cost is dependent upon the cost to Quinn Technologies of having units reconditioned or replaced. This cost plus overhead will be passed on to the consumer.

7. *The product line will be marketed under a unique Quinn Technologies brand name, with individual models being designated by model numbers.* The tentative name for the product line is the Executive Conference Phone. The final brand name will be developed in conjunction with the advertising campaign and must have the following qualities:

   A. *Be preemptive and proprietary.* This will enable it to be trademarked for exclusive Quinn Technologies utilization in the telephone conferencing device product category.

   B. *Be applicable to advertising and promotion.* The name has to have the ability to lend itself to advertising and promotional activities on behalf of the brand.

   C. *Be meaningful to the target market.* The name should have a positive meaning and relevance to the target market of business and residence business users (e.g., increased profit, customer service, and so on).

   D. *Be timeless.* The name should not be one that is likely to be easily dated or become obsolete.

8. *A display will be provided in each retail store to catch the consumers' attention and serve to demonstrate the product line.* Specifically, the objectives of the display are as follows:

   A. *Create interest.* The displays will be located in stores and will be designed to draw the attention of visitors and customers and lead to further investigation.

   B. *Demonstrate the unit.* The display should provide both a working telephone conferencing device and a demonstration of a telephone hook-up to allow for consumer experimentation.

   C. *Be flexible to meet retailers' needs.* The display should be flexible enough to accommodate various-sized stores. It should also use a minimal amount of floor space.

   D. *Have a three-year minimum life.* The display should be designed to provide a minimum of three years' service.

   E. *Dispense brochures.* The display should hold and dispense informational brochures on the various telephone conferencing device models.

F. *Be affordable.* The display, not counting the telephone conferencing device, should be obtainable from an outside supplier for less than $75 per display.

9. *A full-time national program coordinator and nineteen regional product managers (on a part-time basis) will be needed to staff the program.* The national program coordinator will create the annual marketing plan and monitor the overall progress of the program. The coordinator will also be responsible for implementing the marketing plan, coordinating with the regional product managers, and interfacing with the manufacturer of the conferencing devices and the other outside suppliers.

10. *Training will be provided for the customer contact personnel at retail stores.* This training will provide them with overall product knowledge, sales and billing information and procedures, and the replacement policy for defective units. This training will be done by the regional product managers.

11. *The objective of the venture's advertising copy is to build awareness of and demand for the telephone conferencing devices among the target audience.* Specifically, the following points should register with the target audience:

A. *Overall product quality.* The Quinn Technologies' telephone conferencing devices have been designed to be consistent with the quality standards of other products from the company.

B. *Specific product advantages.* Different models have been designed to provide various feature needs, and how those features positively compare to the competition.

12. *The overall objective of the advertising media plan is to obtain broad coverage of the target market (business and residence business users) and to direct special efforts toward selected groups.* Examples of these groups are skilled craft workers, professionals, and the self-employed. Specifically, the media objectives are:

A. *Reach and frequency.* To achieve a minimum reach of 80 percent of the target market an average of three times per month during the introductory period. On a sustained basis, to achieve a reach of 50 percent of the target market an average of two times per month.

B. *Awareness.* To use large ad formats and full color to generate overall consumer awareness that telephone conferencing devices are now available from Quinn Technologies.

    C.   *Appropriate media.* To select and utilize media that will permit full and effective communication of product benefits and the features that are available on the various models.

    D.   *Advertising continuity.* To develop a media plan that will provide continuity of advertising throughout the year.

13. *The overall media strategy will be to use magazines as the primary medium, use supplementary media for specialized markets, and front-end load the plan for maximum introductory impact.* The specifics of this strategy are as follows:

    A.   *Magazines as primary medium.* Magazines are seen as superior to other advertising media for communicating the venture's copy points for the following reasons:

        1. *Selectivity.* Specific magazines can reach the target market selectively.

        2. *Efficiency.* For the telephone conferencing device market, magazines (on a cost-per-thousand basis) most efficiently deliver impressions to the target market.

        3. *Sales development.* Printed media will allow a complete and detailed sales presentation to be made to the target consumer. Sufficient facts can be provided without the time constraints inherent in television and radio.

        4. *Lengthy message requirement.* The complicated copy requirements of this advertising campaign preclude the use of outdoor advertising, radio, and television. Daily newspapers will be considered for use only during the sustaining periods, when no color advertising will be scheduled.

    B.   *Supplementary media.* As supplementary media, industry publications and direct mail will be used to support specialized markets. This will provide increased coverage of groups with high incidences of usage or those who don't normally read a large number of magazines frequently, such as doctors, lawyers, contractors, and so on.

    C.   *Media spending.* Two front-end-loaded spending levels will be tested to determine the optimum amount of advertising required for the venture. The high-level plan will introduce the venture at a $4 million level of national expenditure. During succeeding years, this budget will drop to $2.5 million nationally. The low-level budget to be tested will be exactly half of that for the high-level plan. Table 8-14 summarizes the two national budgets to be tested.

14. *A formal test market is planned for the venture prior to a full national introduction.* The test will last for a period of six months in four cities representing a total of 2 percent of the

TABLE 8-14. Split-Level Advertising Test of National Media Plan

Medium	High-Level National Budget (000)	Low-Level National Budget (000)
Consumer magazines	$3,111	$1,555
Business publications	106	53
Direct mail	194	97
Production	589	295
Total introduction	$4,000	$2,000
Going year	$2,500	$1,250

households in the total United States. At the end of the six months, the results will be evaluated to determine if and how the program should be expanded. The following specific areas will be evaluated:

A. *Volume forecast.* Unit and dollar sales will be measured to determine the viability of the objectives set forth in this marketing plan. If necessary, the sales forecast will be modified after the test market.

B. *Advertising spending.* Two separate levels of advertising will be run during the test market. Two markets will be at the high level of advertising, and the other two markets will be at the low level. The ideal level of advertising will be determined based on the actual sales achieved at each level.

C. *Advertising communication effectiveness.* The degree of success in reaching the target audience and in communicating the proper message will be determined.

D. *Internal effectiveness.* The effectiveness of all levels of the organization involved in the venture will be evaluated to determine the success of the training program, communication channels, and so on.

E. *Overall plan effectiveness.* A miniature version of the total national plan will be launched during the test market. The objective of the research conducted during the test will be to identify any area that should be modified. This will include suppliers, product performance, cost variations, organizational effectiveness, and so on.

15. *Major research and product-testing projects will be conducted during the early stages of the program.* These various projects will seek to develop a tracking system so that actual progress may be measured against the objectives outlined in this marketing plan. The follow-

ing are the types of research and testing projects that will be conducted to refine and track this marketing plan before and during the test market.

A. *Product testing.* Quinn Technologies will conduct bench testing of the prototypes and initial production runs to ensure that they meet the original specifications.

B. *Copy testing.* The advertising copy will be tested in order to determine how well it meets the copy objectives.

C. *Consumer research.* Consumer focus groups will be conducted to determine if any change in consumer usage and attitudes has occurred prior to or during the implementation of the program. In addition, surveys will be conducted to test awareness and effectiveness of the program in particular and the product category of telephone conferencing devices in general.

D. *Internal tracking.* The company will develop and conduct an internal tracking study to determine unit movement and sales for the program as a whole and for each region. This study will serve as a foundation for the annual marketing plan and related sales forecasts.

E. *Test market translation.* From the research conducted during the test market, results will be projected on a national basis and the finalized elements of the marketing plan will be adjusted to reflect this added input.

F. *Ongoing research.* On an ongoing basis, copy testing, consumer research, and internal tracking will be conducted throughout the life of the program.

16. This marketing plan is based on the tentative timetable in Table 8-15.

FINANCIAL PROJECTIONS

1. *Launching a telephone conferencing device program is expected to provide Quinn Technologies with an incremental business opportunity of between $114 and $173 million in revenue and between $19.7 and $28.0 million in before-tax profits between the years 2001 and 2005.* These projections are based upon a multitude of assumptions. The following summarizes these assumptions based on a high and a low level of advertising expenditures.

    A. *The entry of Quinn Technologies into the telephone conferencing device product category is expected to expand the overall national market by 25 to 40 percent in 2002.*

TABLE 8-15. Tentative Venture Timetable

Management presentations for approval	10/1/99
Select national program coordinator	11/1/99
Determine product design	12/1/99
Determine product availability and cost	12/15/99
Decide on brand name	1/1/00
Develop advertising program	1/15/00
Management presentations on regional basis	2/1/00
Product testing completed	2/1/00
Develop collateral material	3/1/00
Complete training for test market	6/1/00
Test market introduction	7/1/00
National expansion	1/1/01

Without Quinn Technologies' entering the market, the normal market growth would result in 2002 sales of 344,000 units and $55 million in national retail dollar sales. With Quinn Technologies' entry on a national basis, the overall market in 2002 is expected to grow to 481,000 units and $77 million based upon the high-level advertising budget, and to 429,000 units or $69 million based upon the low-level budget.

B. *Quinn Technologies' market share is expected to depend on the level of advertising.* Quinn Technologies is expected to obtain a 17 percent market share with the low-level advertising plan, representing 73,100 units and $13.7 million in retail sales. The high-level advertising plan is expected to result in a 21.7 percent market share for Quinn Technologies, with unit sales of 104,400 and retail dollar sales of $19.6 million.

C. *Assuming a 1/1/01 implementation of a national plan, Quinn Technologies expects to achieve a 20.9 percent profit margin (before taxes) for the year 2005 and a cumulative profit margin for the years 2001 to 2005 of 15.0 percent based upon the planning assumptions for the low-level advertising plan.* Table 8-16 provides a financial overview of the results with the low-level advertising plan.

D. *With the high-level advertising plan, Quinn Technologies expects to achieve a 19.3 percent profit margin before taxes for the year 2005 and a cumulative profit margin for the years 2001 to 2005 of 13.2 percent based upon the planning assumptions for the high-level advertising plan.* Table 8-17 illustrates that while the profit margins with the high-level plan are lower, the overall magnitude of the cumulative before-tax profit is $2.6 million greater than with the low-level advertising plan.

TABLE 8-16. Financial Overview
National Low-Level Advertising Plan

Year	Unit Sales	Retail Dollar Sales (Net) (000)	Net Profit Before Tax (000)	PBT as % of Net Sales
2001	950	$ 174	$ (542)	
2002	73,100	13,459	498	3.7%
2003	81,100	14,940	2,612	17.5
2004	90,100	16,583	3,090	18.6
2005	100,000	18,406	3,856	20.9
Total	345,250	$63,562	$9,514	15.0%

TABLE 8-17. Financial Overview
National High-Level Advertising Plan

Year	Unit Sales	Retail Dollar Sales (Net) (000)	Net Profit Before Tax (000)	PBT as % of Net Sales
2001	950	$ 174	($542)	—
2002	104,400	19,194	166	0.9%
2003	116,900	21,498	3,270	15.2
2004	130,900	24,077	4,021	16.7
2005	146,600	26,962	5,206	19.3
Total	499,750	$91,905	$12,121	13.2%

2. *Detailed pro forma five-year profit-and-loss statements are provided for 2001 to 2005.* Tables 8-18 and 8-19 illustrate the anticipated revenue, expenses, and profits for both the low- and high-level advertising plans.

CONTINGENCIES

With a marketing program of this magnitude, it is reasonable to assume that there are a large number of contingencies that could occur. The following is a list of those situations that could occur based on previous company experiences.

TABLE 8-18. Pro Forma Five-Year P&L Statement
National Low-Level Advertising Plan (000)

	2001	2002	2003	2004	2005	Total Projected 2001–2005
Total unit sales	950	73,100	81,100	90,100	100,000	345,250
Gross sales	$178	$13,733	$15,244	$16,921	$18,782	$64,858
Less bad debt @1%	2	137	152	169	188	648
Less 1% allowance for returns	2	137	152	169	188	648
Net sales	$174	$13,459	$14,940	$16,583	$18,406	$63,562
Expenses						
Cost of goods	$181	$ 8,624	$ 9,573	$10,626	$11,559	$40,563
Company overhead	10	731	811	901	1,000	3,453
Advertising/promotions	75	2,000	1,250	1,250	1,250	5,825
System training & information	20	500	100	100	100	820
Displays/display installation	9	235	78	78	78	478
Collateral material	9	183	203	225	250	870
Market research/tracking	120	100	50	50	50	370
Project development	275	325	0	0	0	600
Administrative headcount	17	263	263	263	263	1,069
Total expense	$716	$12,961	$12,328	$13,493	$14,550	$54,048
Net profit before tax	($542)	$ 498	$ 2,612	$ 3,090	$ 3,856	$ 9,514
PBT as % of net sales	—	3.7%	17.5%	18.6%	20.9%	15.0%

1. *Competitors might challenge advertising.* It is not uncommon for one competitor to request that the Federal Trade Commission review another competitor's advertising, the goal being to require corrective advertising. As a preventive measure, all advertising will be approved by the legal department of Quinn Technologies and all advertising claims will be documented.

2. *Current manufacturers might retaliate in the marketplace by modifying their marketing plans.* The following are specific marketing plan elements that could be implemented by competitors:

   A. *Product improvements.* Current manufacturers could modify their own units in order to regain a product advantage over Quinn Technologies products. This could be done by adding features while maintaining current price levels. The contemplated reaction would

TABLE 8-19. Pro Forma Five-Year P&L Statement
National High-Level Advertising Plan (000)

	2001	2002	2003	2004	2005	Total Projected 2001–2005
Total unit sales	950	104,400	116,900	130,900	146,600	499,750
Gross sales	$178	$19,586	$21,936	$24,569	$27,512	$93,781
Less bad debt @1%	2	196	219	246	275	938
Less 1% allowance for returns	2	196	219	246	275	938
Net sales	$174	$19,194	$21,498	$24,077	$26,962	$91,905
Expenses						
Cost of goods	$181	$12,300	$13,776	$15,429	$16,932	$58,618
Company overhead	10	1,044	1,169	1,309	1,466	4,998
Advertising/promotions	75	4,000	2,500	2,500	2,500	11,575
System training & information	20	500	100	100	100	820
Displays/display installation	9	235	78	78	78	478
Collateral material	9	261	292	327	367	1,256
Market research/tracking	120	100	50	50	50	370
Project development	275	325	0	0	0	600
Administrative headcount	17	263	263	263	263	1,069
Total expense	$716	$19,028	$18,228	$20,056	$21,756	$79,784
Net profit before tax	($542)	$ 166	$ 3,270	$ 4,021	$ 5,206	$12,121
PBT as % of net sales	—	0.9%	15.2%	16.7%	19.3%	13.2%

    be to do consumer research to determine the real appeal of the added features, and if necessary modify the Quinn Technologies units or add a new model.

B. *Lower price.* Current manufacturers might try to counter the Quinn Technologies effort by lowering the price of their units. If this happens, no reaction is contemplated unless the price reductions are dramatic and permanent.

C. *Special promotions/discounts.* Special incentives, temporary in nature, might be used to counter the initial entry of Quinn Technologies into the market. No reaction is contemplated unless Quinn Technologies' sales are affected.

D. *Increased advertising.* On either a manufacturer or a retailer level or both, advertising expenditures could be increased. Since advertising efforts are currently deemed to be below the threshold of effectiveness, no reaction will take place unless Quinn Technologies' sales are adversely affected.

E.   *Redirect advertising message.* One of the real alternatives for current manufacturers or retailers is to redirect their advertising message, either against the Quinn Technologies offering or in light of it. It would be rather simple to point out that the consumer can get a comparable device for less from someone other than Quinn Technologies. Any redirection of advertising will be monitored, and, if appropriate, our copy strategy will be modified.

3. *Quinn Technologies might not be able to obtain the product either at a reasonable cost or on a private-label basis.* If the problem is one of cost, a reevaluation of the profit-and-loss statements and the pricing of the conferencing devices will be required. If the current manufacturers can't or won't provide the private label to Quinn Technologies, then manufacturers who are not currently in the business will be contacted. There are many manufacturers who could easily manufacture the needed products.

4. *The viability of the telephone conferencing device market, plus Quinn Technologies' entry, might attract major manufacturers into the market.* Until such an event occurs, it is difficult to determine the exact reaction. The contingency plan calls for tracking a major new entrant's strategy and products and adjusting the marketing plan only if necessary.

5. *A technological change could make the concept of a telephone conferencing device obsolete.* The research conducted for this plan, along with previous studies, indicates that such an occurrence will not find consumer acceptance in the foreseeable future. However, should this occur, an evaluation will be made to determine whether the program should be phased out.

CHAPTER 9

Market Reviews Completed with Online Surveys

Example: Tiffany Table Mats and Napkins

Now that we are in the twenty-first century, the completion of a market review for your marketing plan may have been made easier by the Internet. We discussed in an earlier chapter how to use the Internet to gather secondary information. This can sometimes be more effective than other methods of gathering this information because of the global nature of the Internet. The Internet can sometimes also be effective for gathering primary research data. One example of this is online surveys.

An online survey is similar to a telephone survey, except that it is conducted over the Internet. Rather than answering questions over the telephone, respondents simply fill in a questionnaire on their computer screens. The value of this method of data collection is that it can be done globally and can be done at the participant's leisure. Some respondents actually prefer the anonymity of quietly filling in a questionnaire on their computer rather than giving their answers to a telephone interviewer.

Generally, Internet surveys are conducted by market research organizations that specialize in this type of research. Some of these organizations have preestablished panels of consumers who have agreed to participate in Internet surveys. It is not unusual for panels of this type to have several million members. The panel members are recruited by telephone, by publicity releases, and by advertising banners on different web sites and search engines. The research company generally monitors the composition of the panel, and adjusts it as needed in order to keep the panel balanced in terms of major demographic variables.

If you would like to conduct an Internet survey for your products, you can pull samples for the whole United States, for individual states, or for large metropolitan areas within states. International Internet surveys can also be conducted for a large number of countries around the world. Once a representative sample is drawn, the next step is screening that sample over the Internet to identify users of the targeted product category.

All of the interviewing is completed over the Internet. Normally participants have to enter a unique access code before they can respond to the survey. This prevents people from filling out more than one questionnaire or from taking the survey without being invited. As the survey progresses, the data are transferred to the research company's internal computer. These data are then used to create statistical tables, which are sent to you (the client) either over the Internet or in printed report form.

This chapter includes a marketing plan that identifies an opportunity by demonstrating that textile table mats and napkins are a neglected area in the nation's supermarkets. The plan outlines the best way to develop a profitable business through the supermarket trade. It provides a detailed marketing program, as well as giving volume and profit objectives that would more than double the company's sales and profits in this category.

The market review for the Tiffany Table Mat and Napkin venture was put together with data obtained from secondary sources, company sales information, and information from an online survey. Once the overall market was known, projections were made based on a consumer survey taken over the Internet that enabled the company to forecast sales by geographic region, manufacturer, and trade class. Estimates of spending per household and pricing in the various trade classes were also made.

One of the other interesting aspects of this marketing plan is its use of trade research to help develop the program. The company had had almost no experience with the supermarket trade prior to this venture. In-depth interviews were conducted with supermarket executives in a variety of chains in different geographic locations across the United States. During these interviews, supermarket merchandising managers were asked for their evaluation of the current status of the textile table mat and napkin market. They were then asked for their reactions to a variety of concepts regarding the marketing of this category to consumers as well as to the supermarket itself. Their answers to these questions became an integral part of the marketing plan for the venture.

Marketing Plan for:
Tiffany Table Mats and Napkins
Coil Industries[1]
April 7, 2000

INTRODUCTION

The purpose of this report is to analyze the U.S. market for textile table mats and napkins and to make recommendations concerning what Coil Industries might do to substantially increase its sales of table mats and napkins through supermarkets. This report is divided into the following eight sections:

1. **BACKGROUND.** This section describes the current Coil organization and reviews Coil's current objectives in building expanded sales of table mats and napkins through the supermarket trade.

2. **MARKET REVIEW.** This section reviews the growth and nature of the U.S. market for table mats and napkins.

3. **CONSUMER USAGE AND ATTITUDES.** This section outlines present consumer practices, desires, and expectations regarding the table mat and napkin category in general, and specifically regarding the purchasing of table mats and napkins in supermarkets.

4. **SUPERMARKET PRACTICES AND ATTITUDES.** This section reviews the supermarket trade's current involvement with table mats and napkins and its reactions to alternative marketing approaches.

[1] **Disclaimer:** The specific information in this sample marketing plan was compiled for intended use as an example only. Although this marketing plan is based on actual products from a real company, the specific information in the plan is hypothetical and is not intended to compete with or to divulge proprietary ideas, company structure, or the financial status of any company. The names, numbers, and some of the facts in this marketing plan have been changed because of the confidential nature of the information. The information is intended to be used as a guide only.

5. **CONCLUSIONS.** This section presents key thoughts based on the facts presented in the previous sections.

6. **RECOMMENDATION.** This section makes a recommendation concerning the advisability of Coil Industries' attempting to build a profitable consumer franchise in textile table mats and napkins sold through supermarkets.

7. **MARKETING PLAN ELEMENTS.** These are very specific plans concerning what Coil should and should not do within the framework of the information obtained during the course of preparations for this marketing plan. Additionally, this section provides a fully developed national marketing plan.

8. **FINANCIAL PROJECTIONS.** This section provides a forecasted profit-and-loss statement for the venture.

This document is primarily directed at identifying what Coil should do, in addition to its present marketing activities, to increase its sales of table mats and napkins through the supermarket channel of distribution. The research and plans in this document deal strictly with textile table mats and napkins, not with paper products. The recommendations presented in this marketing plan have been designed as an incremental marketing effort and are intended to be compatible with Coil's present activities through other channels of distribution and in other product categories.

The information required to write this report was gathered in six stages. The stages were designed to provide a systematic understanding of the overall table mat and napkin market from both the consumer and the trade standpoint, as well as to develop specific marketing plans and strategies. The following steps were taken:

1. **INFORMATION GATHERING.** A careful review of marketing plans, cost details, and other information currently available at Coil was conducted. In addition, a careful screening of virtually every available secondary source related to the table mat and napkin market was done. This included information from the Census of Manufacturers, the U.S. Department of Commerce, and dozens of trade publications. Finally, the market review was rounded out with information from a consumer survey taken over the Internet.

2. **INDUSTRY CONTACTS.** Extensive interviews were conducted with manufacturers of table mats and napkins, with the research departments of related trade associations, and with the editors and market research directors of a number of business and consumer publications.

3. **CONCEPT GENERATION.** Based on the information gathered from screening the available market data and interviewing key industry contacts, a series of concepts for alternative marketing approaches was generated. This was accomplished during a series of brainstorming sessions.

4. **MARKET RESEARCH.** Focus group interviews were conducted with consumers to learn more about their willingness to purchase table mats and napkins in food stores and their reactions to the concepts developed. In addition, a special run of a textile panel was purchased to provide statistical breakdowns on a number of important aspects of the overall market. All of this market research information, together with the secondary source information, was used to develop statistical tabulations and estimates of the size of the table mat and napkin market and trends in that market.

5. **FIELD TRIPS.** Fieldwork was conducted in a number of geographic locations throughout the United States. This involved carrying out store checks to personally determine the current status of table mat and napkin product lines in food stores. In addition, interviews were conducted with key executives in leading supermarket chains in the western, midwestern, and southern regions of the United States to obtain their evaluations of the current status of the table mat and napkin market and to determine their reactions to alternative concepts from both the consumer and the trade perspective.

6. **MARKETING PLAN DEVELOPMENT.** Based on the information gathered in the previous five steps, a detailed plan of action was developed, including a step-by-step action plan that should enable Coil to profitably penetrate this incremental segment of the table mat and napkin market.

BACKGROUND

Coil Industries is an aggressive manufacturer of a number of textile lines, including both consumer products, such as infants' knitwear, and institutional products, such as textiles sold to the food service industry. The company believes that despite the difficult economy, it will still be able to increase profits through aggressive market planning, expanded advertising/promotional programs, and a tightening of the overall organizational structure.

One area that Coil plans to emphasize during the 2000/2001 season is table mat and napkin products. The company believes that these products will show considerable growth and high profitability for Coil as a result of a number of recent changes in the marketplace. Primarily, the withdrawal of a major competitor from this market will allow Coil to gain a greater percentage of the total market. In addition, Coil is looking for stronger new product development and special programs to deepen its penetration of the table mat and napkin market.

Coil is currently focusing its efforts on upgrading its line by improving the quality of the product and the packaging. Additionally, plans are now underway at Coil to develop a product catalogue and illustrated promotional sheets as required. As production becomes available, Coil plans to add a new program focused on the department store market, to be sold either direct or through distributors.

One area of special concern to Coil is the concept of expanding table mat and napkin sales through food retailers. Coil believes that this is a neglected area in food stores and that there could be a substantial opportunity for a hard-hitting marketing program. The objective of this plan is to determine the best way for Coil to develop profitable table mat and napkin volume through supermarkets and to establish specific volume and profit objectives for this business. This is to be done through the development of a detailed marketing program that will ensure that Coil meets its agreed-upon objectives.

MARKET REVIEW

1. *The total market for table mats and napkins in 1999 amounted to $113 million in retail sales.* Prior to 1999, the market had been growing at the rate of 6 percent per year, and it is expected to continue growing at the rate of 5 percent per year over the next few years. In 1995, the average household spent $1.64 on table mats and napkins. This is expected to increase by 4 percent in 2000 and by 3 percent in 2001.

2. *Table mat and napkin sales tend to be strongest in the Northeast and North Central geographic regions.* The Northeast and North Central markets account for 58 percent of total

table mat and napkin sales. The Southern and Pacific regions account for roughly 16 percent of total retail sales each, while the Mountain and Southwest regions account for only 10 percent.

The Southern region is extremely underdeveloped. Although 16 percent of total dollar sales are in the South, a comparison of the number of households in the South reveals an index of only 76 percent, showing that fewer dollars per household are spent on table mats and napkins in the South than in any other geographic region. In addition, the South has a smaller percentage of dollar sales than it does of unit sales, indicating a generally lower price level. To a lesser degree, the same trend is apparent in the Mountain and Southwest regions.

The Pacific region of the United States is in many ways opposite to the Southern, Mountain, and Southwest regions. The Pacific region has 12 percent of total unit sales (slightly less than its percentage of households) and 16 percent of total retail dollar sales (somewhat greater than its percentage of households). This indicates that while the Pacific region is slightly underdeveloped in terms of penetration of units, the general price level in the Pacific region is considerably higher than that in the balance of the United States.

3. *The major metropolitan areas tend to generate roughly the same percentage of retail dollar sales as their percentage of total households.* For example, in total, New York, Chicago, and Philadelphia generate $17 million in retail sales, or 15 percent of the total market (which is roughly the same as the percentage of households in these areas). Los Angeles is a unique exception, generating a substantially smaller percentage of unit sales and retail dollar sales than the total number of households.

In both New York and Los Angeles, these products tend to be selling at a higher than average general price level, making the percentage of dollar sales greater than the percentage of units. For example, New York generates 6 percent of total unit sales and 8 percent of total dollar sales, while Los Angeles generates 2 percent of total unit sales and 3 percent of total dollar sales.

4. *As might be anticipated, table mat and napkin sales tend to be concentrated in urban and suburban areas rather than rural areas.* The central cities generate $36 million, or 31 percent of total retail dollar sales; this tends to be slightly higher than the total percentage of households in the central cities. The larger suburban areas generate $48 million in total retail dollar sales, or 43 percent of total table mat and napkin sales, and this also tends to

be greater than the percentage of households in these geographic areas. The smaller suburban areas generate only 26 percent of total table mat and napkin sales and tend to be relatively underdeveloped.

5. *The table mat and napkin market is clearly dominated by three major manufacturers.* These three manufacturers generate total retail dollar sales equal to 58 percent of the total market. The remainder of the market is divided among a number of smaller manufacturers.

6. *Discount stores are the leading outlets for table mats and napkins (27 percent of dollar sales), while supermarkets are a minor factor (only 11 percent of total retail dollar sales).* Outlets such as mail order, specialty stores, and other nonconventional retail outlets are not really in the business. A total of $31 million in retail sales is generated through discount stores, $22 million through department stores, $16 million through national chains, and $19 million through variety stores. Supermarkets account for only $12 million. Specialty stores and mail order vehicles represent only 3 percent of total sales.

It should also be noted that a comparison of unit sales and dollar sales indicates that the price level in department stores and regional chains is slightly higher than that in discount stores and supermarkets. For example, supermarkets generate 13 percent of total unit sales, yet only 11 percent of total retail dollar sales.

CONSUMER USAGE AND ATTITUDES

1. *Table mats and napkins are purchased almost exclusively by women.* In some cases, the husband may accompany the wife while she is purchasing table mats and napkins. It was clearly indicated by the people interviewed, however, that this is a female purchase decision. It was indicated that the female generally made all decisions regarding the type of table mats and napkins purchased. Even in the case of gift purchases, the woman was the actual purchaser.

2. *The quantity of table mats and napkins purchased will vary depending on the number of people in the family, and the amount of entertaining done.* There was a clear difference between heavy and light users of table mats and napkins. Heavy users tended to have large families and generally used a lot of dishes during each meal. These women indicated that

because of the sheer volume of usage, their table mats and napkins tended to wear out or become badly stained more quickly.

3. *For table mats and napkins, brand names were found to be not very important.* A number of the respondents interviewed recognized the major brand names. These respondents indicated, however, that they did not make their purchase decision on the basis of the brand name of the item. They did not even attempt to repurchase the same brand that they had bought in the past—even if this brand ideally suited their desires. Most of the people interviewed felt that they would evaluate a table mat or napkin at the time they were making the purchase and would base this purchase decision on a number of factors, with brand being one of the least important.

4. *The people interviewed indicated that they generally purchased their table mats and napkins in department stores or in discount stores, with only a small percentage making their purchases in supermarkets.* The main reason given for purchasing in discount and department stores was the large selection available in these outlets. Although most of the respondents interviewed realized that table mats and napkins were sold in supermarkets, they generally felt that the selection there was too small to warrant much of their shopping time. Supermarkets would be an acceptable outlet for table mats and napkins purchased for self-use, provided there was a reasonable selection of items and the quality of the products was comparable to that found in discount and department stores.

5, *Approximately 28 percent of total table mat and napkin sales are for gift purposes.* Of total table mat and napkin sales ($113 million), $32 million are for gift purposes and $81 million are for self-use.

6. *Department stores and national chains are the most acceptable outlets for gift purchases of table mats and napkins, while supermarkets are the least acceptable.* Approximately 50 percent of total gift sales are made in department stores and national chains. Discount stores account for 19 percent of gift sales, variety stores for 16 percent, and supermarkets for only 3 percent. Nongift purchases are the most important segment of the market, and discount stores dominate this segment, with 31 percent of nongift sales. Supermarkets also play a significant role in the nongift market, with 14 percent of the retail dollar sales for the segment.

7. *Consumers normally do not plan to give gifts of table mats and napkins unless the recipient has a specific need for them.* Most table mats and napkins that are purchased as gifts are purchased on impulse. The exception to this is where there is a specific need (e.g., weddings or knowledge of the recipient's need for table mats and napkins).

8. *Consumers do not expect table mats and napkins to be on sale and do not wait for sales to make their purchases.* The people interviewed during this research indicated that they almost never see special sales or promotions on table mats and napkins. Because of this, most consumers expect to pay full retail price for table mats and napkins and do not spend a lot of time seeking out bargains.

9. *Ensembles make up a relatively small segment of the total market, accounting for only 12 percent of dollar sales and 10 percent of total unit sales.* Ensembles of table mats and napkins are frequently desired for gifts, but they usually are not wanted for self-use. The consumers interviewed indicated that they would prefer to buy their table mats and napkins individually. When they need a table mat for their own use, they do not want to be forced to buy a napkin as well. On the other hand, if the consumer is purchasing table mats and napkins to give to someone else, a matching ensemble is appealing.

10. *The color of table mats and napkins is clearly more important to consumers than the pattern or design.* Conservative or traditional designs are preferred over unique or fashionable designs. Consumers are primarily interested in coordinating their table mats and napkins with the color theme in their dining room or kitchen. Because of this, it is very important that the overall color of the table mat and napkin does not conflict with the overall color scheme in the dining room or kitchen (wallpaper, appliance colors, and so on).

11. *White, avocado, gold, and brown are expected to be the largest-selling colors for table mats and napkins in 2000.* The research in this study indicates that yellow and gold are increasing in importance, while avocado is decreasing. White as the basic color for table mats and napkins is expected to remain constant at 34 percent of total sales through 2000.

12. *The respondents interviewed in this research indicated that in their opinion, table mats and napkins should not be designed for "high fashion."* The table mats and napkins they preferred most were basic plaids, stripes, and checks; solid colors; or very simple designs, including fruit, flowers, spices, and so on. These consumers were presented with fifteen possible

design concepts, ranging from very traditional to wild and modern. Table 9-1 illustrates that those designs that received the highest preference (highest score) were clearly the most basic.

13. *Consumers generally prefer that table mats and napkins be put on display at retailers without being packaged.* When shopping for table mats and napkins, consumers prefer to be able to feel the cloth so that they can judge its thickness, absorbency, and so on. They believe that if table mats and napkins were to be packaged, they would not be able to make intelligent purchase decisions.

14. *Table mat and napkin sales are concentrated in the smaller families.* Although very large families (six members and over) tend to be the heaviest users of table mats and napkins, the bulk of total purchases are made by one- to three-member families. Table mat and napkin sales are further concentrated in the middle to upper middle income ranges. In addition, these income groups purchase a greater percentage of table mats and napkins than would be normally representative of their share of U.S. households.

15. *Most consumers are not aware of the price of table mats, and will base their price comparisons strictly on the prices of the table mats available in the retail outlet at the time they*

TABLE 9-1. Consumers' Preferred Design Concepts for Table Mats and Napkins

Design Concept	Preference Score
Basic plaids, stripes, and checks	64
Solid colors	62
Flowers	58
Fruit	52
Spices	52
Food recipes	50
Scenes of four seasons	46
Designs by famous artists	46
Old print ads	42
Peanuts characters	42
Pictures of songbirds	40
Authentic reproductions of paintings	36
Children's art	34
Magazine covers	12
Packaged goods pictures	6

Note: Scores based on a 5-point scale ranging from excellent through poor. Highest score indicates most positive reaction.

are purchasing a new one. While most of the people interviewed indicated that they do want to obtain the best bargain possible, they really have no benchmark on which to base this, primarily because the purchase is so infrequent.

16. *There were several factors regarding the purchase of table mats that were common among respondents.* Table mat sales tend to be concentrated in the lower price ranges. Over half of consumers purchase two or three table mats at a time. The majority of table mats are purchased as nongift items.

17. *As with table mats, there were also several consistent factors identified in the purchasing of textile napkins.* Most consumers purchase four or less textile napkins during a single transaction. The most frequent transaction size was two, representing 28 percent of all transactions. Nongift sales make up 88 percent of all textile napkin sales and 87 percent of all textile napkin retail dollar sales.

18. *A good textile table mat or napkin is considered to be one that is attractive, is long-lasting, and won't fall apart after a few washings.* The primary problem with table mats and napkins is that they wear out. They also become permanently stained, or they fall apart after a number of washings. Table mats and napkins that would last longer would be considered to be preferable.

19. *People would be willing to pay more for good table mats and napkins.* A table mat or napkin that lasts longer is considered to be worth more than an inferior table mat or napkin. Because of this, most of the consumers interviewed would be willing to pay more for a good table mat or napkin.

20. *Most consumers use textile table mats and napkins only occasionally, although a small group never uses these items, and another small group uses them every day.* Typically, the average consumer uses textile table mats and napkins approximately once a week or less. For many, the main reason for using textile table mats and napkins is that the family is giving a dinner party, which is not typically an everyday occasion.

Consumer Concepts

Three different consumer concepts were developed and presented to consumers for their reactions. The following summarizes the consumers' overall and specific reactions to each of these concepts.

1. *Consumers had a lukewarm reaction to the concept of purchasing both textile table mats and napkins and paper napkins with coordinated patterns and prints.* The consumers' primary objection to this concept was that they felt that it was impractical to coordinate paper napkins with cloth table mats and napkins because (1) they like to buy whatever brand of paper napkins is on sale and don't want to be locked into a single brand, and (2) they feel that the cloth patterns will eventually fade and will not match the paper once this happens.

2. *Consumers generally reacted favorably to the concept of purchasing table mats and napkins with the latest designs (modern recipes, great paintings, attractive reproductions of fruit or flowers, and so on).* The people interviewed indicated that they liked the idea of being able to select a design that matched their kitchen and/or their individual taste. It was clearly indicated, however, that there would have to be a fairly wide selection of designs to accommodate each consumer's individual desires. Although designer table mats and napkins generally had a wide acceptance, each specific design individually appealed to only a very small group of consumers. Finally, it was indicated that the primary appeal of this concept would be in purchasing for the gift market. Consumers would be much more prone to buy table mats and napkins with modern designs to give away to someone else than they would be to buy them for self-use.

3. *Consumers responded very enthusiastically to the concept of being able to purchase high-quality, basic textile table mats and napkins (i.e., department store quality) at their local supermarket.* It was indicated that this concept filled a primary need in that they would be able to purchase their table mats and napkins conveniently while they were in the food store instead of making a special trip to a department store or discount store. Also, they felt that a supermarket was a logical place to buy table mats and napkins in that consumers are thinking of their kitchen and dining room while they are shopping in the food store.

Although it was clearly indicated that consumers would purchase textile table mats and napkins for their own use in supermarkets, they would hesitate to purchase gift items in these outlets. Generally speaking, most of the people interviewed did not feel it would be acceptable to purchase a gift for someone in a supermarket, as this is generally considered to be a low-status outlet.

There were two problems associated with the supermarket program. First, it was felt that there would be a very limited variety of designs in supermarkets. Consumers felt that they must have at least enough colors to match with their kitchen and dining room. Second, women like to touch and feel table mats and napkins before purchasing them. Consumers felt that in a supermarket program, the table mats and napkins were likely to be all packaged up, and that this would be a negative.

4. *The supermarket concept received by far the most positive reactions from consumers.* Participants in the focus group interviews were asked to rank each concept as their first through third choices. A score was then assigned to each concept based on how many consumers gave it first, second, and third place. The supermarket program received a substantially higher score than any of the other concepts, as indicated in Table 9-2.

SUPERMARKET PRACTICES AND ATTITUDES

1. *Most supermarkets carry at least some textile table mats and napkins; however, the amount of space allocated to this category is generally minimal.* Almost all of the supermarkets visited in preparation for this marketing plan carried at least some table mats and napkins. However, they were usually located on the bottom shelf of one section of a gondola in the housewares section.

Most of the supermarket executives interviewed indicated that they believed table mats and napkins to be a "good, stable business"; however, most of them did very little merchandising of this category. There were a few exceptions to this. A few chains engaged in a major program, displaying table mats and napkins on the equivalent of half of a four-foot gondola section. Generally speaking, however, table mats and napkins were relegated to an unimportant position on a lower shelf, with no more than one four-foot shelf of space.

2. *The table mats and napkins currently carried by supermarkets are at the low end of the quality scale.* Supermarkets are not involved in selling high-quality, high-fashion table mats

TABLE 9-2. **Consumers' Ratings of Alternative Marketing Concepts for Table Mats and Napkins**

Marketing Concept	Preference Score
Supermarket program	62
Designer prints	36
Coordinated kitchen	32

Note: Scores based on consumers' rating in order of preference. Highest score indicates most positive reaction.

and napkins. The type of merchandise currently sold is chosen primarily on the basis of price so that the supermarket can offer a line in the lower price ranges.

3. *Price points on table mats and napkins sold through supermarkets are generally in the low to mid range.* The supermarket executives interviewed were very concerned that their retail prices on these products be competitive. They believed that consumers expect supermarkets to carry this type of merchandise at fairly economical prices.

4. *The retail margins (percentage off retail) on table mats and napkins are currently in the area of 40 percent.* These margins assume no outside servicing. In this case, the supermarket handles the merchandise through its nonfoods warehouse, and all in-store servicing is performed by store personnel. Where a rack jobber is involved (this is seldom), the store will generally net a 25 percent profit.

5. *There are no real standards for performance or profitability of table mats and napkins sold through the supermarket trade.* Most supermarket people do not really know the amount of profit that a given program is generating. They generally use trade margins and inventory turns as their primary indices.

6. *Supermarkets generally do not expect a line of table mats and napkins to be nationally advertised.* None of the supermarket executives interviewed were aware of any nationally advertised brands of table mats and napkins, and they did not feel that national advertising would be necessary on a new brand that they might take on. Most of the advertising for this category is done by the retailer. Almost all of the supermarkets visited were doing at least some advertising of their own on table mats and napkins. This was primarily related to special sales on specific items.

A supermarket would, however, generally expect the manufacturer of table mats and napkins to provide it with allowance money so that it could advertise sales on these products in its regular food ads. There was a mixed reaction to the idea of the manufacturer's providing co-op money to pay for this advertising. The majority of people felt that co-op money would not be necessary. Virtually all the people, however, felt that it would definitely be necessary for the manufacturer to provide allowance money to support price discounts.

7. *As with most nonfood items, the housekeeping on table mats and napkins in supermarkets varies considerably from chain to chain and from one region of the country to another.*

During store checks of table mats and napkins in supermarkets throughout the country, it was found that the housekeeping ranged from excellent to poor. Most of the people interviewed felt that their housekeeping efforts in the nonfood areas were improving substantially; however, they could not maintain a consistently high level of housekeeping. It was indicated, however, that where the racks are very clearly marked and the items are packaged conveniently, with the proper in-packs and so on, their own people can do a reasonably good job of housekeeping. Some chains are especially well equipped to handle housekeeping on nonfood items and do an excellent job in this area.

8. *Most supermarket chains are properly equipped to handle soft goods such as table mats and napkins through their nonfoods warehouse.* All of the supermarket executives interviewed indicated that they were very well equipped to handle the special "pick packing" and other requirements necessary for nonfood items. Most of the table mats and napkins that they currently sell are handled through the warehouse without any problems.

9. *A major new program on table mats and napkins would initially be sold to the appropriate merchandising manager, and then all follow-up transactions would be handled by the appropriate buyer.* During trade meetings, it was indicated that the decision to take on a new and major table mat and napkin program would be made, in most cases, by the merchandising manager. In some cases the manager would discuss the decision with the appropriate buyer to arrive at a joint decision. It was clearly indicated, however, that this decision would be made above the normal buying level. Once the program has been accepted, most follow-up transactions would be made with the buyer.

Trade Presentation of the Coil Venture

During the preparation for the writing of this marketing plan, interviews were conducted with leading executives of seven major supermarket chains located throughout the United States. During each of these interviews, a "straw man" concept on selling table mats and napkins through supermarkets was outlined. This concept had the following key elements:

1. **THE SCOPE OF THE PROGRAM.** The overall concept is to put together a major totally integrated marketing program for textile table mats and napkins, to be launched solely through supermarkets. This will be the largest national program on table mats and napkins ever launched by any manufacturer.

2. **PROGRAM OBJECTIVES.** Supermarkets currently have only a minor share of the total textile table mat and napkin business. The objective of this program is to shift a major portion of the table mat and napkin business to supermarkets. In sum, this program is intended to restructure the table mat and napkin industry so that supermarkets will become the leading retail channel of distribution.

3. **DISTINCTIVE NAME/PACKAGE/DISPLAY.** A traditional supermarket program has very little display impact on the consumer. Table mats and napkins are usually given very little space and are displayed in an area of the store that has very little visibility. This concept will dramatically change the in-store impact by providing a dramatic and distinctive display unit that will fit into the current gondolas. The name and packaging will be tied into the display with a central theme so that the consumer will receive a dramatic, well-coordinated image. In sum, this concept will have a highly visible billboard effect as the consumer is walking through the supermarket, attracting a great deal of interest and resulting in impulse purchasing.

4. **PRODUCT LINE.** The consumer research indicated that although consumers would prefer to buy table mats and napkins in supermarkets, they frequently shop at alternative outlets, primarily because there is very little selection in supermarkets and the product quality is at the low end of the spectrum. This concept will provide the consumer with high-quality merchandise at competitive prices. In addition, this concept will provide an excellent selection of table mats and napkins. Consumers will now be able to find the same quality and selection of basic table mats and napkins in supermarkets that they used to have to go to other, less convenient outlets to find.

5. **DISTRIBUTION.** The product will be distributed through the supermarkets' nonfoods warehouse and sold through a network of food brokers. There will be no servicing in the store by either rack jobbers or manufacturer personnel. The display will be constructed in such a way that the regular in-store personnel can easily maintain the stocking and housekeeping of the rack.

6. **ADVERTISING AND PROMOTION.** In order to allow the supermarket to put merchandise on sale and promote it in its regular newspaper ads, trade allowances will be provided at various times throughout the year. Additionally, there will be a limited amount of national advertising and a manufacturer-sponsored sales promotion program.

7. **MARGINS/VOLUME.** The manufacturer will provide the supermarket with a 40 percent margin (percentage off retail). While the volume per store is not yet known, it is anticipated that this program will generate five to six inventory turns per year.

Trade Reactions

Each supermarket executive interviewed was told that this was a hypothetical program that was still early in the planning stages. They were told that the decision as to whether or not the program would move forward would depend on the results of discussions with them and other people in the industry, as well as a detailed financial analysis. After the overall concept was described, the trade was asked for overall and specific reactions. The following outlines the trade's reaction to the Coil supermarket venture:

1. *The overall trade reaction to the Coil supermarket venture was positive.* Almost all of the supermarket executives interviewed were receptive to the overall concept and felt that this was an area that definitely needed a strong program now. The people interviewed generally felt that it would be possible to shift a substantial percentage of the total business to supermarkets, and they indicated that they would like to participate in such a program. In addition, they felt that the venture was likely to be successful, as there appeared to be no competition at this point in time.

2. *The trade strongly indicated that it would prefer that the items carried in the Coil line be standard rather than premium products.* The executives interviewed felt very strongly that the price points in this category should be competitive with those of other channels of distribution (notably discount stores). Ideally, the prices of these goods in a supermarket would be lower than the discount stores' prices. Because of this, the executives felt that it would not be appropriate to design a program selling premium-priced, high-quality table mats and napkins through supermarket chains.

3. *The supermarket executives interviewed generally felt that a manufacturer-provided display to be inserted in the gondola would be a valuable asset to the entire program.* They felt that a properly designed display would get consumers' attention, would facilitate housekeeping and loading by in-store personnel, and would provide additional motivation for them to take on the new program. In addition to the trade's receptivity, the concept of a display provided by the manufacturer elicited the following suggestions:

A. *It was generally felt that the size of the display should be flexible and that it should fit into the regular gondola section.* Some stores wanted an entire four-foot section, while others wanted only two shelves of the four-foot section. Because of this, it was felt that what was needed was a modular unit with a variable number of shelves that could be adapted to the size of the individual store.

B. *It was unanimously felt that the configuration of the display should be such that it would be very easy for in-store personnel to stock.* The stores' ability to handle the in-store merchandising varied considerably from one chain to another. For example, one chain felt that it would have absolutely no problem maintaining impeccable housekeeping. On the other hand, another chain indicated that housekeeping would vary considerably from one store to another, primarily because some stores in the chain have trouble with housekeeping in the nonfoods areas. The concept of a visual schematic to facilitate easy identification of which products go where was extremely well received, and it was generally felt that this would minimize the problem.

4. *It was generally felt that space would be made available for a new venture like the Coil supermarket program.* Nearly all of the supermarket executives interviewed agreed that they would be able to find space for this program, either by reducing their involvement in another category (e.g., putting it in the soap section and reducing a few sizes of soap) or by shifting items around in the housewares section. In sum, space would be made available for initial distribution, and it would remain available as long as movement appeared to warrant carrying the line.

5. *The trade was generally unable to indicate its requirements for acceptable movement of a textile program.* Generally speaking, the stores interviewed were not aware of their current performance in this category and did not have any rule of thumb by which to measure the performance of a new program. A number of possible guidelines were provided, but even these were very subjective.

6. *A 40 percent margin (percentage off retail) appeared to be a generally satisfactory trade margin on a new table mat and napkin program.* This varied somewhat from chain to chain. For example, one merchandising manager indicated that he would have to have at least a 50 percent margin. Generally speaking, however, a 40 percent margin appeared to be attractive enough to warrant distribution.

7. *The trade indicated a clear preference for a trade allowance program of some type that would permit them to discount in-line merchandise so that it could be put on sale and advertised as such as part of the regular advertising program.* It was clearly indicated by most of the trade people interviewed that they would prefer that sales be provided on regular merchandise carried in the regular line. They felt that this would enable them to continually generate excitement within a normal line. Special merchandise put on sale through dump bins was not nearly as interesting to them as in-line sales. Additionally, they felt that these sales should be provided to them several times during the year (the most preferred number was four).

8. *Most of the supermarket executives interviewed apparently promote table mats and napkins three to four times a year and feel that they get good results from this.* Because they are accustomed to promoting table mats and napkins now, they would feel perfectly comfortable continuing to do this with a new program. Although there were a few exceptions, most people indicated that it would not be necessary for the manufacturer to provide co-op money to pay for the stores' advertising programs. It was generally felt that if a reasonably effective allowance program were offered, the stores would pay for their own advertising, as they do now. The main reason for this negative response to co-op money was that it was frequently found to be a "pain in the neck" to keep track of co-op money and to provide proof of advertisement.

9. *The supermarket trade preferred that the table mats and napkins be packaged in such a way that the in-store personnel would not be required to fold the products.* It was generally felt that if some form of packaging that kept the products in a constantly folded state were offered, this would greatly simplify the in-store housekeeping problem for store personnel. Additionally, it was felt that if the table mats and napkins were packaged in such a way that the consumer could feel the actual merchandise without destroying the package, this would be a significant consumer benefit. Finally, the trade really did not have any preference on a two-pack versus a single pack. It was suggested that a test be conducted on both to determine the advantages of each.

10. *It was suggested that the inventory on the rack consist of eighteen units and the replenishment in-packs consist of six units each.* It was suggested that the case size be six dozen per case, or twelve in-packs. It was generally felt that this combination would be easily manageable, both in the store and in the warehouse.

11. *The supermarket trade strongly recommended that the merchandise be changed, at least in part, approximately four times per year.* The trade felt that it was important to keep the rack "alive" by providing some changes periodically throughout the year. It was indicated that if the merchandise were never changed, it would quickly become invisible to the consumer.

12. *The supermarket trade saw no reason why this could not become a permanent program within the supermarket.* It was indicated that as long as the movement appeared to be satisfactory, the supermarket executives would not consider this to be a temporary program. They were eagerly looking for ways to improve their soft goods merchandising, and this appeared to be an attractive way to permanently put them in the textile table mat and napkin business.

13. *Coil Industries was generally considered to be a major company in this industry, and this added credibility to the entire program.* Most of the people interviewed were familiar with Coil and had a highly favorable impression of the company. It was felt that if Coil Industries were to engage in such a program, it would have a reasonably good chance of achieving success.

CONCLUSIONS

1. *The textile table mat and napkin market is a small but stable market with little potential for expansion.* The total market for table mats and napkins in 1999 amounted to $113 million in retail sales and is expected to grow at the rate of approximately 5 percent per year for the foreseeable future. Consumer research indicated that because of the nature of this product category, there is little potential to explode the market through innovative marketing programs. Consumers tend to require a given number of items in this product category per year and do not appear to be willing to expand this usage, except perhaps on a temporary basis. For example, severe price cutting may induce consumers to buy more table mats and napkins in a given period, but if they do so, they will simply reduce their consumption in the next period. The reason for this is that there is apparently no way to induce consumers to use up (wear out) more products than they are using up currently.

2. *There is some geographic concentration in the table mat and napkin market.* The textile table mat and napkin market provides greater opportunities in the suburban and central city

areas than in rural areas, and greater opportunities in the Northeast and North Central geographic regions than in the South, Mountain, Southwest, and Pacific regions. The Northeast and North Central regions account for 58 percent of total table mat and napkin sales, and the market is clearly concentrated in the major cities (31 percent) and larger suburban areas (43 percent).

3. *There are currently no retail price standards in the table mat and napkin market.* Virtually the same products are sold in the same retail channels of distribution at a myriad of different retail price points. In addition, most consumers have no idea of what the price of a table mat or napkin should be. While they obviously want to obtain the best bargain possible, consumers have no benchmark on which to base textile table mat and napkin retail prices other than the range of merchandise available in any given outlet. The lack of price recognition appears to result from the infrequent purchase of these items.

4. *There is a substantial potential for the sale of textile table mats and napkins through supermarkets.* Although the table mat and napkin market currently is relatively underdeveloped in the supermarket trade (11 percent of retail dollar sales), the potential in supermarkets is substantially greater than this. The basis for this potential can be summarized as follows:

   A. *Major success in a limited number of chains.* Almost all supermarkets carry at least some table mats and napkins. Usually they are located on the bottom shelf of one section of a gondola in the housewares section. A few supermarket chains, however, have been experimenting with large textile table mat and napkin programs with a great deal of success. These supermarkets are putting table mats and napkins on the equivalent of an entire four-foot gondola section, and are generating sufficient sales at retail to justify giving the program this amount of space. The executives of these chains who were spoken with indicated that they planned to accelerate their efforts in the table mat and napkin area.

   B. *Buyers' acceptance.* With one exception, all of the supermarket executives interviewed were receptive to the idea of taking on a major brand of table mats and napkins. They generally felt that they would be willing to devote a substantial amount of space (e.g., four gondola feet) to such a program, and that this amount of space would remain available as long as movement appeared to warrant carrying the line. These retail executives saw no reason why a large textile table mat and napkin program couldn't become a permanent part of their nonfoods section.

C. *Extremely favorable consumer attitudes.* Consumers generally feel that a supermarket is a logical place to buy table mats and napkins because they are thinking of their kitchen and dining room while they are shopping in the supermarket. The only reason given for not purchasing table mats and napkins in supermarkets now was that the selection in food stores was almost negligible. In sum, consumers would rather purchase textile table mats and napkins in food stores than in any other outlet, primarily because of the convenience factor.

D. *Supermarkets are well equipped to handle a table mat and napkin program.* Most supermarket chains are properly equipped to handle soft goods such as table mats and napkins through their nonfoods warehouses. Those that carry them now are not experiencing problems with the table mats and napkins that are presently moving through these warehouses. Additionally, the people interviewed indicated that clearly marked and properly constructed racks for nonfood products enabled their in-store personnel to adequately handle all housekeeping chores.

5. *A carefully selected network of food brokers would be the ideal selling agent to handle a table mat and napkin program through supermarkets.* The key retail executives interviewed generally believed that a rack jobber or manufacturer's detailing service would cost too much for a program in this category, given the small expected dollar volume. They felt that a network of food brokers who are especially well equipped to handle in-store detailing, coupled with the store's ability to assist in this effort, could effectively sell the products at the headquarters level and could also do a satisfactory job at the store level.

6. *There is clearly an opportunity for a branded line of table mats and napkins.* No such line currently exists. Although the table mat and napkin market is currently dominated by three major manufacturers, these three manufacturers have only modest brand recognition in the table mat and napkin categories. Consumers do not generally recognize any current brand of table mats and napkins. More important, consumers do not now make their purchase decision on the basis of the brand name of the item, and do not even attempt to repurchase the brand that they have bought in the past. Because of this, there is clearly an opportunity for a manufacturer to develop a brand franchise through heavy consumer promotion.

7. *Color coordination is the only key consumer benefit that would be meaningful for an entire line of table mats and napkins.* Although there are specific benefits that are important for either table mats or napkins, the research identified color coordination as the most impor-

tant overall consumer benefit. Consumers have a strong interest in coordinating their table mats and napkins with the color theme in their kitchen or dining room.

8. *There is a broad but fairly distinct target market toward which a brand of table mats and napkins could be directed.* Table mats and napkins are primarily purchased by females over twenty-five years old, with two- or three-member families, in the middle income ranges, who have at least a high school education. Additionally, these women are primarily purchasing table mats and napkins for their own use rather than as gifts.

9. *Coil Industries is ideally suited to launch a major program selling a brand of textile table mats and napkins through supermarkets.* Coil has an excellent reputation in the supermarket industry. Nearly all of the people in the supermarket trade who were interviewed were familiar with Coil and had a highly favorable impression of the company. They felt that if Coil were to engage in such a program, it would have a reasonably good chance of achieving success. Additionally, based on its current product lines, Coil is well equipped to produce a line of quality table mats and napkins that would fit well into a supermarket branded program.

RECOMMENDATION

Coil Industries should move now to launch a branded line of textile table mats and napkins to be sold through supermarkets. The following paragraphs detail the rationale for this recommendation:

1. *A branded supermarket program on table mats and napkins offers Coil the opportunity to more than double its current sales and profits in this category.* On an ongoing basis, we believe that a branded textile table mat and napkin program through supermarkets would generate retail sales of approximately $20 million, net factory sales of approximately $12 million, and profit before tax of approximately $1.8 million annually. These forecasts are detailed in the Financial Projections section.

2. *A branded supermarket program offers Coil the opportunity to increase its share of the table mat and napkin market by a substantial proportion.* The objective of the program recommended would be to achieve a 17 percent dollar share of the total textile table mat

and napkin market. While we believe this figure is reasonable, its achievement will more than double Coil's current share of market.

3. *A branded business would be a relatively stable one.* Because this would be a branded item with a sustained consumer franchise, Coil would not be subject to the normal distribution shifts, price cutting, and overall instability of operating in a market without such a brand.

4. *Coil could launch a branded supermarket program without any disruption in its normal day-to-day operations.* By gradually expanding the program to national levels, Coil would have ample time to expand its facilities and make the modest staff additions that would be required to manage a supermarket-distributed brand.

MARKETING PLAN ELEMENTS

1. **PRODUCT LINE.** Coil's product line should provide the consumer with a basic array of textile table mats and napkins for self-use on a day-to-day basis. It should include three types of table mats and three types of napkins (solid color, printed, and striped). Specifically, the products in Table 9-3 should be selected from the present Coil line.

These products should be produced in four basic colors (gold, yellow, brown, and green), and the same colors should be used for each of the table mats and napkins (striped, printed, and solid). In this way, Coil will provide consumers with all their product needs, in a variety of colors that will coordinate with almost any kitchen or dining room.

2. **PRICING.** All table mats should be priced at $2.99. Napkins should be priced at $1.99. These prices will allow Coil the necessary margins to pay for a national advertising and promotion

TABLE 9-3. Product Line Summary

Product	Code Number
Table mat	12500
Table mat	12213
Table mat	12500 (solid)
Napkin	13306
Napkin	13214
Napkin	13300

program, yet will still be acceptable to supermarkets. The food trade believes that this pricing structure is suitable from a consumer standpoint.

3. **PACKAGING.** Coil should not package these products. The cost would be prohibitive, and consumers prefer buying textile products that they can touch. Instead, it is recommended that a special gummed label be developed giving the brand name, pertinent data, and, as necessary, any promotional announcements. The table mats and napkins will be presented to the consumer as they normally are, folded and placed on the rack with an identifying sticker.

   Although a nonpackaged product may create housekeeping problems at the store level, it is believed that these problems can be overcome. Two factors account for this optimism. First, all of the supermarkets visited that were running major textile table mat and napkin programs were successfully doing so without packaging. Second, the display rack (described below) will be an enormous help in maintaining attractive displays.

4. **DISPLAY STRATEGY.** It is recommended that a modular display be developed in two sizes, to be inserted into supermarket gondolas. This display should be created in such a way that it can occupy the top half of a four-foot gondola section in small stores and the entire four-foot gondola section in large stores.

5. **PRODUCT NAME.** It is recommended that Tiffany be used as the brand name for this product. The primary product advantage Coil will have in this program is that it will be providing the consumer with a coordinated line of table mats and napkins in a large variety of colors. The name Tiffany effectively communicates this product advantage.

6. **MARKETING SPENDING.** We recommend a first-year marketing expenditure of $3,957,000 (37 percent of factory sales). Advertising will consume $2,097,000 of this, or 53 percent of the total budget. By limiting commercial production expenditures, the plan is to apply over 90 percent of this amount to working media. Promotion expenditures will total $1,860,000. Almost half this amount will be spent on direct consumer offers (couponing and refunds). Going-year marketing spending is planned at $1,758,000 (14 percent of sales), with $1 million of this amount being spent for consumer advertising.

7. **COPY STRATEGY.** The copy on the display, in the promotional material, and in advertisements should clearly communicate to the consumer that this product provides a coordinated

line of table mats and napkins in a variety of colors. Media efforts should further emphasize that the product line is available in supermarkets.

8. **MEDIA STRATEGY.** Daytime television is recommended as the primary medium for the brand's consumer advertising. At this point, it is envisioned that most, if not all, of the brand's working dollars should be spent supporting thirty-second commercials. Longer spots would be unaffordable. Shorter ones might prove difficult to administer and would not provide the time required to adequately communicate all copy points. Further, it is recommended that the brand's working dollars be flighted. Flighting (the concept of advertising for several consecutive weeks, taking a hiatus, and then repeating the process) enables the efficient use of media funds. The budget established for this brand provides sufficient funds to support three or four flights of five-day weeks each. Naturally, the first of these flights will be the longest in duration and will include the greatest number of commercial announcements. Such front-end loading will help establish the brand quickly and convince the trade of its consumer potential.

9. **PROMOTION STRATEGY.** Promotion efforts will focus on generating consumer trial of the brand. Temporary price incentives (coupons and refund offers) will be utilized to do this. Trade expenditures will be maintained at the minimum levels consistent with attaining the brand's distribution goals.

It is recommended that three consumer promotion events be run in the introductory year. The first should consist of a consumer refund offer. The offer should be announced on a sticker attached to initial distribution quantities. The consumer would mail this coupon to Coil, who, in turn, would mail back a coupon giving the refund amount on the next purchase of a Tiffany product. The second event should consist of a coupon, redeemable at the local supermarket, to be run by Coil in newspapers. The third event should consist of an in-ad coupon to be run in the regular newspaper advertisements of participating retailers.

To support the consumer promotion and to generate trade interest, the trade should receive a first-month introductory offer of one free item with a purchase of twelve. In addition, this event should include an advertising allowance of 10 percent. The second trade event, to take place in Month 4, should consist of a 15 percent advertising allowance on an eight weeks' purchase.

10. **TRADE MARGINS.** Coil should offer the retail trade a margin (percentage off retail) of 38 percent. During the trade meetings, it was indicated that, generally speaking, the supermar-

ket trade shoots for an objective of a 40 percent margin on products such as table mats and napkins. Based on Coil Industries' current experience with what supermarkets are actually getting, it is felt that a 38 percent margin would be acceptable to the trade.

11. **DISTRIBUTION SYSTEM.** Coil should establish a national network of food brokers to handle the selling and maintaining of the table mat and napkin line. The brokers in the network should be paid a commission of 8 percent on gross sales of the product line in their respective areas. A number of food brokers have been interviewed that are well equipped to handle the heavy in-store detailing required for this product category, and they have indicated that an 8 percent commission would provide them with sufficient motivation to properly handle the selling and other related functions.

12. **IN-STORE RACK LOADING.** It is recommended that the Tiffany product be shelved in four-foot racks, each containing the six different product types and the four basic colors indicated earlier. There will be a total of twenty-four stock-keeping units. Large racks, floor to top of gondola, would hold thirty-six units of each item. Smaller racks, using just the top half of the gondola, would hold only eighteen units of each item.

13. **CASE PACKS.** It is recommended that all products be packed six dozen per case, broken down into twelve individual in-packs. There should be six units in each in-pack. If possible, units should be packaged in a cartridge form so that they can be loaded easily onto the racks. With the in-packs packed in units of six, the supermarket warehouse will find it very easy to pick-pack for each individual store.

14. **TENTATIVE TIMETABLE.** Assuming that management approval to proceed with this program is received on April 21, 2000, the advertising should be able to begin on September 1, 2000. The exact timing of these steps will of course depend on a number of factors, including available funds, production capacity, and other management decisions. Table 9-4 gives the details of this recommended timetable.

FINANCIAL PROJECTIONS

It is forecasted that $19.8 million in retail sales and $11.9 million in net factory sales will result in a profit before tax of $1.8 million. This is illustrated in the estimated income statement in Table 9-5 and is backed up in considerable detail in a separate financial plan.

TABLE 9-4. Tentative Timetable

Marketing plan presentation	4/7/00
Marketing plan approval	4/21/00
Start display design and production	5/1/00
Start advertising creation and production	5/1/00
Assign project manager	5/1/00
Creative ready	6/10/00
Product ready for shipment	7/22/00
Start retail placement	8/12/00
Start advertising	9/1/00

TABLE 9-5. Estimated Income Statement for Going Year (000)

Retail sales	$ 19,812
Retail margin (38%)	− 7,529
Gross sales at factory	$ 12,283
Cash discount (2% gross sales)	− 246
Returns (0.5% gross sales)	− 61
Seconds (0.85% gross sales)	− 104
Net sales	$ 11,872
Less: Freight (5%)	− 594
Cost of goods	− 4,416
Package cost ($0.02/unit)	− 569
Gross profit	$ 6,293
Operating expenses	
Advertising	$ − 1,000
Promotion	− 758
Display depreciation (3 years)	− 177
Marketing and administration	− 537
Sales and distribution	− 2,040
Profit before tax	$ 1,781

Retail sales are based on the sales forecast of $19,812,000 at retail prices of $2.99 for table mats and $1.99 for napkins. The display depreciation expense is based on the distribution forecast and assumes placement of 3,291 large racks at $100 each (total of $329,000) and 4,056 small racks at $50 each (total of $203,000), for a total display expense of $532,000. This total cost was divided by a three-year expected life to arrive at an expense of $177,000 annually. Marketing and administration assumes a $300,000 annual expense to cover the regional sales managers plus their expenses and supervision and 2 percent of net sales for corporate overhead. Sales and distribution assumes 8 percent of gross sales for broker expense. Distribution is assumed to be 8.9 percent of net sales.

CHAPTER 10

Focus Groups Can Be the Key to Understanding the Consumer

Example: Craftmaster Hardware Products

Finding the match between your company's resources and the needs and desires of your target customer group is a major mission that must be undertaken by every developer of a marketing plan who is serious about creating a successful venture. It is not always easy to identify this match. Casually asking customers at random may not reveal the true picture. Fortunately, there is a research method that is ideal for this purpose. It is called the focus group. You should become familiar with this important research tool, and should use it to make sure that the ideas for your business match your target customer.

Early identification of consumer practices, attitudes, problems, needs, and reactions to ideas regarding a business venture can help the developer of a marketing plan steer in the right direction. If it is determined that the product or marketing concept does not appeal to the target customer group, then perhaps it will appeal to another group. In this case, it may be possible to redirect the marketing. On the other hand, perhaps some aspect of the product or concept can be changed to make it more appealing to the target group of customers. This identification of a match or mismatch can also be very helpful in forecasting the viability and potential sales of the venture.

Developers of successful marketing plans have often used focus groups early in the development stage to identify customer practices and attitudes. The following is a basic description of focus groups and how they can be used in the development of a marketing plan.

Focus Groups

What Are Focus Groups?

A focus group is a special type of interactive interviewing process in which individuals (technically called respondents) are brought together to discuss a specific topic. The respondents are selected on the basis of carefully thought-out criteria, so that they are exactly the types of individuals who can best relate to the subject. During the group discussions, questions are generally asked by a trained moderator, usually following a preplanned discussion guide. Focus group sessions are usually held in a specially designed facility that has a one-way mirror on one wall, behind which observers can watch the process.

Focus groups should generally be done in a series. It can be dangerous to do just one focus group. A single focus group typically includes from eight to twelve respondents. It is possible for such a group to go off on a tangent, resulting in misleading information. By conducting a series of focus groups, you can check the responses of one group against those of another. Consistent answers between groups help to validate the responses. Another advantage of doing a series of groups is that this enables you to refine the discussion guide. Discussions in the first one or two groups can give you insights that you can use to hone the questions for subsequent groups.

A typical focus group project might involve a series of six groups in three different geographic locations. This provides enough diversity to validate many of the key responses, and it brings in the viewpoints of potential customers in different geographic regions. Naturally, the number of groups will vary depending on the specific nature and size of your marketing mission. If there are a lot of different segments of potential target customers, then more groups may be required. On the other hand, fewer groups may be required if there is only one segment and one geographic region involved.

Also, focus groups cost money, and the number you conduct has to be in proportion to the capital you intend to invest in the development of the marketing plan.

The interpretation of focus group findings is very subjective and is greatly dependent on the ability of the moderator and the interpreter. You are the one who is most interested in identifying the attitudes of consumers, and in determining how your potential customers are reacting to various ideas. You may, however, not be the best person to interpret what respondents are saying during focus groups. People who are listening to consumers' reactions to their own business often hear only what they want to hear. They will grab on to a positive comment and may simply ignore or dismiss the other negative comments. It is usually best to retain the services of an independent expert who has no vested interest and considerable experience in evaluating participants' responses.

Find the Right Respondents to Represent Your Target Customers

The respondents to be included in focus groups must be carefully selected. You must be sure that they really represent your potential target customers and that they are capable of giving you valuable insight. You also want to avoid people who might tip off potential competitors and "professional respondents" who have been to so many focus groups that they are incapable of giving fresh, objective responses to your questions. You should become personally involved in decisions regarding the selection of respondents.

The key to recruiting exactly the kind of respondents you are looking for is the development of a very specific and detailed screening questionnaire. Put a great deal of thought into the questions that will be asked of potential respondents. You will want to know:

■ Whether they fit your target market profile.

■ Whether they have the right income, education, and lifestyle.

■ Whether they work for your competition, or for any other business that might result in a leak of your proprietary information. Examples are advertising agencies, certain related retailers, and market research firms.

Asking such questions beforehand can improve the quality of the information you obtain during the group discussions. You may need a professional moderator to help you develop the best possible screening questionnaire for your purposes.

Psychographic recruiting often helps bring in people who have more than normal insight into the personalities of new business ventures. In this technique, the respondents' thought patterns and habits are matched against the recruiting requirements. For example, you might want only people who have a record of trying new products early, since these are the potential customers who will have to be sold first. This technique can also help you recruit respondents who are unusually good communicators, which will be useful when you are trying to identify their innermost feelings. You can ascertain these qualities in people by including sophisticated psychological questions in the screening questionnaire. Ask your researcher to consider psychographic recruiting.

Where Do You Conduct Focus Groups?

Focus groups are normally conducted in a professional facility designed for this purpose, and the selection of the focus group facility is very important. There are hundreds of alternatives listed in the *Market Research Association Blue Book*, and they can also be found in other sources, such as trade magazines and under Market Research in the Yellow Pages. Facilities vary considerably in appearance and in their ability to effectively recruit the number and type of respondents required. It is a real waste of time and money if half of the respondents are no-shows or do not meet the requirements of the screening questionnaire. These things happen often enough that you should check references carefully before hiring a facility to host your focus groups.

A key function of the focus group facility will be to recruit your respondents for you. The facility's staff will call potential respondents on the telephone and use your screening questionnaire. To ensure that eight people will show up, you should recruit twelve. The facility will normally use lists from its database that represent the general types of respondents you are looking for. If you have particular needs (such as customer lists), you may provide this information to the facility.

What Should You Ask During Focus Groups?

Asking the right questions during focus groups is obviously the key to learning how your potential customers feel about your business venture. Finding out how someone really feels can be quite tricky. It is important that you know what to listen for when respondents are discussing their reactions. Here are three methods that can be valuable in evaluating responses during focus groups.

1. *The collage.* An important step is to determine what image of your product or service your consumers have. A fun and effective technique for finding this out is to have focus group respondents build a collage. By selecting the pictures that will go into the collage and then describing the collage, these people can give you real insight into how they see your business venture.

Focus group respondents like to participate in this type of activity, and generally everyone gets involved. The technique works with consumers of household products and with professional buyers of technical products. It has even been used in groups of potential customers of business-to-business products. Some of these people have not been involved in a "cut-and-paste exercise" like this since they left grammar school, but they seem to be quite enthusiastic about building a collage in a focus group.

2. *Forced relationships.* Sometimes the best way to understand the perceived personality of a new product or service is to force a relationship between the product and something else. It is not always easy for individuals, separately or in groups, to describe what they really feel about a product or service. Therefore, it is sometimes difficult for people to visualize whether a new product or service matches their needs. The forced relationship technique often helps overcome this problem.

In this technique, you ask respondents to force a relationship between your product or service and something totally different. You then ask them why they have chosen this relationship. For example, if you have an idea for a new financial product, such as a new credit card, then you might have respondents try to match your idea with an animal. If you have an idea for a new hair spray, then you might want to have them relate this to a make of automobile. These totally unrelated images can give you very revealing insights into the respondents' perceptions of your new business venture.

A good example of this occurred during the evaluation of a new retail service for a large bank. Respondents in focus groups were asked to pick an animal that reminded them of this new banking concept. Although many animals were mentioned, the lion was the most frequently brought up. When respondents were asked why, they usually said it was because the lion is the king of the jungle, and this concept reminded them of a powerful service offered by a big, dominant bank.

In probing further, it was determined that these potential customers felt that they would not trust the reliability of the new service concept if it were offered by a small local bank. They felt that it required too many resources. In fact, they felt that there were only a few banks that could pull off something of this magnitude, and that the bank doing the research was one of them.

3. *Personality associations.* Many people are reluctant to tell you exactly how they personally relate to a product or service. For example, some women may personally like the idea of buying fake jewelry, but want others to believe that they are the type of person who buys only real jewelry. In a group discussion, therefore, these women may tell you that a certain jewelry concept is great, but is not for them (although internally they really feel that it is for them).

An excellent technique for breaking down this barrier is the personality associations technique. With this technique, respondents are shown a series of photographs of different types of individuals and asked how they feel those individuals would probably react. The particular photographs used will depend on the nature of the concept being evaluated. With a new consumer product for women, for example, you might use a variety of pictures of women in different age groups, in different types of occupations, and with different income levels. Show each respondent a new idea, then ask him or her to select the photograph best representing:

■ The type of person who would be likely to buy the product or service

■ The type of person who would *not* be likely to buy it

Respondents will often tell you things about the person in the photograph that they would never tell you about themselves (although they are really talking about themselves). It is somehow safer to give intimate details about an abstract person than to provide those same details about oneself. This technique enables you to find out many details about potential target customers for your business that would be difficult to obtain through direct questioning.

This chapter gives a marketing plan for selling a branded line of hardware in supermarkets throughout the United States. The plan includes the strategy for a unique distribution program in which the company provides retailers with a complete inventory of hardware products on a distinctive display. Advertising and promotion programs are included, along with the details of a distribution system. The marketing plan is based on consumer needs identified through a series of focus groups. The plan includes these consumer research results along with the results of trade research, marketing objectives, and financial forecasts.

Marketing Plan for:
Craftmaster Hardware Products
Santos International Corporation[1]
July 1, 2002

INTRODUCTION

The purpose of this document is to provide a comprehensive marketing plan for a major new venture in marketing a broad line of hardware products through supermarket organizations throughout the United States. This document is divided into the following seven sections:

1. **BACKGROUND.** This section reviews the background of this project and outlines the steps that led to the development of this marketing plan.

2. **MARKET REVIEW.** This section reviews the nature of the U.S. hardware market and identifies the opportunities for this category in the supermarket environment.

3. **CONSUMER RESEARCH RESULTS.** This section outlines present consumer practices, desires, and expectations regarding the purchase of hardware products in supermarkets.

4. **SUPERMARKET PRACTICES AND ATTITUDES.** This section reviews the supermarket trade's current involvement with hardware products and its reactions regarding accepting distribution of this venture.

---

[1] **Disclaimer:** The specific information in this sample marketing plan was compiled for intended use as an example only. Although this marketing plan is based on actual products from a real company, the specific information in the plan is hypothetical and is not intended to compete with or to divulge proprietary ideas, company structure, or the financial status of any company. The names, numbers, and some of the facts in this marketing plan have been changed because of the confidential nature of the information. The information is intended to be used as a guide only.

5. **MARKETING OBJECTIVES.** This section provides the specific objectives of this venture over the next five years.

6. **STRATEGIC PROGRAMS.** This section presents the specifics of the various plans developed for achieving the marketing objectives of this venture.

7. **FINANCIAL PROJECTIONS.** This section reviews the results of a test of this venture that was conducted in a panel of stores in Alabama, and the sales projections developed based on the results of this test. The section then provides detailed calculations of the cost, volume, and payout of the venture from initial launch to full national expansion. A pro forma profit-and-loss statement is also provided.

This marketing plan is the result of a study that was conducted for the purpose of identifying and developing a major new consumer product opportunity in the hardware category. This project included the following nine steps:

1. **INFORMATION GATHERING.** A careful review of virtually every secondary source that might be appropriate for the proposed venture was conducted. Information was gathered on both the supermarket environment and the market for hardware and other do-it-yourself products.

2. **FIELD TRIPS.** Store checks and in-store interviews were conducted in supermarkets throughout the United States. The purpose of these trips was to identify the extent of hardware programs in the supermarket channel of distribution in various areas of the country. Interviews were also conducted with eighty-five different hardware manufacturers for the purpose of identifying their involvement in the supermarket channel of distribution, as well as obtaining detailed information on their respective product categories. These interviews were conducted during personal visits to the manufacturer's location, as well as during two hardware shows.

3. **CONSUMER RESEARCH.** A series of focus group sessions looking at various aspects of the hardware market and specifically the concept of purchasing hardware products and other do-it-yourself items through the supermarket channel of distribution was held with consumers.

4. **TRADE VISITS.** Meetings were held with supermarket buyers and merchandising managers throughout the United States The purpose of these meetings was to identify their current practices and their attitudes toward the hardware category, as well as their willingness to accept distribution of a new venture in this category.

5. **PRODUCT SOURCING.** Based on this research, a list of products to be included in this venture was assembled. These products represented the fastest-turning products in the hardware category and those that appeared to be appropriate for supermarket distribution. Manufacturers were then contacted and agreements were made for them to supply products for the program.

6. **PACKAGING.** Packaging for the program was designed, and small quantities of packaging were produced by each participating manufacturer. The purpose of this initial production run was to provide product for a test market.

7. **TEST MARKET.** A formal test market was conducted in Birmingham, Alabama, for the purpose of identifying product movement opportunities.

8. **OPPORTUNITY ANALYSIS.** Based on the results of the test market, an analysis was made to determine which products should be included in the program, criteria for selecting additional products, and the overall magnitude of the opportunity based on a sales forecast.

9. **MARKETING PLAN.** All of this research was summarized in the marketing plan, together with the strategic programs and financial projections necessary to launch the venture.

In addition to this research and analysis, this document reflects the input of a broad group of individuals from the marketing community and the hardware industry who were assembled for the purpose of identifying this opportunity. This input was gathered by detailed discussions on this subject, either in individual sit-down sessions, in status meetings, or in group work sessions held specifically for this purpose.

BACKGROUND

The concept of selling hardware products in supermarkets was identified as a significant opportunity. Hardware and other do-it-yourself products are one of the largest segments of the U.S.

economy. Over $8 billion worth of these products is purchased by American families annually, and this is growing at the rate of 15 percent per year. Women make a significant proportion of these purchases, and they would like to buy these products in the supermarkets where they regularly shop. Supermarkets today have not yet developed a response to this need. Their programs in hardware products are very sparse, and the products they carry are generally of inferior quality.

A team of leading manufacturers in the hardware industry was assembled by Santos International Corporation to assist Santos in developing a program for the sale of hardware in supermarkets. It was felt that the advice of these manufacturers would be beneficial in that they could provide real live input from the hardware industry. This team provided broad input on various segments of the market.

It was identified through trade research that the reason supermarkets have not developed strong hardware programs is that the hardware industry is very fragmented. Very few manufacturers in the hardware industry are large enough to be able to put together a major supermarket hardware program. Most manufacturers in this industry are small or specialize in one segment of the industry. Because of this, no one has helped supermarkets accommodate the hardware needs of their customers. Furthermore, it was felt that it would be very difficult for the hardware industry to retaliate against a major new program because of this fragmentation.

Based on this input, the Craftmaster program was developed. By combining the product lines of a number of manufacturers, a full line of high-quality hardware products was assembled. The products selected were the fastest-turning products in the categories that were appropriate for supermarkets. Exceptional packaging was developed for the entire line, together with an in-store display. A direct-to-store distribution system was developed, together with a strong pull-through marketing program.

A test market was conducted in Birmingham, Alabama, with tremendous success. It was found that the supermarket trade was receptive to the idea of a major new hardware program. Consumer sales were 4.64 turns of the display inventory per year. This represented a national opportunity in excess of $150 million in annual wholesale sales. Based on this test, the decision was made to proceed with the implementation of the venture.

Upon completion of one year of intensive research and development, this marketing plan, which summarizes the overall opportunity, was created. The plan demonstrates how the venture will move through each phase until it has achieved distribution throughout the United States.

MARKET REVIEW

1. *The hardware category is one of the largest growth segments of the U.S. economy.* Retail sales of hardware products are currently running at an annual rate of $34 billion nationally. These sales have been growing at the rate of 15 percent annually, and this growth is not expected to taper off in the foreseeable future. Hardware sales are stimulated by the strong do-it-yourself trends that are currently found throughout the United States and in most demographic segments. Do-it-yourself companies have grown at a compound annual rate of 15 to 20 percent over the past ten years. The hardware category has actually grown 50 percent faster than total U.S. retail spending.

2. *Hardware sales even increase during recessionary periods.* During recessions, there is a tendency for people to do more of their own repairs. Many hardware products actually become necessities during these periods. The hardware industry grew 27 percent during the 1974–1975 recession. The current recession's effect on hardware sales is evident from looking at building supply stores. Stores that cater to contractors have grown very little, while stores that who are exclusively consumer-oriented have grown tremendously during this recession.

3. *There is a growing trend toward self-reliance among Americans.* More and more consumers are doing things themselves these days. Some are doing this to save money, while others simply enjoy working with their hands. Over 75 percent of Americans buy hardware every three months. The average person spends $13.50 on hardware during this period. Most analysts agree that the hardware category should continue to grow throughout the foreseeable future.

4. *Supermarkets are one of the most significant distribution channels in the American retailing system.* Supermarkets do over $228 billion in retail sales annually. Most of these sales are concentrated in larger outlets. There are 137,000 supermarkets throughout the United States.

5. *Consumers do not generally shop for hardware products in supermarkets.* National Family Opinion conducted a large survey this year among 1,427 consumers. Consumers were asked about their normal practices in purchasing hardware products. Only 3 percent of this sample shopped for hardware products in supermarkets. Approximately 4 percent shopped for hardware products in drugstores, and 40 percent bought hardware products in discount stores. Approximately 53 percent of consumers in this study shopped for hardware products in specialty or other stores.

6. *Supermarkets have a very small share of overall hardware sales.* All supermarkets together did $30 million in hardware sales during 2001. This is less than 1 percent of all sales. Despite the size of the supermarket channel, supermarkets are not really participating in the hardware category. Supermarkets did over $4 billion in general merchandise sales last year, yet only 0.7 percent of this was in hardware.

CONSUMER RESEARCH RESULTS

1. *Consumers purchase hardware and other do-it-yourself products for a broad variety of reasons.* Saving money obviously plays a major role in these purchases. In addition, however, many consumers gain a great deal of personal satisfaction from fixing or building something themselves. Many enjoy working with their hands. Do-it-yourself projects are often found very therapeutic. Finally, a number of consumers do projects themselves simply because it is difficult to find outside help.

2. *It is the wife who typically conceives a household project.* She is frequently at home more often then her husband, and thus has the time to develop ideas for home improvement. She will collect data on major projects, and will often think through how a project is to be completed. The wife will then either carry out the project herself or convince her husband to do the work. Projects that are completed by the wife are often minor projects that do not require expertise that she does not have. Many women, however, are beginning to tackle more and more complex projects.

3. *Hardware products are currently purchased by both men and women.* Women will generally purchase products for their own do-it-yourself projects or from a list provided by their husbands. Women not only are concerned with purchasing the right products, but would

like to be able to purchase them in as convenient a location as possible. Men are also interested in shopping convenience; however, they are willing to spend more time evaluating product alternatives, seeking out information, and shopping for dollar savings from alternative hardware products.

4. *The concept of a well-known brand name for hardware products is generally preferred by consumers.* Consumers feel that brand names make it easier to identify quality products. Many people feel that major companies that have well-known brand names will stand behind their products better than producers of unknown brands. Many consumers are willing to pay a slightly higher price for a branded than for a nonbranded product. Some consumers use brand name products as a benchmark and then select a lower-priced alternative.

5. *Consumers could recall very little manufacturer advertising for standard household hardware products.* Stanley was the only name frequently recalled in this category. Most of the advertising seen by consumers was from retailers. They remembered advertising of sales both on television and in print.

6. *Normal household projects require a broad range of hardware products.* Several different types of products are generally required for a typical project. Some are already on hand, but many others must be purchased at the time of the project. The most common products mentioned by consumers during focus groups were hand tools, paintbrushes, fasteners, adhesives, and plumbing devices.

7. *Consumers felt that retailers that are in the do-it-yourself business needed to carry a broad product selection.* Consumers do not generally enjoy shopping around for hardware products. They would prefer to go to one location for all their needs. Locations where they typically shop for hardware products are hardware stores, discount stores, and building supply stores. They shop at these outlets because they feel confident that all the products they need will be there at the time of the shopping trip.

8. *Most consumers are currently unaware that supermarkets carry hardware products.* A few consumers have seen hardware products in supermarkets, but they have not purchased these products. The reason is that they felt the selection was very poor, and they were concerned about the quality of the hardware products in the supermarket being inferior.

9. *The concept of selling hardware products in supermarkets was very well received by consumers.* Both men and women felt that it would be very convenient to buy standard household hardware products in supermarkets. This would eliminate an extra trip or an additional stop during a routine shopping trip. Consumers generally felt that this would be a very valuable addition to supermarkets' product offerings.

10. *Consumers recommended that a supermarket hardware program offer a complete selection of quality products.* These would primarily be medium-quality products for routine household projects. Ideally they would have a well-known brand name and would be well organized for easy shopping. Most consumers indicated that if a basic line of hardware products were offered in supermarkets, they would purchase these products.

SUPERMARKET PRACTICES AND ATTITUDES

1. *The supermarket trade views hardware as a major product category.* Virtually all of the supermarket executives interviewed felt that hardware was a significant product category. They generally felt that although these items turned very slowly, they could be profitable because of the high profit margins attached to the hardware category. Because of this, they felt that this category was appropriate for supermarket distribution, as long as the line was broad enough to generate sufficient overall dollars.

2. *Many supermarkets have unsuccessfully attempted to establish a hardware business in their stores.* Almost all of the supermarkets visited during this study carried at least some hardware. Generally these were small sections with a very limited selection of product. Many supermarkets simply carried a few items scattered around the store. The only major exception to this was in Los Angeles, where a major distributor had established a strong hardware business in supermarkets. Many nonfood merchandisers have tried to establish a hardware section. They have developed plans for four or eight feet of space, but they have found that they were unable to maintain this program because of a lack of manufacturer assistance.

3. *The overall reaction to this venture by supermarket executives was very positive.* The venture was seen as solving a major problem for supermarkets. The supermarket would be provided with a complete hardware department and with a product line covering its customers' basic needs. Because the company would be providing supermarkets with ongoing assistance in

marketing and in maintaining the program at store level, executives saw this as a workable program. Many executives felt that this was the only way in which they could successfully enter the hardware category.

4. *Supermarkets typically felt that the venture would eventually have to take over their entire hardware business.* Many organizations indicated that they would put the new brand in alongside whatever programs they might currently have. Once it proved successful, however, they would prefer to eliminate their existing program. In sum, supermarkets would really like to turn over the unique requirements of purchasing and marketing hardware to an outside expert company.

5. *The supermarket trade felt that the operators of a supermarket hardware program must provide them with a line that is complete enough to cover all their needs.* Many supermarkets wanted to be able to provide "a miniature hardware store" for their customers, but this would have to fit into the space that they had available. In some cases this was four feet of space, while in other cases the supermarket could provide eight feet. It was felt that Santos International Corporation must have a broad enough product line to accommodate the various size stores.

6. *A permanent section for hardware products must be created within the supermarket.* The trade would like to allocate a fixed area within the stores for hardware. The objective would be a permanent ongoing department. To accomplish this, the venture must provide the stores with a plan-o-gram that will enable them to create this permanent section.

7. *Store service would be a critical factor for a hardware venture.* The primary problem that supermarkets have had in the past with hardware has been ordering the product. Store personnel have tended to neglect these departments, resulting in empty pegs and eventually the elimination of the section. It was felt that the new Santos International program must provide assistance in setting up the display initially and in ordering product on an ongoing basis. This will ensure that the display is kept full at all times. In most cases, store personnel will be able to take product from the back room of the store and place it on pegs on the display once it has been ordered.

8. *The most viable physical distribution system was felt to be UPS drop shipments to each individual store.* Several distribution options were discussed with the trade. Using the super-

markets' own warehouses was not felt to be a viable option because the hardware line has too many individual items. It was recommended that a distributor's warehouse be used so that the distributor could pick-pack orders for each individual store. Custom orders could then be shipped to each individual store by UPS. It was felt that store personnel could effectively receive the merchandise and put it on the displays.

9. *The supermarket trade liked the idea of putting all the hardware products it sold under a common brand.* The trade was told that all products in this program would be under the one brand. Packaging for all products would be similar, and the entire brand would be advertised. The reaction to this concept was quite positive. Executives felt that the new advertised brand would be perceived as a major national brand and would help generate incremental sales for their stores.

10. *The major conclusion from the research with supermarket executives was that hardware would be an excellent addition to the supermarkets' nonfood departments.* Supermarkets are looking for high-margin products. Nonfood products help to increase overall profits, and hardware was felt to fit this profile. It was generally felt that the new hardware brand from Santos International Corporation could become an excellent new business for supermarkets.

MARKETING OBJECTIVES

1. *To create and maintain, over the next five years, a highly profitable consumer product business marketing a line of basic household hardware products through supermarkets nationally.* It is intended that this be a permanent ongoing major business, staffed with a product management team that is dedicated to perpetuating the brand's existence and continuously expanding the brand's sales and profits.

2. *To achieve a strong reputation among consumers as a high-quality brand of hardware products that is sold in supermarkets.* The goal is to become known as a brand of high-quality products for routine household do-it-yourself projects and to become known as a brand that is conveniently located at the local neighborhood supermarket.

3. *To become the only brand of hardware products in most of the major supermarkets throughout the United States.* The Craftmaster concept solves a major supermarket trade

problem. Therefore, the goal is for Craftmaster to become so valuable to supermarkets that they do not feel it is necessary for them to carry any other brand of hardware products. In sum, the goal is to become the dominant force in selling hardware products through this very important channel of distribution.

4. *To lock up the key hardware manufacturers as the source of product for the supermarket program.* Santos International Corporation does not intend to go into the business of manufacturing hardware products. The company intends to be a key force in marketing other manufacturers' products under its own brand name. Therefore, it is Santos's goal to make sure that the manufacturers of its products make products of excellent quality, yet at competitive prices.

5. *Over the next five years, to obtain distribution in supermarkets throughout the country.* The plan is to carefully manage growth by systematically rolling out the program in key markets throughout the United States. This will reduce the risks involved in expanding too rapidly, and it will enable Santos to expand the organization in an orderly manner.

6. *To successfully launch the venture on the east coast of the United States during 2003.* The goal is to achieve distribution during 2003 in 5,301 stores located between Boston and Washington, D.C. This means that by the end of 2003, Santos International Corporation will be solidly in the hardware business in supermarkets.

STRATEGIC PROGRAMS

1. *The initial Craftmaster product line will consist of an assortment of basic hardware items appropriate for supermarket distribution.* It will provide a broad line of the fastest-turning products in the hardware category. The objective is to provide the supermarket shopper with a line of products appropriate for do-it-yourself projects. The typical supermarket will be offered seventy-six different products that will completely fill a four-foot gondola section.

2. *Larger supermarkets will be offered a fuller product line.* There are a number of supermarkets in the United States that are large enough to accommodate a major line of hardware products. These stores will be offered the basic four-foot product line, plus an additional four-

foot expanded section. This expanded section will include 104 additional fast-selling products.

3. *All products will be marketed under the Craftmaster brand.* This name is applicable to do-it-yourself products, and it has been trademarked for exclusive use by Santos International Corporation. The name is catchy, can provoke consumer interest, and has a timeless quality.

4. *The entire Craftmaster product line will be packaged in a coordinated manner.* Hardware products that are currently sold in supermarkets come from a variety of different manufacturers. The packaging of these products has many different colors and designs. Because of this, the hardware category in supermarkets is confusing and unattractive. All Craftmaster packaging will have uniform graphics that convey a high-quality image. All products will appear to be one major national brand. This will be unique among hardware products in supermarkets.

5. *The Craftmaster packaging will not interfere with the manufacturers' normal operations.* The products sold as part of this program will come from a variety of different manufacturers with different packaging machines. The objective is to minimize expense at each manufacturing location. Because of this, Craftmaster will use the existing basic package of each manufacturer. The only change in the packaging will be the graphics. Therefore, each manufacturer can continue to use its own machinery, carton sizes, and so on.

6. *The Craftmaster in-store display is created from existing store fixtures.* Each store will be asked to allocate either a four-foot or an eight-foot gondola, depending on whether the supermarket is accepting the basic program or the expanded program. The display will then be plan-o-grammed. Each peg on the display will be assigned to a specific product type. Signage will then be placed on the gondola. The result is an attractive hardware display that is well organized for shopping convenience.

7. *The Craftmaster display can be tailored to fit the needs of virtually any supermarket.* There is an amazing variety in the sizes and types of supermarket outlets. The Craftmaster display can fit into any of these different types of stores. The display can be put at an end aisle or in-line, with adequate inventory for replenishment. Most stores will require displays in four-foot increments. Three-foot sections can also be created if that is required to meet the needs of a particular store.

8. *Craftmaster products provide excellent consumer value.* The products that have been selected for this program provide excellent quality levels for household tasks. These products will generally be superior in quality to similar products found in supermarkets today. Extremely expensive products (professional level) have not been included in this program, as they do not fit the profile of the typical supermarket shopper. Pricing of Craftmaster products will be competitive with that of similar-quality products in other channels of distribution.

9. *The trade margins have been set to represent an excellent profit opportunity for the supermarket.* Pricing has been established to enable supermarkets to earn a 40 percent margin (percentage off retail price) on the entire product line. This is considered to be an excellent profit level in the supermarket environment. Distributors participating in this program will earn a 25 percent margin off the wholesale price to the supermarket. Distributors are required to pay for store service out of their margins. The store service will run from 8 to 10 percent of the wholesale price, netting the distributor between 15 and 17 percent. These are considered to be acceptable margins by distributors.

10. *Consumer advertising will be used to build the Craftmaster brand.* Most hardware products are not advertised. The typical hardware brand is too small to justify the expense of any significant level of advertising. Craftmaster has the advantage of selling a number of different hardware products under the same brand. The combined revenue of all these different products provides a significant fund for advertising. Santos International Corporation has allocated 20 percent of the revenue received on the Craftmaster brand to advertising expense. This will enable the brand to spend in excess of $2 million on advertising on an annual basis.

11. *The overall objective of all Craftmaster advertising will be to build the sales of Craftmaster hardware products in supermarkets.* The goal is to become the major source of hardware in the supermarket channel of distribution. Therefore, the advertising will be geared to telling consumers that they can now buy these products in supermarkets. It is intended that this strategy will help shift sales from other outlets into the supermarket channel of distribution. The other major objective of the advertising will be to identify Craftmaster as a quality brand of do-it-yourself products.

12. *The Craftmaster brand will fully exploit the opportunity for sales promotion that supermarkets provide.* Supermarkets provide an excellent vehicle for sales promotion, in that they

utilize virtually every promotion device available: coupons, rebates, contests, and so on. These promotion techniques are not typically used for hardware products because they are not always acceptable in the traditional channels of distribution. This provides the Craftmaster brand with a unique opportunity. Santos intends to utilize this as a way of outpromoting the hardware industry.

13. *The Craftmaster brand will use promotion as a vehicle for obtaining and maintaining distribution and for ensuring strong consumer sales.* The marketing plan has allocated 10 percent of the income from Craftmaster sales for sales promotion activities. This will yield over $1 million on an ongoing annual basis for promotion.

14. *The Craftmaster concept provides a tremendous opportunity for publicity.* Do-it-yourself products is one of the largest retail product categories. Major supermarket distribution of this category will now be available for the first time. This will provide a major new consumer benefit. These facts are genuine news, and are the basis for a substantial public relations campaign.

15. *The Santos International Corporation will launch a major public relations campaign with the introduction of the Craftmaster brand.* The theme of this campaign will be that the company is making a broad line of quality hardware products available to consumers in convenient supermarket locations. Press conferences and meetings will be held with all segments of the business and consumer press. Appearances will be scheduled on national and local television programs and on radio broadcasts. Feature articles will be generated in national and local print media. This publicity will be used to supplement the advertising, and to create a sense of urgency and excitement about the launch of the Craftmaster brand.

16. *The Craftmaster brand will be introduced to the trade in such a way as to create the impression that this introduction is a major new marketing event.* Supermarket buyers tend to react very favorably to new brands that are associated with powerful consumer pull-through programs. In many cases the supermarket buyers will feel that they must accept distribution of this new brand simply because most of their customers will be looking for these products in the buyers' stores. Supermarket executives do not like to miss out on those products that they feel their customers know about and want to buy on a regular basis. The introduction of the Craftmaster brand will be done in such a way as to make buyers feel that they have no choice but to accept distribution.

17. *During the Craftmaster sell-in, each supermarket will be exposed to a series of powerful sales activities.* The campaign will begin with a pre-sell meeting with each buyer to introduce the concept. The buyer will then be invited to attend the actual sell-in presentation. The next step will be a major PowerPoint presentation to each supermarket organization. The entire buying committee will be invited to attend this presentation, which will be a dramatic, highly persuasive show that will convince the buying committee that it must accept distribution of the program. Finally, a third sales meeting will be held with each organization for the purpose of closing the sale.

18. *A national organization will be created to manage the implementation and ongoing activities of the Craftmaster brand.* This organization will create all marketing plans, it will obtain and maintain distribution, it will coordinate all manufacturing activities, and it will ensure a profitable operation. The following outlines the responsibilities of each management position:

   A. *Vice president of sales and marketing.* The vice president of sales and marketing is the chief marketing officer for the brand. This person will create ongoing marketing plans on a periodic basis, direct the advertising agency and all other outside marketing organizations, and supervise the three zone sales managers and will be responsible for the entire sales organization. New and ongoing product sales are the vice president of sales and marketing's primary responsibility.

   B. *Operations managers.* There will be two operations managers. They are the primary link between the sales organization and the manufacturing organizations. They will ensure that the products are packaged properly, and that they are shipped in a timely manner. They will evaluate data from the sales and servicing organizations to ensure that the entire physical distribution system is flowing smoothly. They will also provide the primary quality control for all Craftmaster products.

   C. *Zone managers.* There will be three sales zone managers. They will supervise the distributing organizations as well as the three district managers in each zone. Zone managers are responsible for obtaining new distribution and for ongoing sales in each zone. They report to the vice president of sales and marketing.

   D. *District managers.* There will be a total of nine district sales managers, with three located in each zone. They will supervise the servicing organizations and will be the primary contact with supermarket buyers. District managers will obtain new distribution and will contact supermarket organizations on a regular basis. They report to the appropriate zone managers.

19. *All manufacturers will sell the products directly to a series of outside distributors.* Several distributors that will actually purchase the product on an ongoing basis in various areas of the United States have been lined up. These distributors will receive purchase orders for each store from the service organization. They will then ship the products and invoice each store. Replenishment stock for the warehouse will be ordered by the distributor directly from the manufacturers. The distributor will actually be the manufacturer's customer. Distributors will be supervised by sales zone managers in their respective territories.

20. *A national service organization will be the primary contact with each store.* Acme Support Services, Inc., has been appointed as the Craftmaster service organization. Acme has a national organization of 1,200 people located throughout the United States. It will contact each store on a regular basis to take replenishment orders. It will also set up each store for the first time. This organization will be supervised by the district manager in each appropriate area.

21. *A number of manufacturers have been commissioned to manufacture product for the Craftmaster brand.* Manufacturers have been selected based on their ability to produce a quality product and to provide the large quantities that will be required as this program is rolled out nationally. In addition, pricing from each manufacturer must be competitive. All of the manufacturers selected thus far are leaders in their respective industries.

22. *Each manufacturer will pay Santos International Corporation a commission of 10 percent of net factory sales on all products sold under the Craftmaster brand.* This will be on net prices to distributors. Each manufacturer thus far has signed an agreement indicating that the manufacturer has the right to sell product to our distributors under the Craftmaster brand. Each manufacturer will use Craftmaster packaging graphics. This 10 percent commission is the primary income to the Santos International Corporation.

23. *The plan is to have the entire brand management team in place by the middle of January 2003, and to have the initial stores set up and begin advertising by October 1, 2003.* Beyond this, the plan will unfold according to the rollout schedule indicated in the next section of

this marketing plan. Table 10-1 outlines the timetable for the launch of the Craftmaster brand during 2003.

FINANCIAL PROJECTIONS

Test Market Results

1. A test market was conducted in a panel of stores in Birmingham, Alabama, for the purpose of gathering data to be used in developing the Craftmaster sales forecast. Eighty-two different products were placed in a five-store test. The movement of each product was tracked every other week for eight weeks. There was no advertising placed during this test. The following results were obtained:

   A. *Product movement.* The movement of product varied greatly from one class of product to another. Fifteen fasteners turned at an annual rate of 7.09 times. This was the fastest-turning segment of the product line. Roller frames/covers turned at the slowest rate, which was 0.88 times. The results of the test clearly indicated that the products in the

TABLE 10-1. Venture Timetable

	2003 Completion Dates
Brand management team in place	1/17
Produce sales materials	2/11
Complete pre-sell meetings	4/8
Manufacturer product samples	4/11
Write sell-in presentation	4/11
Complete sell-in presentations	
—Boston	4/15
—Hartford	4/22
—New York	5/13
—Philadelphia	5/20
—Baltimore	5/27
—Washington, D.C.	6/3
All purchase orders to manufacturers	7/15
Ship product and displays to distributor	8/26
Set up all stores	9/30
Start advertising	10/1

original line needed to be adjusted. It also provided a basis for selecting products on an ongoing basis.

B.   *Turns forecast.* Based on the results of the five-store panel test in Alabama and basic adjustments made to the content of the product line, the overall line is forecasted to turn 4.64 times per year. This figure will be used for all future forecasting until actual movement is identified. Products found to move slower than 4.64 times per year will be eliminated from the program.

2. *It is estimated that the Craftmaster program will eventually achieve distribution in 30,000 supermarkets throughout the United States.* This represents 22 percent of all supermarkets. It is felt that all 30,000 stores will receive the basic four-foot product line section. Ten thousand of these stores will also receive an additional four-foot section containing the expanded product line.

3. *It will take four years to roll out the Craftmaster program to the entire United States.* It is felt that it will take the first six months of 2003 to prepare sales materials and actually contact each organization. During the third quarter of 2003, the product will actually be set up in 5,301 stores.

4. *During 2003, distribution will be obtained along the east coast of the United States.* This will include distribution in six markets stretching from Boston to Washington, D.C. This area encompasses 17.56 percent of U.S. households. To achieve distribution in these markets, a total of ninety-eight presentations will be made to supermarket buyers.

5. *The national sales forecast for 2003 for all products included in the Craftmaster program is $7.4 million in net factory sales.* This is made up of $5.3 million in sales of product from the basic four-foot section and $2.1 million in sales from the expanded section. The total net factory sales in 2007 is forecasted to be $114 million. Table 10-2 gives the national sales forecast for the basic section and the expanded section from 2003 through 2007.

6. *The national sales forecast for the basic four-foot section is made up of pipeline sales plus consumer sales.* For 2003, it is estimated that the pipeline sales will be $3.2 million in wholesale sales. This is simply the amount of dollars that will be required to fill each of the 5,301 displays. Consumer sales assume that the display will turn at an annual rate of 4.64 times. In 2003 the inventory in the stores will be available only during the last quarter of

TABLE 10-2. National Sales Forecast ($000s Omitted)

	2003	2004	2005	2006	2007
Basic Section					
Wholesale sales	7,087	29,207	73,859	107,561	108,780
Net factory sales	5,315	21,906	55,395	80,671	81,586
Expanded Section					
Wholesale sales	2,836	11,687	29,553	43,038	43,526
Net factory sales	2,127	8,765	22,165	32,278	32,644
Total Program					
Wholesale sales	9,923	40,894	103,412	150,599	152,306
Net factory sales	7,442	30,671	77,560	112,949	114,230

the year. Total wholesale sales for each year beyond 2003 have been adjusted to allow for inflation at the rate of 6 percent annually (conservative estimate). Net factory sales for 2003 are 75 percent of wholesale sales, because the distributor's margin has been subtracted.

7. *It is estimated that the expanded four-foot section will generate $2.1 million in net factory sales for 2003.* The calculations for identifying consumer sales and pipeline sales on the expanded section are similar to those for the basic four-foot section.

8. *During the beginning of 2003, $130,000 will be invested in the development of marketing tools and in the initial ninety-eight sales presentations.* This development expense will pay for the creation and filming of a television commercial, as well as the preparation of the formal sales presentation to be used during sell-in meetings. Ten thousand dollars will be invested in elaborate presentation equipment, which will include a computer and projector. It is estimated that $50,000 will be required to pay for travel expenses, meals, room rentals, and so on, to put on ninety-eight major sales presentations.

9. *On an ongoing basis, it is expected that the pretax profits generated from the Craftmaster program will be in excess of $6 million.* During 2003, a loss of $383,000 is expected; this is the investment required to launch the brand. It is expected that the brand will generate a profit of $1 million during 2004 and will remain profitable in subsequent years.

CHAPTER 11

Using Online Consumer Qualitative Research

Example: Eagle Central Air Conditioners in Taiwan

This chapter provides a marketing plan for expanding the sales and distribution of a Chinese manufacturer of central air conditioners in Taiwan. One of the interesting aspects of this marketing plan is its use of the Internet to develop a qualitative understanding of consumer usage and attitudes. Internet research can be very useful when research respondents are sparse or difficult to find because they are scattered in a lot of different locations. When the Internet is used, it really does not matter where the respondent is located. In the case of this marketing plan, there were very few central air conditioning consumers in Taiwan at the time the plan was written, and they were located all over the island. Clearly the most efficient research method in this case was the Internet.

The qualitative research method used for the development of this marketing plan was the *time-extended online depth interview* technique. The interviewing procedure included time-extended online interviews that used a "bulletin board" discussion format to conduct a moderator-facilitated discussion. These time-extended online depth interviews lasted three days with each respondent, who logged on twice each day. Exposing each respondent to a small series of questions twice each day enabled the respondents to give more thought to each question. This approach also enabled the moderator and company management personnel to provide input throughout the series of interviews.

The moderator guided the discussion by introducing the topics from the discussion outline and posing follow-up questions. Throughout the process, the moderator continued to encourage participants to provide the greatest possible amount of detailed information about any and all of their experiences, thoughts, feelings, attitudes, decision-making processes, and behaviors that were pertinent to the purposes of the study.

The time-extended online depth interview has many of the same benefits as the traditional face-to-face depth interview or focus group. Because respondents can review the moderator's questions and post their answers at their convenience, time-extended online depth interviews enable the recruiting of respondents who would not be able or willing to participate in the traditional face-to-face qualitative research on the same topic.

Furthermore, time-extended online depth interviews give the respondents more time to reflect on their answers and therefore can produce more thoughtful and in-depth comments than any other form of qualitative research—including both traditional and online interviews and focus groups. Similarly, the extra time available to the moderator (and to the clients, who can observe the time-extended online depth interviews that are in progress on their own computers) allows the moderator to ask more reflective and insightful follow-up questions than would be practical in other types of qualitative research.

For Eagle central air conditioners, all interviews with central air conditioning consumers in Taiwan were conducted over the Internet. The overall objective of the research was to develop a profile and obtain an understanding of the habits and practices of purchasers of central air conditioners for their homes. A questionnaire was prepared for the interviews that provided information meeting all of the objectives of this project. The questionnaire included approximately thirty to thirty-five unstructured questions. A database of approximately 350,000 Internet users in Taiwan, of which 2,000 were purchasers of central air conditioners, was then purchased. The completed interviews were taken from this sample.

An e-mail invitation was sent to all of the potential respondents asking them to complete a short screener. They logged on and answered a few questions to confirm that they were qualified. They were then told about the survey and asked if they would be willing to participate. Those participants who answered yes were told that they would receive notification of their selection shortly (so that the company could control how many people were interviewed).

A full report was prepared after completion of the interviews. The full report included detailed findings and an analysis of the results. Full transcripts of the interviews were also provided with the report. The entire project was completed in approximately six weeks. This research was done early in the process of developing the marketing plan, enabling the company to design programs around the needs of its target group of consumers.

Marketing Plan for:
Eagle Central Air Conditioners
Zhenzhou Electric Company[1]
July 1, 1999

INTRODUCTION

The purpose of this document is to analyze the residential central air conditioning market in Taiwan and to provide a marketing plan for the Zhenzhou Electric Company to use to expand its sales to this market. This report is divided into the following sections:

1. **BACKGROUND.** This section details the current Zhenzhou organization in China and reviews the present strategy for competing in the Chinese central residential air conditioning market.

2. **MARKET REVIEW.** This section reviews the growth and nature of the central residential air conditioning market in Taiwan, including the present and anticipated competitive environment.

3. **CONSUMER USAGE AND ATTITUDES.** This section reviews the desires and expectations of current Taiwan consumers, as well as their acceptance of the idea of purchasing central residential air conditioners through various nontraditional channels of distribution.

4. **DEPARTMENT STORE PRACTICES AND ATTITUDES.** This section reviews the department store trade's current involvement with central residential air conditioners in Taiwan, and its attitudes toward the product category.

[1] **Disclaimer:** The specific information in this sample marketing plan was compiled for intended use as an example only. Although this marketing plan is based on actual products from a real company, the specific information in the plan is hypothetical and is not intended to compete with or to divulge proprietary ideas, company structure, or the financial status of any company. The names, numbers, and some of the facts in this marketing plan have been changed because of the confidential nature of the information. The information is intended to be used as a guide only.

5. **CONCLUSIONS.** This section presents strategic implications based on the facts presented in the previous sections.

6. **MARKETING PLAN ELEMENTS.** This section presents very specific and able to be acted upon plans for what Zhenzhou should do within the framework of the information presented in the previous sections.

7. **FINANCIAL PROJECTIONS.** This section provides detailed calculations of the sales projections and the anticipated costs associated with a residential central air conditioner program in Taiwan.

The scope of this report is primarily directed at identifying what Zhenzhou should do to expand its central air conditioner sales to Taiwan, in addition to its present marketing activities in China. The recommendations presented in this report have been designed to function as an incremental marketing effort and are compatible with present plans for the present air conditioning business. In addition, this report deals only with the residential segment of the central air conditioning market and does not comment on the new construction or builders' market, except where appropriate for clarification reasons.

The information required to write this marketing plan was gathered in three stages. The first stage involved three field trips to Taiwan, during which extensive discussions were held with two major Taiwan advertising agencies, three major department stores, and a major appliance dealer. Second, the available market research on central air conditioners in China was reviewed and then updated with a Taiwan survey of recent air conditioning purchasers and potential customers in the Taipei area. Finally, an Internet survey of purchasers and potential purchasers of central air conditioners in Taiwan was conducted.

BACKGROUND

Sales of Eagle central air conditioners in China are currently handled by the Zhenzhou Electric Company in Zhenzhou, China. The present air conditioning company started in 1990; first-year sales were $6,330,000, increasing each year to a 1998 sales level of $16,000,000. At the end of 1995 the company reached its break-even point, and it is now operating in the black. United States dollars are used throughout this marketing plan to simplify comparisons for the reader.

The air conditioning company is headed by a general manager, who has delegated the responsibility for sales to a national sales manager and five field sales representatives. The main sales thrust since 1990 has been to the residential market through heating and cooling contractors. The company now plans to penetrate the central air conditioning market in Taiwan. Thus far, however, strong efforts by well-entrenched competitors have limited Zhenzhou's ability to achieve an effective level of penetration.

In an effort to circumvent the heating and cooling contractors in Taiwan, in 1997 Zhenzhou conducted an experiment in Taipei that attempted to penetrate the residential market by selling through major appliance dealers. The test never got off the ground because of certain insoluble problems with the installing subcontractors.

Because of the dramatic growth of the residential segment of the central air conditioning market in Taiwan, and because of the inability of the Zhenzhou Electric Company to penetrate this market through traditional contractors, it has been decided to evaluate a nontraditional approach to entering the market. There are two specific reasons for this decision. First, there is the proven ability of the Zhenzhou service group in China to launch an effective installing organization. It is felt that this same type of organization can be organized in Taiwan, thereby permitting Zhenzhou to circumvent the traditional distribution channels. Second, there would be an obvious difficulty in obtaining a large network of major heating and cooling contractors in Taiwan as a result of the solid entrenchment of competitors.

As a result of these considerations, Zhenzhou decided to develop a nontraditional method of penetrating the residential segment of the air conditioning market in Taiwan that would run concurrently with other sales thrusts in China. Thus, the objective of this marketing plan is to provide a distribution plan that will generate incremental sales and result in a deep penetration of the rapidly expanding market for central air conditioners in Taiwan.

MARKET REVIEW

The Taiwan market for central residential air conditioners has been growing at the rate of 40 percent per year for the past three years. This growth rate is expected to continue at least through 2005. The recent upsurge in the sale of central residential air conditioners can be accounted for by the heavy promotion campaigns waged by the utilities, air conditioning manufacturers, and local dealers and distributors beginning in 1996. These promotion efforts were triggered by the "Spring into Summer Campaign" that the local utilities launched in 1976 in order to get increased power usage in the summer.

Although the Taiwan market for central residential air conditioners is still very new, a number of identifiable characteristics are beginning to emerge. The following are features of the Taiwan central air conditioning market as it has developed thus far:

1. *Of the total central air conditioning market, sales to the residential segment alone were over 19,000 units in 1996.* Because of the newness of central air conditioning for Taiwan customers, a replacement market for central residential air conditioners has not yet developed. However, it is expected that after 2000 central residential air conditioners will begin to be replaced, and that this segment of the market will emerge strongly. Table 11-1 illustrates the growth of the residential segment of the central air conditioning market from 1994 through 1999, using a projection of a 40 percent per year growth rate.

2. *Because of the small percentage of homes in Taiwan that are currently air conditioned, it is feasible for the growth of this market to continue for some time.* According to the utility company, 64 percent of homes located in areas of Taiwan where air conditioning would be desirable have forced-air heat, and yet only 5 percent of these homes currently have central air conditioners.

3. *Central air conditioning dealers usually base their decisions concerning which brand to sell on three things.* The first of these is the margins provided by the manufacturer. The second is the amount of advertising and other promotional support available. The third is the availability of special incentives, such as trips, contests, and so on, to dealers. Conversely, dealers usually do not select the manufacturer based on the quality of the brand. The primary reason for this is that there are very few perceptible differences in product at the consumer

TABLE 11-1. Forecasted Unit Sales of Central Residential Air Conditioners in Taiwan

1994	94,170
1995	132,680
1996	192,290
1997	269,210
1998	372,890
1999	527,650

level. Although there are some technical differences between the units provided by one manufacturer and those provided by another, the home air-conditioner consumer usually does not understand these differences, nor are they very important to this consumer.

4. *Traditionally the primary channel of distribution for central residential air conditioners is the heating and cooling contractor.* Some sales are obtained through fuel oil dealers, department stores, and other nontraditional channels. The major channel in Taiwan, however, is the heating and cooling contractor.

5. *The procedure used by these contractors in selling air conditioners is fairly uniform throughout Taiwan.* The consumer generally responds to an ad in the local newspaper, after which a representative of the contractor goes out to the consumer's home and makes an estimate. If a sale is made, the contractor sends out a team to install the air conditioner. Follow-up servicing is done by the contractor as needed.

6. *Over 90 percent of the Taiwan air conditioning market is controlled by six manufacturers.* Although the shares of market, the strengths and weaknesses, and the business practices of these manufacturers do differ, they have the following things in common:

    A. *Central air conditioning manufacturers are extremely trade-oriented rather than consumer-oriented.* Generally speaking, all central air conditioning manufacturers are competing for the same basic pool of dealers. Their objectives are to (1) convince as many of these dealers as possible to carry their brand of air conditioner and (2) convince as many dealers as possible to push their brand over a competitive brand.

        In Taipei, for example, nearly all of the dealers in the phone book carry more than one brand of air conditioner, and some carry as many as three or four. In visiting two of the major contractors in Taipei, it was noticed that each of them had manuals and promotional materials from nearly every manufacturer of air conditioners on a back shelf. The contractors explained that although they generally emphasize one brand of air conditioner at a time, they are capable of selling almost any brand of air conditioner available in Taiwan, and they do change brands from time to time depending on changing margins and other types of dealer incentives.

    B. *Taiwan central air conditioning manufacturers have very little control over their contractors.* As indicated earlier, an air conditioning contractor is an independent business-person and therefore has a great deal of flexibility concerning the brand and type of air conditioners he or she will sell, the number of options to include, and even the quality of service to be provided. Because of this, most manufacturers are forced to rely heavily on the judgment of the individual contractor.

This lack of control is even greater with smaller manufacturers. Smaller manufacturers, who have fewer and relatively less lucrative incentives, are frequently forced to accept any distribution channel they can get. In these cases they have virtually no control because dealers will simply shift to another brand if any requirements are placed on them that do not meet with their approval.

C. *Because of the independence and instability of the contractor network in Taiwan, manufacturers generally do not place a great deal of emphasis on national brand advertising.* Instead, most advertising monies are generally funneled to the contractor on a co-op basis. The contractor then places his or her own ads in the Yellow Pages and local newspapers, and leads are generated from this advertising.

In interviews with local contractors, it was explained that even when a consumer requests a specific brand of air conditioner, the contractor can usually convert this consumer to another brand by simply telling the consumer that "although the brand selected is a good one, it simply is not the right brand for his or her house." Because of this, national brand advertising has not proved successful when the traditional channels of distribution are used.

CONSUMER USAGE AND ATTITUDES

General Research Findings

The average Taiwan central air conditioning consumer is male, is over thirty-five years old, considers himself to be either a professional or a white-collar worker, and is a family man living with his wife and at least two children. This consumer owns his own home, which is over six years old. The key purchasing characteristics of the average Taiwan central residential air conditioning consumer can be characterized as follows:

1. *As might be expected, by far the overwhelming reason for purchasing a central air conditioner is to overcome the heat and humidity during the summer.* Although a small number of consumers (17 percent) indicated that they purchased an air conditioner because of

allergies or respiratory problems, and a few (7 percent) had previously owned a central air conditioner, the prime reason for purchase was the weather.

2. *The final decision to purchase a central air conditioner is generally made by the husband.* In this purchase situation, the wife generally plays the role of the influencer. In some cases (26 percent), the wife even telephones for the original estimate. However, the wife is clearly not the decision maker and almost never closes the sale.

3. *At the time of purchasing a central air conditioner, the consumer usually does not have any other form of air conditioning in the house.* Although a small percentage (22 percent) of those purchasing a new central air conditioner were replacing a window unit, generally speaking purchasers were not trading up from window units to a central unit.

4. *Over 85 percent of central air conditioning consumers make their actual purchase within three months of the time they made their original decision.* In other words, although central air conditioning is not generally purchased on impulse, the entire cycle between original decision and installation is completed within one season.

5. *After the original decision to purchase a central air conditioner has been made, most consumers do at least some shopping.* Approximately 32 percent of the people in Taiwan who purchased a central air conditioner in 1999 obtained estimates from two separate contractors, and 39 percent received estimates from three or more contractors.

6. *A number of the people in Taiwan who purchased central air conditioners did no shopping before they purchased their air conditioner.* Approximately 28 percent of Taiwan central air conditioning consumers did not shop around, but bought their air conditioner from the first contractor they contacted.

7. *Most of the people in Taiwan are not familiar with central air conditioning or the process they would have to go through in order to make such a purchase.* Because of the small percentage of homes that have central air conditioners (5 percent), consumers are unable to discuss the purchase with neighbors who have gone through the process already. About the only research they are able to conduct is reviewing advertising on central air conditioners and discussing it with their local contractor.

8. *Over 68 percent of recent central air conditioning purchasers were unaware of any advertising of central residential air conditioning.* Of those who had seen or heard advertising, the major medium remembered was newspaper.

9. *The market for central residential air conditioners in Taiwan is not very price-sensitive.* Over 70 percent of those who purchased a central residential air conditioner in 1998 made their purchase decision on the basis of something other than price. Most purchase decisions were made on the basis of the credibility of the contractor, the knowledge of the person doing the estimating in the home, or the brand name.

10. *Most of the people in Taiwan who purchased a central residential air conditioner felt that the final installed cost was about what they expected it would be.* The average person in Taiwan fitting the profile of the target market feels that a central residential air conditioner will generally run between $2,000 and $2,300, depending on the size of their house. Those with very large homes recognize that the cost will be substantially greater.

11. *Nearly all recent purchasers (98 percent) did not feel that they had to wait until it was time to replace the furnace before they bought a central residential air conditioner.* Air conditioning is considered to be an entirely separate purchase.

12. *Almost 70 percent of those who purchased an air conditioner in 1998 paid cash.* Of those purchasing on credit, the major source was a credit card or bank loan.

Nontraditional Distribution Channel Findings

Although currently nearly all residential central air conditioners are sold through heating and cooling contractors, there are a number of nontraditional channels that either are now being used or theoretically could be used in the future. Past experiments by the Zhenzhou Electric Company demonstrated that air conditioners could be sold through major appliance dealers. In addition, major department stores in China are now selling a limited number of air conditioners. Theoretically, air conditioners could also be sold directly by the manufacturer, or by discount stores. The following summarizes the consumer's reaction to each of these nontraditional channels:

1. *Potential central residential air conditioning consumers and recent purchasers of a central air conditioner feel that they would not be willing to purchase a central air conditioner in*

a discount store. A primary reason for this is that they feel that the discount store could not be counted on to stand behind the unit if something were to go wrong. Although these consumers recognize that they could conceivably save money by buying their central air conditioner from a discount store, they feel that a central air conditioner is a major addition to their home, and therefore they would rather forgo the savings and deal with an organization that has a reputation for backing up the sale if later problems arise.

Consumers feel that even if their central air conditioner were guaranteed and completely backed up by the manufacturer, they still would prefer not to buy a central air conditioner from a discount store because of these stores' generally poor reputation for service. In sum, customers feel that the function of a discount store is to provide them, at a discount, with products that require no post-purchase service. In the case of a central air conditioner, this negative was increased substantially because of the fact that the air conditioner would actually be installed in the home. Because of this, the organization responsible for the initial sale is felt to be extremely important, and discount stores simply do not fit into this category.

2. *The concept of buying a central residential air conditioner directly from a major manufacturer was extremely well received by both recent purchasers and potential purchasers.* The major reason for this preference was that consumers felt that by buying directly from the manufacturer, they would realize a savings because of the elimination of the margins usually provided to the "middleman" channel of distribution. In addition, they felt that if the manufacturer were standing behind the sale, the consumer would be able to obtain faster and more reliable service and maintenance than through any other channel.

3. *Taiwan consumers reacted negatively to the concept of purchasing central air conditioners through major appliance chains.* Generally speaking, Taiwan consumers associate major appliance chains with discount stores. They feel that these organizations are impersonal and that store personnel would not be knowledgeable about air conditioning. Also, they feel that these organizations have no experience with products that require major installation and long-term service.

This negative consumer reaction to the appliance chain concept holds true even if the manufacturer were to do the installation and service, and were to train the appliance salespeople in its factory. Taiwan central air conditioning consumers want to be able to go to the organization where they originally purchased their air conditioner if they have any problems. Although they realize that the manufacturer would also be backing up the sale, they feel that obtaining recourse through the manufacturer would be difficult and that obtaining recourse through the appliance chain would be impossible.

4. *The concept of purchasing central air conditioners through small, independent, and (importantly) local appliance dealers with the factory doing the installation and the appliance dealers being factory trained was well received by Taiwan consumers.* The main reason for this was that small neighborhood appliance dealers have a reputation for very personal service. Consumers felt that they would be able to go back to their local appliance dealer and obtain satisfactory recourse should they experience problems with their air conditioning unit. Although they recognized that the actual servicing would be done by the manufacturer, they felt that the appliance dealer would take a personal interest in their problem and would pursue the manufacturer until satisfactory recourse was obtained.

5. *The concept of purchasing central residential air conditioners through major department stores was enthusiastically received by Taiwan consumers.* Over 40 percent of the potential customers interviewed indicated that they would be very likely to purchase a central residential air conditioner through a major department store. The major reason for this enthusiastic response was their confidence that a major department store would stand behind its service and installation until any problems were corrected to the consumer's satisfaction. Although these retail outlets are very large, they have been successful in establishing an outstanding reputation among Taiwan consumers for backing up any sales they make. About the only real negative associated with purchasing through department stores was these stores' general unfamiliarity with the product category. However, there was a strong segment of the market that felt that this negative was overcome by these stores' willingness to stand behind the purchase.

6. *Consumers typically felt that with a department store program like the one described to them in a concept statement, they would actually receive a double guarantee.* Their installation would be backed not only by the chain, but also by the manufacturer. In addition, consumers felt that having the appliance salespeople attend a factory school would overcome some of the doubts that they had about the store's product knowledge. In sum, consumers were so enthusiastic about this approach to the sale of central air conditioners that they would be willing to pay a slightly higher price (i.e., $100) for this "double guarantee."

DEPARTMENT STORE PRACTICES AND ATTITUDES

Two of the three major department stores in Taiwan are now selling central residential air conditioners, although most consumers are unaware of this. Both department stores are currently selling central residential air conditioners under their own private label. Although they are doing a limited amount of consumer advertising, these stores are now primarily relying on the ability of their appliance department's salespeople to generate leads from walk-in traffic. The installation of the air conditioners that they sell is in both cases handled by a subcontractor.

During interviews with merchandisers at both department stores, several problems associated with their current air conditioning programs were described. The following is a summary of their attitudes toward the central residential air conditioning category.

1. *Department stores are currently receiving a weak selling effort at store level because of a lack of product knowledge on the part of the salespeople and small commissions relative to the effort involved compared to the sale of other products in the appliance department.* These appliance salespeople have never been trained on the benefits of a central air conditioner, its technical characteristics, or other aspects of the purchase that the consumer frequently questions them about. Because of this, many appliance salespeople are reluctant to bring up the subject of central air conditioners with consumers, and when they are specifically asked about them, they do not feel confident that they can properly answer the questions. In addition, these salespeople do not find it economically practical to make a great deal of effort to learn the answers to consumers' questions on their own. A top appliance salesperson in Taiwan can earn $75,000 a year by pushing major appliances heavily. The effort required to make a small commission on an air conditioning sale is difficult to justify. This is especially true when there is no obvious way to learn the answers to these questions.

2. *Both of the department stores involved in the sale of central air conditioners are experiencing major problems in coordinating their subcontractor network.* Both of these organizations are extremely concerned about their reputation for service among their customers. The performance of their subcontractors is frequently not up to their generally high standards. Installations are not always done on time and sometimes are not done properly, and the net result is frequent complaints by customers.

3. *Because of the problems with their appliance salespeople and with their subcontractors, these stores are reluctant to spend a great deal of money on advertising.* Because of this, they get very little call-in business. They typically feel that the potential sales of central residential air conditioners are far greater than the sales they are actually achieving. However, without a well-trained, highly motivated sales force and a smoothly functioning installing organization, they find it difficult to justify a heavy advertising campaign.

4. *All three major department stores in Taiwan indicated that the right type of program could alleviate many of their current problems, and would receive their active support.* One of these chains felt that the right type of program run exclusively through that chain would be able to capture a minimum of 10 percent of the Taiwan central residential air conditioning market. The chain's primary basis for this confidence was that it has been successful in capturing 10 percent of the market for every major appliance it has aggressively pursued. For example, its current share of appliance sales in Taiwan is now greater than 10 percent. The chain feels that the only reason it does not now have 10 percent of the central air conditioning market is because of its unwillingness to actively pursue the market as a result of installation problems and the lack of support by its sales force.

5. *This chain feels that the right program from the right manufacturer would overcome these problems.* Given the right program with the right partner, this chain feels that it would pursue the market very aggressively, and there is no question in its mind that it would be capable of achieving at least a 10 percent market share.

CONCLUSIONS

1. *The Taiwan market for central residential air conditioners is now providing central air conditioning manufacturers with strong growth possibilities that are likely to continue, at least into the foreseeable future.* Over 192,000 units were installed in residences in 1996, and this increased to over 527,000 by 1999. This growth rate is expected to continue.

2. *Because of the solid entrenchment of the current air conditioning manufacturers within the existing channels of distribution, the ability of a new manufacturer to obtain distribution rapidly is severely limited.* Existing central residential air conditioning dealers are very sensitive to high margins and trade incentives. All six of the current major competitors are

directing almost their entire marketing efforts toward traditional trade outlets and distribution channels rather than toward the consumer. Because of this, the competition for these channels is extremely rigorous, and they are almost impossible for a low-volume new entry to penetrate.

3. *Launching a consumer-oriented promotion or motivation program, while using the traditional heating and cooling contractor as the channel of distribution, would be almost a fruitless effort on the part of the manufacturer.* Because of the ability of heating and cooling contractors to shift the consumer to any brand they desire because of the contractors' perceived expertise, consumer motivation programs lose their impact when the consumer reaches the point of purchase.

4. *Because of the newness of central residential air conditioning in the Taiwan market, consumers are totally unaware of how to go about buying a central air conditioner.* Because of this, a consumer-oriented advertising campaign could have a substantial impact. Once the consumer decides that he or she would perhaps like to install a central residential air conditioner, the consumer has very few sources from which more information can be obtained. The consumer's neighbors generally do not have central air conditioning, the consumer is generally unaware of any central air conditioning advertising, and during the early stages of the purchase cycle, the consumer is eagerly seeking information.

5. *Advertising in the Taiwan market can be done efficiently as a result of the distinctness of the target market.* The average Taiwan central air conditioning consumer is an upscale family man who owns a fairly expensive home located in one of a number of distinctly separate "pocket" areas throughout Taiwan. Because of this, the consumer is fairly easy to reach through selective media and a selectively designed copy strategy.

6. *Because the average Taiwan consumer completes the entire purchase cycle within one season, a strong sales organization, aggressively following up on initial leads, would be practical in Taiwan.* Because the average Taiwan air conditioner consumer makes his final purchase within three months of the time he originally decides to buy an air conditioner, if he could be identified early in the purchase cycle, it would be practical for a sales organization to continue to pursue this consumer until the final purchase is made.

7. *Because of the combination of (a) the difficulty of obtaining distribution of new products in traditional air conditioning outlets, (b) the potential effectiveness of consumer advertis-*

ing, and (c) the feasibility of a strong consumer sales force, a manufacturer that was attempting to penetrate the Taiwan market would appear to be justified in using nontraditional channels of distribution. Nontraditional channels would enable a new entry into the marketplace to circumvent completely the majority of the barriers established by well-entrenched present competitors.

8. *Selling central residential air conditioners through discount department stores or through major appliance chains would not be feasible as a result of the consumer's unwillingness to purchase through these channels because of their low credibility in terms of follow-up service.* A manufacturer attempting to penetrate the Taiwan market through these channels would have to overcome this strong barrier of consumer nonacceptance.

9. *Although it would be feasible from a consumer standpoint for a new manufacturer to launch a direct sales program, the risks attendant on this would seem to be greater than would be warranted by the long-term potential benefits.* This is because of (a) the relatively large commitment of fixed costs required, (b) the inability of a new manufacturer to forecast sales based on historical data, and (c) the obvious long-term pull required to become established this way vis-à-vis the potential retaliatory tactics that could be used by already entrenched competitors.

10. *Although it would be practical to sell central residential air conditioners through small independent appliance dealers if the factory were willing to conduct training seminars for these dealers and handle the installation and follow-up service, the major problem with this approach also appears to be the large fixed cost investment required to achieve consumer awareness and set up the installing organization.* In addition, it would not be practical for a manufacturer that was attempting to sell through these outlets to rely on leads generated by walk-in traffic, because the walk-in traffic factor in small appliance dealers is relatively negligible.

11. *The most practical nontraditional channel available to a manufacturer attempting to penetrate the Taiwan central residential air conditioning market is major department stores, combined with a training program for these stores' appliance salespeople and factory installation and service.* This method of distribution receives extremely high acceptance by consumers and is available to a new manufacturer because of the advantages to the department store.

MARKETING PLAN ELEMENTS

1. *The Zhenzhou Electric Corporation should launch a central residential air conditioning program exclusively through the largest department store chain in Taiwan.* The program should include installation and service by the Zhenzhou Service Group and Zhenzhou-provided training for the department store's appliance department salespeople. The following are the principal reasons for making this recommendation:

   A. Obtaining local and national distribution would be greatly facilitated, and heavy consumer awareness would be generated through extensive advertising by the department store and an extensive sales effort directed at the large numbers of walk-in traffic.

   B. Zhenzhou could rapidly become a major factor in the central residential segment of the air conditioning market, very probably obtaining a 10 percent market share during its first season in Taiwan. This is based on this department store's *proven* success at obtaining a 10 percent share of the appliance business in any given category, and on the wide acceptance of such a program by consumers.

   C. Going exclusively through this department store chain would provide the chain with a much stronger motivation to sell Zhenzhou air conditioners. Zhenzhou should anticipate that the department store's support will be much stronger in terms of both advertising support and sales effort.

   D. By providing the department store with factory installation and service, Zhenzhou not only would solve the department store's problems with subcontractors, but also would provide its customers with the "double guarantee" (which the department store could capitalize on in its ads).

   E. Such a program not only would be profitable on a national scale, but would achieve a payout in the first year. In addition to the high profitability of such a program, the department store would take on the burden of both the initial investment required to maintain the sales organization and the advertising costs.

2. *Zhenzhou should employ the following tactical plans in entering the central residential air conditioning market in Taiwan.* These plans are a radical departure from the normal ways of marketing central air conditioners in Taiwan, and they should effectively differentiate Eagle central air conditioners from the Zhenzhou Electric Corporation from other central air conditioners in the market.

A. *Factory training.* The program should provide factory training for the department store salespeople to equip them to sell air conditioners effectively, answer any questions the consumer might have, and teach them how to do estimating in the home.

B. *Training seminars.* A series of training seminars for appliance salespeople should be developed and conducted prior to implementation of either the promotion activities or the advertising. It is estimated that an appliance salesperson can be effectively trained in approximately two weeks; however, the organization of these training programs should begin immediately.

C. *Factory installing and servicing.* Installing and servicing of the air conditioner should be completely handled by the factory.

D. *Warehousing.* The warehousing of the air conditioning units should be handled by Zhenzhou and not by the department store. Because the physical movement of the actual unit will be directly from Zhenzhou to the consumer, through the Zhenzhou servicing organization, it would not be practical to warehouse the units at the department store. In addition, the motivation of the department store management will be increased because the store will not have to invest in inventory.

E. *Fixed-cost installation.* A single fixed cost should be established for the installation, so that the estimating can be done by the appliance department's salespeople. Establishing a fixed installation cost will make the estimating job relatively simple, as the only real variables will be the size of the unit and the accessory options.

F. *High commissions.* The program should be profitable enough for the store to enable it to pay its sales force a high commission relative to that paid on other major appliances, thereby significantly increasing the salesperson's motivation.

G. *Store credit.* The financing of the air conditioning unit and the installation and service should be handled by the department store chain.

H. *Store estimating.* The appliance salesperson should have complete control over the entire sale, including the initial sale, in-home estimating, and follow-through until the close is made. Specifically, the salesperson should go out to the consumer's home, conduct a thorough in-home survey, and then recommend the size of system that will exactly fit the requirements of the home. He or she will explain how the system works, what the installation will involve, and how much the system will cost. If the consumer decides to order, the salesperson will put in a call to Zhenzhou reserving the equipment and the staff needed for the installation. Zhenzhou will then install the system.

I. *Merchandising support.* The factory should provide the store with merchandising devices such as a display, wall banners, and pins for the salespeople to wear. Specifically, a freestanding display should be placed in the appliance department of each department store. The display should be designed to achieve high visibility. Brochures explaining the program should be inserted into special slots on each display. A button inviting inquiries about central air conditioning should be worn by each salesperson in the appliance department.

J. *Advertising program.* The advertising department of the chain should do the advertising; however, the factory should provide the chain with guidance on media selection because of its greater knowledge of the consumer. Full-page ads should be placed in media reaching every area of the potential market. The message in this advertising should promise the fastest, most efficient, guaranteed home air conditioning system available anywhere.

K. *Store Margin.* The store should receive a 35 percent margin on the unit itself and an additional 15 percent margin on the installation. Out of this, the store should pay for all advertising and for the commission to the salesperson.

L. *Eagle brand name.* The department store should be required to use the Eagle brand name on all Zhenzhou Electric air conditioners.

FINANCIAL PROJECTIONS

1. *A marketing program wherein a manufacturer would sell central residential air conditioners through a major Taiwan department store appears to offer an excellent profit potential.* On a national basis, this would generate sales of $72,304,000 and would yield an income before tax of approximately $14,526,000.

2. *On the average sale of a central residential air conditioning unit at $1,645.00 retail, the margin to the department store at 35 percent off retail would be $575.00. This would give the manufacturer a sales-billed figure of $1,070.00 per unit.* At a retail installation price of $355.00 and a 15 percent margin to the department store, factory sales billed would be $302.00. In sum, at a total retail installed price of $2,000.00, the manufacturer would realize sales billed of $1,372.00 per unit. This is illustrated in Table 11-2.

TABLE 11-2. Retail Sales Versus Sales Billed

Retail unit price	$1,645
Less 35% margin	575
Sales billed	$1,070
Retail installation Price	$355
Less 15% margin	53
Sales billed	$302
Total retail price	$2,000
Total sales billed	$1,372

3. *In addition to these variable costs, the central air conditioning manufacturer would incur fixed costs for promotion, dealer training, sales and distribution, and initial project development.* Although these costs would vary considerably depending on the forecasted volume, the following generalizations can be made:

   A. *Promotion costs for this program will consist largely of providing one display for each outlet for the purpose of attracting walk-in traffic.* The maximum cost of these displays will be approximately $10,000 on a national basis. This cost would provide a cardboard display for each store.

   B. *The cost for training appliance salespeople will be approximately $30,000. This will provide seminars for all salespeople employed by the department store chain.*

   C. *Sales and distribution costs for this program will run about 9 percent of sales billed for the installing organization and 10 percent of sales billed for the facility providing the air conditioning units.* This cost would cover the sales maintenance of a large department store and the warehousing of product and its delivery to the home.

   D. *Project development cost for this program will be $55,000.* This will include the cost of writing training manuals, supervising the development of the department store's advertising campaign, and modifying the original plan as sales begin to develop.

4. *The net effect of these expenses is that at a retail total installed price of $2,000 per unit and at a 10 percent share of market, the Zhenzhou Electric Corporation should expect to earn approximately $14,526,000 in income before tax in the year 2000.* Table 11-3 gives a forecasted P&L.

TABLE 11-3. Taiwan Central Residential Air-Conditioning
Forecasted Profit and Loss for 2000 (000)

	Air-Conditioning Sales	Consumer Service	Total
Unit sales	52,700	52,700	52,700
Sales billed	$56,389	$15,915	$72,304
Product/installation cost (70%)	39,472	11,140	50,612
Net sales	16,917	4,775	21,692
Promotion	10	—	10
Dealer training	20	10	30
Sales and distribution	5,639	1,432	7,071
Product development	45	10	55
Total marketing	5,714	1,452	7,166
Income before tax	$11,203	$ 3,323	$14,526

CHAPTER 12

Using Ethnographic Research to Understand Consumers

Example: Twinkle Baby Shoes

In this chapter, ethnographic research was used to develop a summary of consumer usage and attitudes in the baby shoe category. The objective was to understand the detailed habits and practices of mothers of infants as they related to the purchasing and usage of baby shoes. The procedure involved in-home discussions with respondents about their habits and practices, with videotaped observations of where the respondents kept baby shoes and how they were used included. The interviews were conducted in three cities: Boston, Chicago, and Los Angeles. A total of twenty-four interviews were completed.

There are times when the objectives of a research project call for identifying subtle emotional dimensions that are almost impossible to uncover by simply asking questions. Participants may not even recognize their own behavior patterns and motivations. These are the times when ethnographic research should be the technique of choice, as was the case with Twinkle Baby Shoes.

Like projects involving traditional qualitative research, this project began with the identification of specific objectives. A screener was then created to recruit *key informants* who fit the requirements. These were respondents who were very knowledgeable about baby shoes and were able to clearly communicate with the ethnographers. A battery of psychographic questions was included in the screening questionnaire to help in identifying these respondents. The respondents also agreed to allow the researchers to videotape them in their home. A specialized recruiter network was used to carry out this unique recruiting.

As with focus groups or in-depth interviews, a discussion guide was written to ensure that all of the research objectives were covered with each consumer. In addition to questions, this guide also included a storyboard outline of the observations to be completed with the respondent. The objective was to observe as many aspects of the respondent's life as possible, then focus on the respondent's usage of and attitudes toward baby shoes. The verbal interview was conducted simultaneously with the videotaped observations to enable the respondent to explain her activities.

This chapter provides a marketing plan to sell a line of infant's shoes in retail stores under the brand name Twinkle Baby Shoes. The plan includes a detailed action program for each step necessary to bring the marketing program from management approval to implementation. The marketing plan is based on the completion of a detailed market review and on ethnographic research that identified a significant niche opportunity in the infant's shoe category.

The Twinkle Baby Shoes venture is an example of a business built around a positioning of the product as "fun" in order to stimulate repeated purchases of baby shoes by parents and as gifts by friends and relatives. Twinkle Baby Shoes are fun to wear and fun to give for holidays and special occasions. This chapter shows how the ethnographic research was used to discover the premise on which the complete marketing plan was based.

Marketing Plan for
Twinkle Baby Shoes
Accola Shoe Corporation[1]
December 1, 2001

INTRODUCTION

The purpose of this report is to develop a five-year marketing plan for a venture to sell a line of infants' shoes in retail stores throughout the United States. This report is divided into the following sections:

1. **BACKGROUND.** This section details the activities that led up to the development of this venture, and reviews the specific objectives and methodology used in completing this marketing plan.

2. **MARKET REVIEW.** This section reviews the size and nature of the U.S. infants' shoe market.

3. **CONSUMER USAGE AND ATTITUDES.** This section outlines present consumer practices, desires, and expectations concerning the infants' shoe category.

4. **TRADE PRACTICES AND ATTITUDES.** This section reviews the trade's current involvement with infants' shoes and its reactions to alternative marketing approaches.

5. **CONCLUSIONS.** This section outlines the strategic implications of the findings from the market review, the consumer research, and the trade research.

---

[1] **Disclaimer:** The specific information in this sample marketing plan was compiled for intended use as an example only. Although this marketing plan is based on actual products from a real company, the specific information in the plan is hypothetical and is not intended to compete with or to divulge proprietary ideas, company structure, or the financial status of any company. The names, numbers, and some of the facts in this marketing plan have been changed because of the confidential nature of the information. The information is intended to be used as a guide only.

6. **FIVE-YEAR MARKETING PLAN.** This section presents a specific and detailed action program for each step necessary to move this venture from management approval to implementation.

7. **FINANCIAL FORECASTS.** This section presents pro forma profit-and-loss statements for the program.

BACKGROUND

A project to investigate the potential of a new incremental marketing opportunity for the Accola Shoe Corporation was started during the fourth quarter of 2001. The overall objective of this project was to develop a marketing plan that Accola could use to market a line of infants' shoes in retail stores throughout the United States. The specifics of this objective were as follows:

1. **MARKET PROFILE.** A review of the overall infants' shoe market was conducted. The purpose of this review was to enable the venture to focus on those product segments with the greatest potential.

2. **CONSUMER USAGE AND ATTITUDES.** Research was conducted to identify consumer attitudes toward infants' shoes.

3. **TRADE PRACTICES AND ATTITUDES.** Past and current experiences that the retail trade has had with the infants' shoe market were identified. In addition, the criteria that the trade uses in making distribution allocations, as well as any problems that it may have been encountering, were also identified.

4. **FIVE-YEAR MARKETING PLAN.** Based on the previous research, a specific and detailed action program was developed for each step necessary to bring the venture from management approval to implementation.

The information required to write this marketing plan was gathered in five stages. Each stage was designed to provide a systematic understanding of the overall infants' shoe market from both the consumer's and the trade's standpoints and, finally, to permit the development of specific marketing plans and strategies. The following specific steps were taken:

1. **AVAILABLE INFORMATION SEARCH.** A review of all the available data that were pertinent to the preparation of this program was conducted. In addition, an exhaustive screening of industry data was done.

2. **STORE CHECKS.** Store checks were conducted in a representative group of retail stores throughout the country. During these store checks, identification was made of product lines carried, breadth of trade involvement in infants' shoes, and so on.

3. **CONSUMER RESEARCH.** Extensive qualitative market research was conducted with consumers on the subject of infants' shoes. The purpose of this research was to develop an understanding of consumer attitudes in general and to explore both specific concepts and reactions toward alternative product lines.

4. **TRADE PROBES.** Interviews were conducted with key executives in retail organizations throughout the United States. Meetings were held with executives at various levels within these organizations, including buyers, merchandising managers, and members of senior management. Organizations of different sizes were contacted, as were similar organizations in different geographic areas. The purpose of these interviews was to identify both trade interest in an infants' shoe program and the trade's requirements if such a program were to be developed.

5. **MARKETING PLAN DEVELOPMENT.** Based on the information gathered in the previous steps, a detailed plan was developed, including a step-by-step action plan that should enable Accola to profitably penetrate this incremental segment of the infants' shoe market.

MARKET REVIEW

1. *The total market for infants' shoes in 2000 amounted to $470 million in retail sales.* Sports shoes was the largest segment of the reported infants' shoe market in terms of dollar sales. Sports shoes represented $250 million in retail sales, or 53 percent of total dollar sales. Dress shoes represented the largest segment in terms of unit sales, with 61 percent of total unit sales. Table 12-1 summarizes the retail dollar sales and unit sales in dozens of this selected portion of the infants' shoe market.

TABLE 12-1. 2000 Selected Infants Shoe Market
Units and Retail Dollar Sales (000)

Item	Retail Dollar Sales	% of Total	Unit Sales (Dozens)	% of Total
Sports shoes	$250,000	53%	2,450	28%
Sandals	45,000	10%	960	11%
Dress shoes	175,000	37%	5,440	61%
Total	$470,000	100%	8,850	100%

2. *Discount stores represent the largest trade channel for infants' shoes in terms of retail dollar sales.* Discount stores account for 32 percent of overall retail dollar sales. Department and specialty stores are the second largest trade channel for infants' shoes, representing 29 percent of total retail dollar sales. Sears and Penney together make up a substantial segment (26 percent) of the infants' shoe market. All other trade channels represent only 13 percent of total retail dollar sales. Table 12-2 outlines the retail dollar sales in the infants' shoe category by trade channel.

3. *The geographic dispersion of the infants' shoe market varies by geographic area as well as by product type within each area.* The New York sales district has the highest sales of sports shoes and sandals. On the other hand, the San Francisco sales district has the highest sales of dress shoes. Table 12-3 provides the unit sales in dozens for sports shoes and sandals versus dress shoes for each sales region.

4. *A substantial number of consumers purchase infants' shoes for their own children's use as well as for gift purposes.* These usage patterns vary considerably from one type of product to another. Dress shoes are generally purchased for the consumer's own children's use.

TABLE 12-2. Infants' Shoe Market by Trade Channel (000)

Trade Channel	Retail Dollar Sales	% of Total
Department and specialty stores	$136,300	29%
Discount stores	150,400	32%
Sears/Penney	122,200	26%
Other	61,100	13%
Total	$470,000	100%

TABLE 12-3. Selected Infants' Shoe Market by Geographic Region

Sales	Sandals and Sports Shoes		Dress Shoes	
	Unit Sales (Dozens) (000)	% of Total	Unit Sales (Dozens) (000)	% of Total
New York	1,709	26.7	238	9.7
Philadelphia	730	11.4	273	11.1
Cleveland	134	2.1	69	2.8
Boston	499	7.8	198	8.1
Los Angeles	410	6.4	125	5.1
San Francisco	1,338	20.9	713	29.1
Dallas	230	3.6	191	7.8
Denver	115	1.8	66	2.7
St. Louis	358	5.6	225	9.2
Chicago	499	7.8	203	8.3
Atlanta	378	5.9	149	6.1
Total	6,400	100.0%	2,450	100.0%

About 85 percent of all unit sales were for the consumer's own children. Sandals are also frequently purchased for the consumer's own children, representing 65 percent of total unit purchases. Sports shoes are evenly divided between own use and gift purchases. Table 12-4 provides a breakdown of gift versus own use purchases by product type.

CONSUMER USAGE AND ATTITUDES

1. *Baby shoes were considered by consumers to include both basic and fanciful items.* When asked about various baby shoes in their homes, respondents said that they viewed certain styles of shoes as "basics." These shoes were purchased on a routine and frequent basis. Other types of baby shoes were considered to be "fancy". These shoes were typically purchased or received as gifts associated with special occasions—from baptisms to the baby's first birthday.

2. *Baby shoes were a popular gift item. Most mothers received baby shoes as gifts, especially for the first-born child.* These gifts supplied up to 50 percent of a child's first-year needs. Sometimes, gifts were received that for one reason or another could not be used. In reviewing the respondents' inventory of baby shoes, it was noted that there were often a number

TABLE 12-4. Selected Infants' Shoe Market Gift Versus Own Use Purchase

	Sports Shoes		Sandals		Dress Shoes	
Transaction	Unit Sales (Dozens) (000)	% of Total	Unit Sales (Dozens) (000)	% of Total	Unit Sales (Dozens) (000)	% of Total
Gift purchases	1,225	50%	336	35%	816	15%
Own use	1,225	50%	624	65%	4,624	85%
Total	2,450	100%	960	100%	5,440	100%

of shoes that appeared to have never been worn. Respondents indicated that they did not feel that these shoes were really practical, or they could not be used because of the child's size or sex.

3. *Sizing of baby shoes was considered to be inconsistent.* When asked about specific baby shoes that had never been used, several respondents indicated that the actual size of the shoe was different from the size indicated and that therefore the shoe could not be worn. Sizing was a major complaint of many of the mothers interviewed. One respondent said, "Sizing is insane—it makes no sense whatsoever." It was often felt that the sizes of baby shoes were not consistent between manufacturers, and in some cases were not even consistent within the same brand.

4. *A large portion of baby shoes were purchased by mothers.* Frequently, baby shoes that were received as gifts covered only the newborn sizes or the first few months. Other shoes received as gifts were not felt to be practical. Even "hand-me-downs" could not always be used because of differences in the size or sex of children. For these reasons, there was a large requirement for mothers' purchases of baby shoes.

5. *Many mothers considered shopping for baby shoes to be entertaining.* When asked where specific baby shoes were purchased, mothers indicated that many of the shoes had been bought during special trips that were really social events. One respondent indicated that she felt it was "more fun to buy shoes for the child than for yourself." Many respondents indicated that they enjoyed shopping for their infant's shoes. Some arranged special trips just for this purpose. It was often felt to be "a great way to get out of the house."

6. *The baby shoes purchased during recreational shopping were typically "fancy" rather than "basic" shoes.* During these in-home interviews, respondents were asked about each of the

different types of baby shoes in their homes. In most cases, the "basic" shoes were purchased during routine shopping trips. The "fancy" shoes either were received as gifts or were purchased during special trips that were considered to be fun-filled recreational activities.

7. *Many of the respondent's favorite "fancy" baby shoes were associated with special occasions.* One of the advantages of this ethnographic research was that the researcher was in the home and had the opportunity to ask questions about specific baby shoes. Respondents were asked to pick their favorite baby shoes, and then explain why these were their favorites. In some cases the favorite shoes were associated with holidays such as Christmas, Valentine's Day, and Easter. In other cases they were associated with special occasions such as birthdays, a christening, a baptism, or even a memorable baseball or football game.

8. *Baby shoes were purchased in a variety of retail outlets.* For those baby shoes that had not been received as gifts, respondents were asked where they purchased each of the different baby shoes in their homes. Many of these shoes were purchased in outlets that specialize in children's shoes and clothing. Department and discount stores were also popular outlets for purchasing baby shoes. Other outlets mentioned were toy stores, drugstores, and supermarkets. A variety of factors influenced where the mother would shop, including good selection, price, and convenience.

9. *Most respondents indicated that they generally preferred national brands of baby shoes over unknown brands.* It was observed, however, that nonnational brands were often included in the baby shoe inventories of the respondents visited. When asked to explain this, respondents indicated that they would purchase an unknown brand if the quality of the shoe could be examined and seemed appropriate and if the design of the shoe was of interest. Another factor warranting consideration of an unknown brand was a lower price point.

10. *Most of the respondents in these in-home interviews recalled seeing advertising from both manufacturers of baby shoes and stores selling baby shoes.* Advertising by manufacturers was seen as creating a quality brand image in the mind of the mother. One participant stated that "manufacturers' ads plant in your head that it's a good brand." Advertising by retail outlets was felt to announce a sale. These advertisements were felt to be strongest when a particular brand was featured on sale. Most respondents indicated that they do respond to store advertising, and that an ad will motivate them to go to a particular store.

TRADE PRACTICES AND ATTITUDES

1. *In an effort to provide a wide variety for their customers, retailers are constantly searching for new programs.* The trade believes that a key to attracting new customers to their stores is variety. Without variety, the retailer runs the risk of losing customers. Therefore, the trade is generally receptive to new products and ideas.

2. *Most of the retailers interviewed recognized the rising birth rate.* The trade recognizes the growth in many infants' products, including shoes, toys, diapers, and baby food. Because of this, many retailers have expanded these departments. Growth is also seen in children's food products.

3. *The trade believes that infants' shoes are a growth category.* Among retailers, it is generally believed that the infants' shoe category is growing. Many feel that this category should be evaluated, and would be receptive to a new program.

4. *A new line of "special occasion," "fun" baby shoes was seen by the trade as a great idea.* The trade viewed this as creating a whole new business for stores. Some retailers felt this was "a long time overdue." This concept seemed to hit an emotional "hot button," and it was universally felt that the concept should be pursued.

5. *Displays creating a complete "fun" infants' shoe section were preferred.* Most retailers preferred a four-foot in-line display. An eight-foot or twelve-foot display might be used in larger stores, while a two-foot display might be used in smaller stores. The display should be flexible enough to accommodate various store formats, with a forty-eight-inch height for low-profile stores and a sixty-six-inch height for high-profile stores.

6. *Trade evaluations of an infants' shoe program would be subjective.* There was no fixed rule on performance requirements. The key was generating enough incremental profit to justify the space. A trade profit of $40 per store per week was mentioned by some retailers, and this can be used as a benchmark for a four-foot section.

CONCLUSIONS

1. *A niche can be created by positioning the line as shoes that are fun to buy, fun to give, and fun to wear.* A large portion of the baby shoes identified during the in-home interviews had

been received as gifts or were purchased during recreational shopping trips by mothers. Most of the baby shoes received as gifts and bought during recreational shopping fit the "fun" positioning. Baby shoes are a popular gift item, and this positioning would be appropriate for gifts of baby shoes, which account for up to 50 percent of a child's first-year needs. Baby shoes bought during recreational shopping were also a large portion of the in-home inventories.

2. *A "fun" product line should consist of "fancy," rather than "basic," baby shoes that are appropriate for holidays and special occasions.* Many of the respondents' favorite baby shoes were associated with special occasions. These special occasions included holidays such as Christmas, Thanksgiving, and Easter and special occasions such as birthdays and a christening or baptism. The shoes' designs should include such images as Santa Claus, Christmas trees, and Easter bunnies, as well as short messages such as "happy birthday."

3. *The sizing of each different model of baby shoe should be consistent with that of other models in the line to eliminate a current negative in the category.* The sizing of current baby shoes was felt by many respondents to be inconsistent, both between manufacturers and even within the same brand. The sizing of all Twinkle Baby Shoes should be consistent.

4. *A "fun" product line should be distributed in stores where recreational shopping is typically done.* These include stores that specialize in children's shoes and clothing and department stores. Discount stores, drugstores, and supermarkets currently sell baby shoes. These types of stores, however, were mainly felt by respondents to be appropriate for basic baby shoes that are bought during routine shopping trips.

5. *Consumer interest and distribution opportunities can be maximized with a brand that is nationally advertised and promoted.* Most respondents indicated that they preferred national brands of baby shoes over unknown brands. Brand advertising and store advertising would help build excitement for the Twinkle Baby Shoes brand and would help to maximize sales and distribution.

FIVE-YEAR MARKETING PLAN

1. *The Accola Shoe Corporation should develop and launch a national program to sell a new line of "fun to wear and fun to give" infants' shoes.* The findings of the research in this

document clearly indicate that such a new infants' shoe program offers the company the opportunity to increase its share of the infants' shoe market by a substantial proportion. We believe that such a program will generate ongoing sales on a stable basis. We also feel that the cost of launching such a program will not be prohibitive for the company. Finally, we believe that Accola can launch such a program on infants' shoes without any significant disruption to its normal day-to-day operations.

2. *The product line for the new line of infant's shoes should be made up of "fancy" baby shoes that are most appropriate for holidays and special occasions.* This should include dress shoes, sports shoes, and sandals. The most popular current colors should be utilized, including white, blue, pink, yellow, and brown.

3. *The pricing of this new product line should be kept to as few price points as possible.* The prices recommended are $6.99 at retail for dress shoes, $3.99 for sports shoes, and $1.99 for sandals. These prices were evaluated during national store checks, and were found to be competitive. All of the financial forecasts in this marketing plan are based on these prices.

4. *The licensed name* Twinkle Baby Shoes *is recommended as the brand name for this program.* This name comes from an established manufacturer that has high credibility within the infants' categories. It is believed that a licensed brand name will be of substantial assistance in gaining distribution. A licensed name will reduce the required consumer advertising for the program. It will also be much less expensive to utilize a licensed name than to create a famous brand name through expensive advertising on a national basis.

5. *A modular in-store display is recommended for the program.* This display should provide an insert for the in-line store shelving. This insert must accommodate stores with both three-foot sections and four-foot sections. The display should provide a uniform look for all stores. It should include an attractive header sign that clearly identifies this section of the store as being for infants' shoes. The display must be provided free to the retail trade, as this is the customary practice in these channels of distribution.

6. *It is recommended that a consumer and trade promotion and advertising program be developed for the infants' shoe line.* This program should include trade allowances, advertising, and publicity. Upon introduction of the line, a strong effort should be launched to motivate the trade to take the line into distribution. At the same time, consumer advertising and

promotion should be launched to strongly introduce the program at the onset. Finally, a publicity program should be coupled with the advertising to supercharge the introduction. A second flight of similar activity is recommended for month 8, so that the program is revitalized during the second half of the first year.

7. *It is recommended that the heaviest funds be allocated to advertising and promotion during the introduction of the program.* This will provide the maximum opportunity for distribution and sell-through of the program. It is recommended that, of this front-end loading for month 1, $924,000 be spent on promotion and $572,000 be spent on advertising. During month 8, it is recommended that all monies be spent on promotion. Table 12-5 summarizes the recommended spending during year one.

8. *Television advertising is recommended during the introduction of the program.* The purpose of this television advertising will be to give consumers the news about the new line as well as to show them what display to look for when they go to the store to shop for infants' shoes. In addition, this television advertising can be put on diskettes to be used in sales meetings with the trade. The concept of television advertising has been found by the sales force to be the most powerful vehicle for sell-in with the trade.

9. *The initial trade promotion should provide the trade with an incentive to take the initial display into distribution.* It is recommended that an initial buying allowance be provided, giving the trade one free product with every twelve purchased. In addition, an advertising allowance of 10 percent of the initial purchases is recommended. This will enable the trade to participate in announcing the introduction of this exciting new program to their customers. Table 12-6 provides an example of the costs of this initial trade promotion.

TABLE 12–5. Year One Promotion Plan Cost (000)

	Month 1	Month 8
Promotion:		
Trade	$ 799	$190.5
Consumer	125	412.5
Total	$ 924	$603.0
Available for advertising	$ 572	$ 0.0
Total money	$1,496	$603.0

TABLE 12-6. Initial Trade Promotion

	Total Dollars (000)
Factory "sell-in" volume	$4,616
Cost of:	
Buying allowance @ 1 free with 12	384
Advertising allowance @ 10%	
(90% trade performing)	415
Total cost	$ 799

10. *Upon introduction, a fifty cents off next purchase promotion is recommended.* The purpose of this promotion is to provide trade excitement and to motivate the consumer to purchase the line on an ongoing basis. Consumers will receive a sticker on every pair of shoes telling them that they may mail in a proof of purchase and receive a fifty-cent coupon that can be used for their next purchase. Coupons that will be good the next time they shop for infants' shoes will then be sent to the consumer.

11. *During the second six months, a fifty-cent in-ad coupon is recommended as a consumer promotion.* The trade will be provided an advertising allowance on ten weeks' purchases of product. In addition, the trade will be authorized to place a fifty-cent coupon, which is store redeemable, in advertisements. This will enable the trade to participate in a pull-through consumer promotion.

12. *It is forecasted that the Twinkle Baby Shoe program will receive distribution in a total of 9,801 retail outlets.* The retailer will require a 33 percent margin off retail price. Distributors will take 25 percent off the retailers' price. This is equal to approximately 17 percent off retail price for the distributor. A 2 percent cash discount will also be required by the trade.

13. *To effectively manage national distribution to 9,801 stores, a sales-specific organization will be required to handle the ongoing activities of this large distribution network.* Each member of the sales organization should have a unique and distinct function. The following organization has been designed to ensure that all 9,801 stores plus the supporting service organizations will be appropriately supervised. Specifically, the different functions are outlined as follows:

   A. *National sales manager.* This individual has the primary and overall responsibility for development and implementation of all sales activities. The national sales manager is responsible for the construction of volume forecasts and annual sales plans. Additionally, he or she has line responsibility for the entire sales organization to ensure that the objectives and results of the marketing and sales plans are achieved.

B. *Zone managers.* Each of the three zone managers is responsible for three district managers and an average of twenty service organizations. In addition, the district managers are responsible for approximately 266 retail headquarters within each of their zones. The zone manager is responsible for achieving overall distribution and volume objectives in his or her geographic territory. The zone manager also bears the responsibility for recommending the addition or deletion of promotion or marketing plans in order to maximize the venture's volume and profit from his or her geographic area.

C. *District managers.* Each district manager bears the responsibility for the overall performance and accomplishments of approximately seven service organizations. In this respect, the district manager is responsible for providing ongoing supervision, evaluation, and motivation of his or her individual service personnel. The district managers will be expected to work at retail level, both with service personnel and on his or her own, to determine the effectiveness of the service persons' efforts. The district manager will also assist his or her service people in making headquarters calls and sales. If necessary, the district manager will have the responsibility for recommending the termination of an individual service person and for the screening process to determine his or her replacement.

D. *Service personnel.* The individual servicing organizations will bear the primary responsibility for introduction and ongoing selling and servicing activities at headquarters and retail levels.

14. *It is estimated that the national sales organization can be operated for 5 percent of net sales.* On a going-year basis, this cost would be approximately $1,270,000. Table 12-7 outlines the direct and indirect costs of the national sales organization on an ongoing basis.

FINANCIAL FORECASTS

1. *The total annual forecasted sales for the Twinkle Baby Shoes program on a national basis is $52 million in retail dollar sales.* It is assumed that sales will vary by store size. In $12 million and over stores, an average of $130 per store per week is forecasted; $110 per store

TABLE 12-7. Projected Going-Year Sales Expenses (000)

Headcount Costs:	
National sales manager @ $60,000	$ 60
3 zone managers @ $45,000 each	135
9 district managers @ $30,000 each	270
3 secretaries @ $16,000 each	48
Total	$ 513 ·
Headcount welfare plan @ 26% of income	$ 133
Overhead expenses @ 52% of salaries and welfare	336
Travel expenses—13 managers @ $1,846/month	288
Total	$1,270

per week is forecasted for $8 to $12 million stores; $100 per store per week is forecasted for $4 to $8 million stores; and $70 per store per week is forecasted for $2 to $4 million stores.

2. *It is recommended that the initial inventory on each display be 166 items with a retail value of $703.34.* This level of inventory will represent over a one month's supply in a typical store. This is felt to be sufficient, because a typical store will be serviced on at least a weekly basis.

3. *It is felt that the pipeline sales on introduction of the program on a national basis will amount to approximately $5 million in sales at factory levels.* This represents the inventory to be placed on displays in 9,801 stores and backup inventory at the warehouse. Warehouse inventory is assumed to be 50 percent of display inventory. Table 12-8 outlines the calculated pipeline sales for the introductory year at retail prices.

4. *Based on the forecasted $52 million in annual sales at retail, the venture will account for a total of 11 percent of the overall infant's shoe market.* The program will generate a 7.9

TABLE 12-8. Pipeline Sales Calculations for Introductory Year at Retail

Number of stores	9,801
Inventory/display	$ 703
Total display inventory	$ 6,890
Warehouse inventory (50% of display inventory)	$ 3,445
Total pipeline sales—$ retail	$10,335
Total pipeline sales—$ net factory (49% retail)	$ 5,064

percent share of the sports shoe market and a 7.7 percent share of the dress shoe market. The share of the sandal market will be 41.7 percent. These shares assume virtually no increase in the overall market size.

5. *On an ongoing basis, it is estimated that the infants' shoe program will generate slightly over $2 million in annual profit before tax for the Accola Shoe Corporation.* This profit assumes gross sales at factory to be 50 percent of retail sales. A 2 percent cash discount is included, as well as 0.5 percent of gross sales for returns and allowances. Advertising and promotion is assumed to be 6 percent of net sales. Displays will be purchased at approximately $100 each, amortized over a three-year period. Sales cost is assumed to be 5 percent of net sales, and distribution cost within the Accola organization is assumed to be 6 percent of net sales. Royalties assume that the program utilizes a licensed brand name. Table 12-9 gives an estimated income statement for the going year.

6. *It is felt that it will take three years to achieve the going year sales level.* It is forecasted that total sales will reach the $41 million level during Year 1 and will gradually build to $49 million in Year 2, and finally to $52 million in Year 3. Pipeline sales will all occur during Year 1. Table 12-10 illustrates how the program will be expanded if national distribution occurs all at one time.

TABLE 12-9. Estimated Income Statement for Going Year

	Going Year	
	$ (000)	%
Retail sales	$52,112	—
Retail margin (33% retail sales)	17,197	—
Distributor margin (17% retail sales)	8,859	—
Gross sales at factory	$26,056	—
Cash discount (2% gross sales)	521	—
Returns and allowances (0.5% gross sales)	130	—
Net sales	$25,405	100%
Cost of goods	15,751	62%
Gross profit	$ 9,654	38%
Operating expenses		
Advertising/promotion	$ 1,524	6%
Display depreciation (3 years)	326	1%
Marketing and administration	1,270	5%
Sales and distribution	2,795	11%
Royalties (6% net sales)	1,524	6%
Profit before tax	$ 2,215	9%

Notes: 1. Retail sales are based on the national sales forecast.
2. Cost of goods is an estimated average of all products provided by the Accola Shoe Corporation.
3. Display depreciation assumes an average display cost of $100 in 9,801 stores depreciated over 3 years.
4. Marketing and administration includes sales management and corporation overhead.
5. Sales and distribution includes broker expense (5%) and normal Accola distribution expense (6%).
6. Royalties are for use of the name "Twinkle Baby Shoes."

TABLE 12-10. Prototype Income Statement
Total National Expansion Based on $52,112,000 Going-Year Retail Sales (000)

	Year 1			Year 2			Year 3
	1st Half	2nd Half	Total	1st Half	2nd Half	Total	& Going
Retail sales	$20,438	$20,602	$41,040	$23,268	$26,238	$49,506	$52,112
Factory net sales							
Consumer	5,992	8,998	14,990	11,354	12,804	24,158	25,405
Pipeline	3,982	1,056	5,038	–	–	–	–
Total	9,974	10,054	20,028	11,354	12,804	24,158	25,405
Available (15%)	1,496	1,508	3,004	1,703	1,921	3,624	3,811
Spending							
Advertising/promotion	1,496	603	2,099	681	769	1,450	1,524
Profit before tax	–	$ 905	$ 905	$ 1,022	$ 1,152	$ 2,174	$ 2,287

CHAPTER 13

The Role of Trade Research in Marketing Planning

Example: Selecto Housewares Boutiques

Many marketing plans result in strategic programs designed to either obtain new distribution or achieve improved performance in existing retail outlets. Many of the marketing plans in this book have called for increased shelf space for product lines, focused on improved in-store visibility, or been intended to add value to retailer relationships. When these plans call for a change in retailers' behavior, it makes sense to identify retailers' attitudes toward these changes before they are included in the marketing plan.

You have seen in previous chapters in this book how companies have gone to great lengths to identify consumers' attitudes. A similar process can be used to determine trade practices and attitudes. Normally the process includes a series of in-depth face-to-face interviews with retailers. Because these people are generally quite busy, these interviews normally take place in the retailer's office.

These trade interviews can be conducted by the sales force during regularly scheduled sales calls. For most of the projects discussed in this book, however, trade interviews were conducted through a process outside of the normal sales operations. The interviews were typically conducted by consultants or marketing managers. In some cases top management was included in the interviews. This separate interviewing process was used to emphasize the importance of the meetings and to eliminate any effect of politics related to the ongoing operations.

This chapter provides a marketing plan for the expansion of a line of housewares products in supermarkets. The plan presents research results demonstrating that retailers who have switched to this housewares program have increased their revenues and total profit dollars from housewares sales 59 percent, with a unit volume improvement of 42 percent. There are two reasons for this increase in sales. The first is a distinctive display unit consisting of a series of two-sided rotating towers that provide much more display space than a flat rack wall unit. The second is a cleaver grid system that enables new housewares products to flow through each grid position without the store's having to change any of the information on the item in its computer. This allows for a constant flow of new products, which stimulate impulse sales. The complete marketing plan is included along with financial projections.

This chapter provides an excellent example of how trade research can be used to discover a premise around which an entire marketing plan can be created. By conducting a national series of in-depth interviews with supermarket executives, Zion Housewares Corporation discovered that many supermarkets were interested in taking advantage of impulse opportunities in the housewares category, but were hampered by a lack of available retail shelf space. Based on this research, Zion was able to solve the supermarkets' problem by creating the Selecto Housewares Boutique, which doubles the retail space by utilizing rotating racks. In sum, the new displays enable consumers to see something new every time they visit the participating supermarket. Zion was able to significantly increase its sales through supermarkets by providing the consumer with a constantly changing series of alternatives in the housewares category.

Marketing Plan for:

Selecto Housewares Boutiques

Zion Housewares Corporation[1]

January 15, 2001

INTRODUCTION

The purpose of this report is to develop a five-year marketing plan for a venture to sell a line of Zion Housewares Corporation's products in major supermarkets throughout the United States. This report is divided into the following sections:

1. **BACKGROUND.** This section details the background that led up to the development of this venture and reviews the specific objectives and methodology used in completing the marketing plan.

2. **SUPERMARKET PRACTICES AND ATTITUDES.** This section outlines present trade practices, desires, and expectations concerning the housewares category in supermarkets, as well as trade reactions to various marketing alternatives. This section also identifies trade attitudes toward accepting distribution of a Zion Housewares program.

3. **PANEL TEST RESULTS.** This section summarizes the results of a panel test in Seattle, Washington, and in Dallas, Texas, of a new Zion Housewares program designed for supermarkets.

4. **CONCLUSIONS.** These are key thoughts on opportunities for housewares in supermarkets in general, on the results of the panel test, and on what this means in terms of an overall opportunity for the Zion Housewares Corporation.

[1] **Disclaimer:** The specific information in this sample marketing plan was compiled for intended use as an example only. Although this marketing plan is based on actual products from a real company, the specific information in the plan is hypothetical and is not intended to compete with or to divulge proprietary ideas, company structure, or the financial status of any company. The names, numbers, and some of the facts in this marketing plan have been changed because of the confidential nature of the information. The information is intended to be used as a guide only.

5. **FIVE-YEAR MARKETING PLAN.** This section presents a specific and detailed action program detailing each step that is necessary to bring this venture from management approval to implementation.

6. **FINANCIAL FORECASTS.** This section provides a forecast of the financial opportunity for Zion Housewares Corporation from expanding distribution in supermarkets nationally.

BACKGROUND

A project investigating the national distribution and sales potential for Zion housewares products was started during February 2001. The overall objective of this project was to prepare a marketing plan for the Zion Housewares Corporation aimed at expanding its distribution to national levels. The specifics of this objective were as follows:

1. **DISTRIBUTION POTENTIAL.** The number of supermarket organizations throughout the United States that would be both capable of and interested in taking on the Zion line was to be identified.

2. **SALES POTENTIAL.** A test market was to be conducted in a group of supermarkets. The purpose of this test was to identify the sales potential per store per week of each item in the Zion housewares line. This information was to be used to forecast the national volume potential of expanded distribution.

3. **MARKETING PLAN.** Based on the results of the distribution and sales investigations, a marketing plan was to be developed demonstrating how Zion should expand from a regional to a national level.

The information required to write this report was gathered in five stages. Each stage was designed to provide a systematic understanding of the overall housewares market from the trade's standpoint and to enable the development of specific marketing plans and strategies. The following specific steps were taken:

1. **MARKET REVIEW.** The project began with a complete review of the overall market for housewares in supermarkets. This included a review of data within the Zion Housewares

Corporation that were pertinent to the preparation of this program. In addition, an exhaustive screening of industry data was conducted.

2. **STORE CHECKS.** Store checks were conducted in a representative group of supermarkets throughout the country. During these store checks, the product line carried, the store's breadth of involvement in housewares, and the nature of the store's overall housewares program were identified. Photographs were taken during most of the store checks to provide a permanent record of the stores' housewares programs.

3. **TRADE PROBES.** Interviews were conducted with key executives in supermarket organizations throughout the United States. Meetings were held with executives at various levels within these organizations, including buyers, the directors of general merchandise, and members of senior management. Organizations of different sizes were contacted, as were similar organizations in different geographic areas. The purpose of these interviews was to identify trade interest in a Zion program, as well as the trade's requirements for such a program. In addition to retail executives, food brokers were contacted to identify their interest in participating in a Zion program.

4. **IN-STORE TESTS.** An in-store test was conducted in a panel of supermarkets in Seattle, Washington, and in Dallas, Texas. The purpose of this test was to determine the movement of a complete eight-foot section of Zion housewares products in supermarkets. The development of this panel test was completed in five separate steps. The following specific steps were taken:

   A. *Test organization.* Arrangements were made with two major supermarket chains to provide one test store each in Seattle and Dallas. Arrangements were also made with a distributor in each market to handle the store servicing aspects of the test. In each case, the existing eight-foot housewares rack was removed and replaced with the Zion program.

   B. *Displays.* Two eight-foot rotating displays were designed and manufactured for the test stores. These displays included rotating towers within each display to increase the holding capacity. In effect, each display held nearly sixteen feet of housewares in only eight feet of space.

   C. *Store setup.* Arrangements were made for the local distributors, as well as Zion personnel, to properly set up each test store for the experiment. In both cases, the display replaced the store's existing eight-foot housewares program.

D. *Test measurement.* Each distributor was instructed to perform weekly counts of the merchandise sold off each display. These weekly store counts were transmitted to Zion Housewares Corporation, where the order was pulled and the data were recorded. Zion then produced an invoice delineating the sales of each item on the rack each week. The Zion invoices were used as the basic recording data to tabulate movement reports. The test began in Seattle on November 10, 2000, and in Dallas on December 1, 2000. The tests were concluded on January 15, 2001.

E. *Data analysis.* The data were formatted in such a way that an analysis of the overall display, of each category within the display, and, finally, of each product within the display could be conducted.

5. **MARKETING PLAN DEVELOPMENT.** Based on the information gathered in the previous steps, a detailed plan was developed, including a step-by-step action plan that should enable Zion to profitably expand to national levels of distribution.

SUPERMARKET PRACTICES AND ATTITUDES

1. *Supermarket chains can be divided into major and minor housewares vendors.* Supermarkets that are major vendors have extensive housewares departments. These departments can range from eight feet of space in the store all the way up to over fifty feet. These major housewares vendors often use a number of different housewares suppliers. In some cases these major vendors buy from housewares distributors, while in other cases they buy directly from housewares manufacturers. Supermarkets that are considered to be minor housewares vendors generally limit their housewares selection to pegged housewares. These chains frequently have only one housewares supplier, and this is generally a distributor.

2. *Boxed and pegged housewares are viewed differently by the supermarket channel.* Pegged housewares are handled more successfully by supermarkets. Generally, one supplier handles the entire pegged housewares business. This is either a rack jobber or a supplier of a program similar to the current Zion Housewares program. Boxed housewares present a much more difficult problem in the supermarket environment. Space allocation is more difficult, and housewares selection becomes more critical. Most of the dissatisfaction mentioned in the interviews conducted with supermarkets in this study focused on boxed housewares.

3. *Supermarkets compare housewares profits directly with the profits from other nonfood categories in their stores.* Major housewares vendors feel that housewares generally outperform many of the other nonfood items in their stores. This justifies the major amount of space they allocate to housewares. Minor housewares vendors feel that housewares provide marginal performance. They find it very difficult to justify expanding the amount of space devoted to housewares. Some of these vendors have eliminated housewares for this reason.

4. *Many supermarket chains have turned housewares over to a distributor rather than handling this category through their warehouse.* This is especially true with pegged housewares. These chains allow the distributor or rack jobber to make all of the day-to-day decisions on housewares merchandising. Many of these chains have established a grid system exactly like the one currently used by Zion Housewares. Most programs rotate stock frequently. Both warehoused programs and programs that were handled on a direct-store-delivered basis were found.

5. *Direct-store-delivered programs are almost always fully guaranteed.* Most direct-store-delivered programs are handled by rack jobbers, and guaranteed sale terms tend to be standard practice in the rack jobber industry. With a guaranteed sale, any items that don't sell are simply returned to the distributor. The stock in these programs is constantly rotated, and damaged goods are picked up and credited to the store.

6. *Many retailers rejected distribution of the traditional Zion housewares program because they felt that they already had a similar program.* A presentation of the concept of taking on Zion Housewares products using the system that Zion Housewares now uses in its existing supermarkets was made to a number of supermarket executives. Many of these people saw the Zion Housewares program as nothing new. They felt that housewares was not a new category for supermarkets. The Zion Housewares system was viewed as already available. Some stores saw Zion Housewares as simply another rack jobber. Other supermarkets saw their programs as being bigger and more sophisticated than Zion Housewares' program. A few retailers felt that Zion Housewares was not of interest to them simply because they did not like housewares, period.

7. *A few of the retailers interviewed demonstrated interest in taking on the standard Zion Housewares program.* Some of these chains were not familiar with the grid system that Zion Housewares uses, and saw this as something new. These chains saw a possible opportu-

nity to warehouse housewares themselves. Others were dissatisfied with their current housewares programs and saw Zion Housewares as a possible replacement for their existing supplier. Some of the chains interviewed were simply looking for a competitive proposal.

8. *Many of the supermarket chains interviewed would consider discontinuing their existing housewares suppliers if they found a better alternative.* A few chains were quite loyal to their long-term suppliers of housewares and other products. Most chains, however, did not feel that their housewares supplier was irreplaceable. For strong enough reasons, most of the supermarket chains interviewed would consider switching suppliers. In some cases, these people were looking for better prices, while in other cases they were looking for improved service. A few retailers indicated that they were always looking for "a better deal."

9. *Many of the supermarket executives interviewed recommended that the product on the current Zion housewares display be tightened.* The executives were shown a photograph of the current Zion Housewares display. This was an eight-foot section on pegboard. Most people had a neutral reaction to this display. A header sign was seen as a possible improvement. The negative reactions generally centered around wasted space. These retailers indicated that they do not allow loose displays in their stores. Their other pegged displays look very tight, with the carded products neatly aligned very close to one another. They would expect the housewares supplier to achieve this same tightness.

10. *Most food brokers and distributors were interested in working with Zion Housewares Corporation.* The new Zion program was shown to a number of food brokers and distributors that could carry housewares, but currently did not. The distributors saw the Zion system as quite appealing. They felt that the system would enable them to enter the housewares business without having a great deal of experience in the category. Most food brokers do not now carry housewares. These people saw housewares as an incremental business.

11. *Some of the supermarket executives interviewed wanted Zion to provide them with a proposal on a full housewares program.* These supermarkets were not loyal to their current supplier. They welcomed the idea of Zion's bidding on their entire housewares department. This bid would be compared to their current situation, and a decision would be made as to whether or not to switch to Zion.

12. *With the current Zion Housewares system, both a warehouse and a direct-store-delivery system must be available to the supermarket.* The warehouse facilities of supermarket chains

vary considerably across the country. Some chains have a warehouse that is appropriate for distributing housewares. The Zion Housewares system is ideal in this situation. The grid system and product rotating system enable the supermarket to enter the housewares business without a full housewares buying department. Other supermarket chains have inadequate warehouse facilities for a housewares program. Many of these chains have no nonfood warehouses or in some cases, no warehouse at all. For these organizations, a direct-store-delivery system must be offered.

13. *Whatever type of direct-store-delivery program is used in the supermarket environment, it must be competitive with rack jobbers.* Damaged merchandise must be picked up and credited to the store. Goods must be preticketed with price stickers for each individual chain. Slow-moving items must be rotated out and eliminated from the display. Some form of guaranteed sale must be provided to the supermarket organization.

14. *A system for removing existing housewares when a new Zion housewares program is installed must be provided.* Most chains already have a housewares program. In some cases, these housewares are on a guaranteed sale basis. This makes replacement relatively easy, as the supplier simply takes back the housewares. In other cases, the supermarkets own the housewares. In these cases, an arrangement must be made to remove the existing housewares from the store and to provide some form of financial compensation to the retail chain.

15. *Each supermarket chain would test a Zion program in a few stores prior to its implementation chainwide.* Most retailers feel that it would be necessary for Zion Housewares to provide them with some data from a traditional test market. In addition, each chain would also want to retest the program in its own stores. These people feel that they must be able to compare the sales in their own stores to the test market data. Because of this, a test should be incorporated into every new sale prospect, and should be considered a standard procedure in entering a new chain.

16. *It was indicated that incentives would be necessary in order to justify initial tests in a new supermarket organization.* The supermarket trade views testing as a disruption to normal operations. An expense is incurred, in the form of both labor and paperwork. Free product or a trade allowance is often given to these retailers for tests. Guaranteed profits are also

sometimes provided. Zion Housewares must plan on some form of compensation to the trade for initial testing.

17. *Switching housewares suppliers was indicated to be a rather slow process.* Supermarket chains generally do not modify all their stores at the same time. First, a new program, such as housewares, is presented to supermarket management. A test in a few stores is then the next step. This is followed by expansion of the program into larger stores. Eventually, the remaining stores are folded in. The entire process of going from zero distribution to the entire chain can take up to a full year.

PANEL TEST RESULTS

1. *A panel test of a new Zion Housewares program was conducted in two large supermarkets.* The first supermarket was in Seattle, Washington, and the second store was in Dallas, Texas. A total of eight feet of shelf space was allocated to the test in each store. Existing housewares were removed from that eight-foot section in both stores. A six-spinner display was placed in each store. Each display had approximately 720 housewares items. The inventory value at trade prices was approximately $800 per store. The test ran for nine weeks in Seattle and for six weeks in Dallas.

2. *Supermarket reactions to the Zion tests were quite favorable.* Supermarket executives liked the panel test program. The display was the primary "hot button." They liked the way the display looked in their stores, and many favorable comments were received from store personnel as well as from customers shopping in the stores. The display was felt to make the program unique. It was felt that the Zion Housewares "boutique" program outsold the stores' previous housewares program.

3. *A number of operational problems with the display were identified during the panel test.* The six towers were located too close together in the prototype displays. This closeness prevented the towers from rotating properly. Housewares were constantly falling off of the displays, causing the packaging to be ripped and crushed. Restocking by the distributors took far too much time. This display did not have enough holding power because of the short hooks used. This frequently resulted in lost sales because of out-of-stock situations.

4. *A number of solutions to the display difficulties were identified during the panel test.* The display concept was considered very important by the supermarket people. They felt that rotating towers would provide maximum use of the store's shelf space. However, they felt that the number of towers should be reduced from six to four. Fewer towers would provide the ability to use longer pegs, which would increase the overall inventory. The bins at the bottom of the towers were felt to be too small, and should be enlarged to, again, improve holding power. The overall expense of the display was found to be high, and should be reduced.

5. *Products did not all sell evenly on the displays in the panel test.* In general, there was a fairly steady drop-off from the best-selling products down to the least-selling products. Products were also ranked by unit sales. The ranking of products by unit sales varied considerably from the ranking of products by retail dollar sales. Although there was a similar spread from the best-selling products to the least-selling products in terms of unit sales, the position of the actual products in these rankings differed.

6. *Within each housewares category, the majority of the sales were accounted for by the few top-selling products.* Almost a third of the sales of domestic housewares products were generated by the ten top-selling products. The top four imported housewares products generated over a third of the sales within that category. The top two domestic staples represented over 40 percent of the sales in that category. Nearly half of the seasonal goods sold were the top two products.

7. *Sales in the panel test stores varied from one week to another.* In Seattle, weekly sales ranged from $492 and $368 on the high side to $138 on the low side. These numbers were partially affected by special situations involving shipping times. Dallas sales were somewhat more consistent.

8. *During the panel test of the Zion Housewares boutique, the average store generated weekly sales of $209.28.* The supermarket in Seattle did considerably better, with average weekly sales of $241.79. The store in Dallas generated weekly sales averaging $176.77. The average store generated unit sales of 118 units per week.

9. *The average monthly sales per linear foot was $28.* This figure is computed by multiplying the average sales per week of $209.28 by 4.3 weeks, to arrive at sales per month. This figure

is then divided by an average of thirty-two feet of linear shelf space, to arrive at $28.12 average monthly sales per linear foot.

10. *The average dollar margin on the products sold in the panel test displays compares favorably with the margin on many other typical supermarket products.* The Zion Housewares boutique generated an average dollar volume margin of $11.25 per month. This is higher than the margin on many other supermarket products, such as canned cat food, vitamins, denture adhesives, mouthwash, chewing gum, and shaving cream. Frozen pizza, ready-to-eat cereal, and deodorants are examples of supermarket products that generate a higher average dollar margin than the Zion Housewares boutique.

CONCLUSIONS

1. *Broad-scale distribution is not available with the current Zion Housewares program.* Housewares in supermarkets are not considered new. Retailers have been exposed to a variety of different programs. The current Zion Housewares program is considered just another housewares program. There were a small number of exceptions to this in various parts of the country; however, the number was not great enough to consider broad-scale distribution opportunities.

2. *A dramatically new program is needed to get the trade interested in a Zion product line.* Zion Housewares must differentiate itself from other housewares suppliers. A program is needed that looks totally new, helps solve current trade problems, and gives supermarkets a reason to shift from their current housewares supplier to Zion Housewares. In sum, a revolutionary new approach to marketing housewares is needed.

3. *The boutique display that was used during the panel test did differentiate the Zion program from standard housewares programs.* The trade responded quite favorably to the display concept. Supermarket employees believed that it made the housewares department look brand new and improved the look of the stores. The display served as a focal point for the entire program. The trade saw the display as a reason to make a change. This was partly because of the attractiveness of the display. The rotating tower made the Zion Housewares program a unique entry into the supermarket's nonfood business.

4. *The boutique display also enabled the trade to better utilize shelf space.* The biggest problem in the supermarket industry is available space. There are constant demands for increased space within the supermarket, and the amount of space is fixed. The Zion Housewares boutique display was seen as a solution to the trade's continuing need to find additional space. The spinners were viewed as literally doubling the amount of available space within that eight-foot section. This extra space utilization provided a powerful motivation for the trade, and should be the basis for a Zion Housewares marketing campaign.

5. *With the right marketing program, Zion has many opportunities for expanded distribution in the supermarket channel.* There are a number of potential new customers throughout the United States. Some of these organizations are ready for a new push on housewares with the right program. Others are simply tired of their old supplier. Although many people were not interested in taking on a program that they viewed as the same as the one they already had, many organizations indicated that they would be interested in switching housewares suppliers for an exciting new marketing venture.

6. *The display boutique program included in the panel test demonstrated the potential to become a viable program.* The Dallas store averaged $176.77 per week from this program, and the Seattle store averaged $241.79 per week. The trade considered these results to be an improvement over the existing situation. Both supermarket organizations indicated interest in expanding the Zion Housewares program within their chains. The distributors involved in the panel test were also interested in expanding the panel test program.

7. *In developing expansion plans, Zion should plan on a step-by-step sales approach.* Taking on a new program is a major decision for a supermarket chain. The initial step is for the buying committee to review proposals submitted by the housewares suppliers. Each new customer would probably require a test prior to broad-scale expansion. This would be followed by gradual expansion within the chain. A somewhat custom approach will be required for each supermarket account.

8. *Food brokers should be included in an effort to gain distribution for the Zion Housewares boutique program.* Food brokers are in contact with every major supermarket chain in its respective markets every week. This frequent exposure is ideal for identifying prospects and making initial sales efforts. Brokers also provide ideal follow-up on sales prospects and

management of the account once it is sold. Brokers generally have strong credibility with chain management, and their expense is on a variable-cost rather than a fixed-cost basis.

9. *Distributors should be included as part of the overall Zion Housewares boutique program.* Zion Housewares Corporation can distribute product to some retail accounts in appropriate geographic areas. Where this is not possible, distributors can perform the same function. Seattle is an excellent example of this, because it would be geographically unwise for Zion Housewares to attempt to service that market. In addition, some retailers will do business only with certain distributors because they do not want additional suppliers coming into their stores. In these cases, it is absolutely necessary for Zion Housewares to use a distributor. The boutique program fits many distributors' requirements, and many of them view the Zion Housewares program as incremental business. Finally, distributors can assist in the difficult task of selling in new accounts.

10. *Food brokers can also be used to assist in store servicing.* Most large food brokerage organizations have a field servicing force. These people are routinely in every supermarket, either weekly, biweekly, or monthly, depending on the store size. Because of this, brokers can be used to offset distribution gaps. When there is no distributor, product can be shipped directly to stores via UPS. Orders can be taken by broker personnel, and product can be put up on the shelves by store people. This system can enable Zion Housewares to cover those parts of the country that it cannot service itself, or where there is no distributor available.

11. *A substantial profit opportunity exists in each new retail chain account.* Many supermarket chains have between 25 and 200 stores in a market. Each store represents potential sales roughly equivalent to the panel test results. Because there are many potential retail chains across the United States, Zion Housewares has a strong opportunity to grow. Growth not only represents improved profitability, but also represents security in broad-scale distribution.

12. *Zion should proceed to implement a housewares boutique program on a national basis.* The display should be the centerpiece of the program because of its ability to completely differentiate Zion Housewares from other suppliers. Trade incentives should be built into the prices so that effective merchandising can be achieved. Food brokers should be added to the sales force to help in selling and maintaining the program. Distributors should be included for those accounts in the geographic areas where Zion Housewares cannot service stores

itself. A step-by-step rollout plan should be launched that increases the program in manageable bites.

FIVE-YEAR MARKETING PLAN

1. *It is recommended that Zion Housewares Corporation move to launch a national program, using the boutique concept developed for the panel test to sell its products through supermarkets.* From the research included in this document, it has been determined that a boutique program offers Zion Housewares the opportunity to increase its share of supermarket distribution by a substantial proportion. It is believed that such a program will help to generate sales on a stable basis. This marketing plan will show that the cost of launching a boutique program would not be prohibitive to Zion Housewares. Finally, it is believed that Zion Housewares could accomplish the launching of a boutique program without any significant disruption of its normal day-to-day operations.

2. *The entire program should be centered around the display concept developed for the panel test.* This display differentiates Zion Housewares from other housewares suppliers. It provides the trade with a reason to switch to Zion Housewares, and it improves the housewares department's in-store look. The display also increases the amount of merchandise that can be put in the housewares section. In sum, the display becomes the basis of the sales and marketing campaign.

3. *An eight-foot display with rotating towers is recommended.* Towers provide the trade with the perception of space savings. The trade believes that approximately sixteen feet of product can be placed in an eight-foot section with the towers. This is a powerful selling point. The display also looks very unusual within the housewares industry. Four spinners are recommended for each eight-foot section. The recommended budget is $420 per display, with the initial forty displays costing $630 each.

4. *The product line for the boutique program should focus on pegged housewares.* All of the product should fit on the rotating display, with bulk housewares being placed in bins at the bottom of each tower. The housewares selection should be made up of the fastest-moving domestic and imported housewares products.

5. *The current Zion merchandising system using a grid should be used on the display boutique.* Each location on the display should have a unique slot number. The first row should consist of locations A-1, A-2 . . . A-32, and so on. Each additional row should follow the same pattern. These slot numbers should be included on each package, and also on all order sheets and price sheets. Warehouse slots should use the same numbers.

6. *The long-term packaging should include the Zion logo.* The eventual goal should be to present Zion Housewares as a manufacturer, rather than a distributor. It is recommended that the packaging eventually be custom made for Zion Housewares. The card sizes should be designed to fit the display, and each card should have the Zion Housewares logo printed on it. This will make the Zion Housewares program stand out, and will simplify the process of selling through distributors.

7. *The products on the boutique should be rotated periodically to keep the display fresh.* The core product will remain basically fixed throughout the year. Some product changes should be made each quarter, however. This will cause the consumer to view the Zion Housewares display as a dynamic system. The stores and distributors will not be affected by product changes because of the grid system. Card sizes, pricing, and location numbers will all remain the same. This will mean that no decisions will be required of either the distributor or the trade on an ongoing basis.

8. *Price levels should be increased to include marketing expenditures.* Current housewares industry pricing is set at commodity levels. The retailer buys at the lowest possible price, and there is no money left for displays or promotions. Currently, the best supplier is simply the cheapest. It is recommended that the Zion Housewares system offer an alternative. It should be a first-class housewares department for the supermarket that promotes its products just like any other successful nonfood program.

9. *The Zion boutique should offer a superior value, even though the pricing has been increased.* Because of the premium display, it is believed that the consumers will perceive the housewares being sold as being of superior quality. Rotating the housewares and promoting them throughout the year will ensure that the feeling of newness will always surround the program. Co-op advertising and publicity will help stimulate this feeling of newness and excitement. The trade will receive higher profits because of the premium pricing. Because of the planned high servicing levels, current labor costs will actually decrease.

10. *It is recommended that the pricing be simplified from that of the normal housewares industry.* The base price should include all of Zion Housewares' costs and profit requirements. All marketing expenditures should be added to this base price. Fixed expenses, such as displays and introductory allowances, should be designed to be paid off within a one-year period. It is recommended that all products carry the same margin. This means that the distributor would generally get a 35 percent profit margin on every product in the line. Similarly, retailers would generally get a 40 percent margin on all products throughout the line. This means that the entire display will carry the same margins.

11. *Retail pricing on the Zion boutique program will be higher than on the current system.* The current housewares industry does not include marketing expenditures in its pricing. The new system will build in a total marketing campaign. The trade will be provided with advertising, promotion, and displays. Funds will be provided for a national sales force through food brokers. Because of this, the consumer price will be inflated slightly. This should not affect impulse purchases, and we do not believe that it will affect Zion's net factory sales.

12. *The name "Selecto Housewares Boutique" is recommended for the program.* It is recommended that the Selecto name be legally registered as a trademark. This will result in Zion Housewares Corporation's legally owning the name. The name should then be used as a consumer brand name. This means that the name will be featured prominently on display headers, and eventually on all packaging. The name will also be used in all consumer advertising, promotion, and other publicity. All sales brochures and other trade communication devices will also use this registered trademark.

13. *Trade promotion is recommended to enhance distribution.* Trade promotion is customary in the supermarket industry. Introductory allowances on new programs help to offset the initial cost to the trade of taking on a new program. Advertising allowances permit trade participation in promoting new brands. Trade promotion makes Zion Housewares competitive with other suppliers of nonfood products to supermarkets. This maximizes the overall distribution opportunities for Zion Housewares.

14. *It is recommended that distribution be opened up with a sell-in allowance in the form of free goods to the trade.* The purpose of this allowance will be to help get initial distribution. This allowance will be used in lieu of buying back the trade's current inventory. The allowance will also help reduce the costs to the trade of changing housewares programs. Giving

the trade free goods could provide a value to the trade at retail prices equal to twice the cost to Zion Housewares Corporation.

15. *Consumer promotion should be part of the sales program for the Zion Housewares boutique.* A full calendar should be laid out for the trade at the time of the sell-in presentation. Each quarter should have a new promotion. This will include on-pack coupons, dump bins with special promotional products, and special features on the display itself. Point-of-purchase material should also be used to flag promotions. Finally, these promotions should be featured in co-op ad slicks given to the trade along with advertising money.

16. *The advertising should consist primarily of a co-op program.* It is recommended that 5 percent of sales be accrued as a market development fund for each market the program is in. This money will be used to pay for the advertising. The trade will be provided with ad slicks outlining what Zion Housewares wants the trade to say in that advertising. Quarterly allowances will be paid to the trade to run these advertisements based upon the 5 percent accrued money. It is recommended that this advertising be tied in to the consumer promotion.

17. *A public relations campaign to boost the advertising is recommended.* Zion Housewares should become part of a national publicity tour launched on the subject of nonfood products in supermarkets. The Zion Housewares boutique would be used as an example of a new nonfood product in the supermarket. This will provide exposure on television, on radio, and in print. Tapes and reprints of articles will be given to the trade. The consumer exposure will help sell product at the store level, while trade exposure will help generate interest in taking on the program in distribution.

18. *A variety of distribution systems will be required for the boutique program.* In some cases, it will be appropriate for Zion Housewares to distribute the product to stores the way it currently does. In other cases, a local rack jobber will be required. In many areas the use of a UPS system will be required. In this case, orders will be taken by local food brokers, and then distributors will ship the orders directly to the store via UPS. The final alternative will be chain warehouses, which will be necessary in some areas.

19. *A network of food brokers will be required.* The food brokers will help Zion Housewares to gain initial distribution. They will also help broaden distribution on an ongoing basis. The

brokers will present quarterly marketing programs to chain management, and will oversee the program in each store. The brokers will be paid a 5 percent commission for this service. In some cases, brokers will take orders at the store level, and will be paid an additional fee by the distributor for doing this.

20. *A separate sales organization is recommended for the boutique program.* A network of twenty food brokers will be required to roll the program out. They will service eighty head-quarters locations and two thousand retail stores. All of this will be pulled through approximately ten regional distributors. This will require a separate sales function.

21. *Two additional people will be required to manage the expanded boutique program.* After the program is launched, a national sales manager will be required, who will maintain constant sales supervision for the program. We envision the sales manager's being assisted by a marketing assistant, who will provide internal coordination of the program.

22. *A formal sell-in presentation to launch the program is planned.* Replacing eight feet of in-store space is an important event to the supermarket trade. Several retail executives within each chain will have to approve the decision, and, in some cases, the approval of the entire buying committee will be needed. Because of this, a formal presentation to launch the program is recommended. This presentation should dramatically explain the benefits of the program. It should place proper emphasis on the importance of the program, and it should demonstrate all of the benefits.

23. *Sales literature will be required as part of the sell-in presentation.* The development of a four-page brochure to describe the program is recommended. The brochure should also include a picture of the display that will be used. Price sheets will be part of this package. The package will also include the promotional calendar and the initial advertising slicks, coupons, and so on. The trade will keep this package after the formal presentation has been concluded.

24. *Activities should be started now to ensure that the program can be launched into the first rollout markets by April 1, 2001.* It is recommended that the program be started with forty stores on 4/1/01. In order to accomplish this, it will be necessary to begin broker meetings in February. The other key dates recommended for the program include the following:

Launch publicity and initial promotion on 4/11/01, begin expanded sales campaign 5/2/01, and begin second rollout 7/1/01.

FINANCIAL FORECASTS

1. *It is forecasted that the Selecto Housewares Boutique program will eventually receive distribution in a total of 2,000 supermarkets throughout the United States.* This would be 4.7 percent of all supermarkets and would represent 7.3 percent of the over $12 million a year stores and 3.5 percent of the $8 to $11.9 million a year stores.

2. *Based on the panel test results, it is believed that the new boutique will eventually achieve total annual retail sales of $21.3 million.* This assumes that the $12 million and over stores will continue to do $242 per store per week in retail sales. Similarly, this assumes that the $8 to $11.9 million stores will continue to do $177 per store per week in retail sales. This means that in the total 2,000 stores forecast, overall sales will be $410,000 in sales per week and $21,320,000 in annual sales.

3. *When the program is fully rolled out to national levels, a net profit before tax on an annual basis of $1,922,000 is forecasted.* The going-year assumptions include a retail margin of 40 percent of retail sales and a distributor margin of 35 percent of trade sales. This would generate gross sales at factory of $8,477,000. As will be outlined shortly, the pricing recommended will result in a cost of goods of 59.25 percent. This will generate a gross profit annually of $3,454,000. Assuming 18 percent for marketing, this will generate 22.75 percent for profit, or $1,922,000.

4. *An annual budget of $175,000 is recommended for the sales administration expense.* This assumes a salary level of $60,000 for the sales manager and a $30,000 salary for a marketing assistant. A 50 percent overhead factor is assumed for office and other expenses, and $40,000 a year for travel expenses is also assumed.

5. *Using the Dallas test store as an example, it is assumed that the total inventory on the boutique display of 719 items will have a trade value of $807.47.* It is recognized that this will be adjusted when the display is modified; however, this inventory level will provide an excellent vehicle for developing pipeline cost assumptions.

6. *Based on an assumed inventory value of $807.47 at trade cost, it is envisioned that the total inventory for all 2,000 displays will be $1,614,940.* In addition, it is envisioned that there will be a warehouse inventory at distributors of 50 percent of this value, or $807,470. This will result in total net factory pipeline sales of $1,574,000 for the Selecto Housewares Boutique.

7. *It is recommended that the cost of goods be calculated based on a price that will yield Zion an ongoing profit after the first year of 12.45 percent of net sales.* If the program were to be rolled out in 300 stores over a one-year period, this would generate sales of $841,000 during the first half of the year because of pipeline sales. During the second half of the year, net factory sales will be $636,000, making total sales for the year $1,477,000.

8. *It is recommended that Zion Housewares begin by budgeting a profit for this year of $184,000, or 12.45 percent.* This profit will be less during the first half of the year than it will for the second half of the year. Displays and introductory allowances will all be taken during the first half of the year. Other marketing expenses will be a fixed percentage of sales. This means that the total expenses for the first half of the year will be $315,000, leaving $498,000 for cost of goods. Similar calculations for the second half result in cost of goods being $377,000, or, in each case, 59.25 percent. It is felt that the pricing should be set to build advertising and other marketing expenses above cost of goods to generate a net profit at the end of the first year of 12.45 percent.

CHAPTER 14

Putting It All Together

Example: New Top Plastic Laminates

After you have completed all of the research required for developing a clear understanding of the overall environment in which your marketing plan will be operating, it is time to begin putting the final plan together. At this point, you should have completed a market review that clearly outlines the size and nature of the market, the market's history and trends, and competitive activity in the market. You should have developed a good understanding of the practices, desires, and expectations of consumers in your product category. You should also have identified retailer practices related to your product category as well as their attitudes toward the methods of distribution specified by your marketing plan.

It is now time for you to draw your conclusions as to what you feel are the key points identified by this research, together with their strategic implications. As outlined in Part 1 of this book, you should look through your research findings to identify elements that match some of the key factors in other marketing plan success stories. Are there any consumer negatives or consumer problems that you might eliminate with your new venture? Are the benefits of your product or service important to your consumers? Can you create a plan that will be convenient for your consumers and retailers? Is your offering truly effective or preemptive?

After you have completed your analysis, drawn your conclusions, and made your planning assumptions, it is time to develop specific objectives for your marketing plan. These should be logical objectives that make sense based on your research findings and the conclusions you have drawn from these findings. Your marketing objectives should state specifically what you are trying to accomplish with your marketing plan. As the plan is implemented, you should judge the success of the plan on the degree to which it accomplishes these marketing objectives.

The elements of your marketing plan should now flow from your research findings, conclusions, and marketing objectives. Your marketing plan should include a description of each of the key elements. Examples of key elements that should be included are the product line, the brand name, packaging, pricing, sales and distribution methods, and marketing communications. A timetable for the implementation of your marketing plan should also be included.

This chapter focuses on a marketing plan for a new line of plastic laminates. This plan provides a good example of how the developer started with a review of the overall market for the different types of plastic laminates in the various channels of distribution. The plan then moves to a review of consumer attitudes toward the plastic laminate category, followed by trade attitudes toward the category. Conclusions are then drawn from this research, indicating that a retail venture for JPK Counter Top Corporation should be an excellent expansion opportunity. These conclusions are followed by specific marketing objectives, a description of all of the marketing plan elements, and then a set of financial projections.

Marketing Plan for:
New Top Plastic Laminates
JPK Counter Top Corporation[1]
March 1, 2001

INTRODUCTION

The purpose of this document is to provide a comprehensive marketing plan for a line of plastic laminates to be sold through retail outlets in the United States. This document is divided into the following eight sections:

1. **BACKGROUND.** This section reviews the background of this project and outlines the steps that led to the development of this marketing plan.

2. **MARKET REVIEW.** This section reviews the growth and nature of the retail segment of the plastic laminate market. A detailed profile of the market for sheet laminates, post-formed countertops, and roll laminates through each of the principal retail trade classes is provided.

3. **CONSUMER RESEARCH RESULTS.** This section outlines present consumer practices, desires, and expectations regarding the concept of purchasing plastic laminates in retail stores.

4. **TRADE PRACTICES AND ATTITUDES.** This section reviews the retail trade's current involvement with plastic laminates and attitudes toward the product category.

[1] **Disclaimer:** The specific information in this sample marketing plan was compiled for intended use as an example only. Although this marketing plan is based on actual products from a real company, the specific information in the plan is hypothetical and is not intended to compete with or to divulge proprietary ideas, company structure, or the financial status of any company. The names, numbers, and some of the facts in this marketing plan have been changed because of the confidential nature of the information. The information is intended to be used as a guide only.

5. **CONCLUSIONS.** These are thoughts based upon the facts presented in the previous sections.

6. **MARKETING OBJECTIVES.** This section provides the specific objectives of this venture over the next five years.

7. **STRATEGIC PROGRAMS.** This section presents the specifics of the various plans developed to accomplish the marketing objectives of this venture.

8. **FINANCIAL PROJECTIONS.** This section provides detailed calculations on the cost, volume, and payout of the venture from initial launch to full national expansion. A pro forma profit-and-loss statement is also provided.

The information required to write this marketing plan was gathered in nine stages. These stages were designed to provide a systematic understanding of the overall retail market for plastic laminates and for the potential that this market may provide. The following specific steps were taken:

1. **INFORMATION GATHERING.** A careful review of technical and marketing information available in company files was conducted. In addition to this information, a screening of virtually every available secondary resource related to the plastic laminate market was done. This information was provided by an outside research organization that was hired to conduct a specific study of this market category. A clipping service was retained to obtain copies of advertisements placed by retailers in selected areas throughout the United States.

2. **INDUSTRY CONTACTS.** Interviews were conducted with seven manufacturers of plastic laminates, with the research departments of related trade associations and government agencies, and with the editorial staffs of a number of industry publications.

3. **FIELD TRIPS.** Store checks and in-store interviews were conducted in key geographic areas throughout the United States. These store checks were conducted in thirteen cities that represent a cross section of the U.S. market. A total of 135 stores in various trade classes were personally visited.

4. **TELEPHONE SURVEYS.** In order to broaden the base of the store checks conducted during this study, additional telephone surveys were conducted. Telephone interviews were con-

ducted with a total of 323 retail outlets. These included 81 hardware stores, 67 lumberyards, 51 home improvement centers, and 124 discount stores.

5. **MARKET PROFILE.** Based on an analysis of the information gathered from the 458 telephone surveys and store checks, a statistical profile of the U.S. market for plastic laminates sold through retail outlets was developed. This model was designed to provide a complete picture of the total market and all of its logical segmentations.

6. **CONSUMER RESEARCH.** A series of six focus group sessions was held with consumers regarding various aspects of the plastic laminate market, as well as specifically with the concept of purchasing plastic laminates in retail stores.

7. **TRADE VISITS.** Meetings were held with retail buyers throughout the United States. The purpose of these meetings was to identify the buyers' current practices and attitudes toward the plastic laminate category, as well as their willingness to accept distribution of a new venture in this category.

8. **PREPARATION OF CONCLUSIONS AND MARKETING OBJECTIVES.** Based on an analysis of the market profile, consumer research, manufacturer and trade practices, and trends in the industry, specific conclusions and marketing objectives concerning the opportunities that this market could offer, as well as what would have be done to capitalize on these opportunities, were prepared.

9. **MARKETING PLAN.** All of this research was summarized in this marketing plan, together with the strategic programs and financial projections necessary to launch the venture.

BACKGROUND

The JPK Counter Top Corporation currently sells the bulk of its products to the traditional market for high-pressure laminates, including builders and fabricators. JPK believes, however, that there may be a larger market for plastic laminates through retail channels of distribution. This project was commissioned to determine whether JPK could be successful in finding a significant incremental market for its products through retail channels of distribution.

Because of its concentration in traditional market segments, JPK has very little information on the exact size or nature of the market for plastic laminates through retail trade classes. The decision was made, therefore, to conduct a study that would determine the scope of the retail market, the success that manufacturers of plastic laminates had had in selling their products through retail channels of distribution, and what JPK would have to do to achieve significant incremental volume through that market segment.

In order for JPK to develop a full understanding of the retail market for plastic laminates, it was decided that this study should include an evaluation of all retail trade classes participating in this market. In addition, this study was to include a detailed analysis of the market for high-pressure laminate sheets as well as for post-formed countertops and low-pressure laminate rolls. Finally, this study was to examine sales through retail outlets to do-it-yourselfers (home-owners) as well as to professional users (contractors, builders, and so on).

MARKET REVIEW

1. *The primary retail channels of distribution for plastic laminates are discount stores, home improvement centers, hardware stores, and lumberyards.* There are significantly more hardware stores than any other of these types of retail outlets in the United States. Lumberyards rank second in terms of the number of outlets, and home improvement centers and discount stores rank third and fourth, respectively. Table 14-1 provides a breakdown of the number of retail outlets in each of these four trade classes by geographic region in the United States.

2. *Home improvement centers and lumberyards tend to stock plastic laminates to a significantly greater degree than discount stores or hardware stores.* Approximately 91 percent of

TABLE 14-1. Number of Selected Retail Outlets by Type and Geographic Region

Region	Discount Stores	Home Improvement Centers	Hardware Stores	Lumberyards
Northeast	1,486	1,145	5,252	2,850
North Central	1,845	2,877	8,671	4,357
South	2,047	2,079	6,862	4,663
West	999	1,443	3,641	1,888
Total	6,377	7,544	24,426	13,758

Source: Estimates based on data from directories (*Discount Merchandiser, National Retail Consumer Reports, Chain Store Age*), and U.S. Census Bureau publications.

home improvement centers and 45 percent of lumberyards stock plastic laminates. Only 7 percent of discount stores and 3 percent of hardware stores stock this product category.

3. *Retail outlets also vary in the type of plastic laminates they stock.* Approximately 80 percent of home improvement centers stock sheet laminates, 70 percent stock post-formed tops, and 45 percent stock roll laminates. Lumberyards also tend to stock sheet laminates to a greater degree than post-formed tops or roll laminates. Hardware stores carry only sheet laminates, and discount stores primarily carry roll laminates.

4. *The amount of annual movement of plastic laminates through retail outlets varies dramatically from one trade class to another, and between the various product types.* Home improvement centers and lumberyards generally sell significantly more sheet laminates than any other type of plastic laminate. Discount stores tend to move more roll laminates than any other product type. Hardware stores generally sell only sheet laminates. Table 14-2 provides a breakdown of the average annual movement of a typical retail outlet in each trade class.

5. *The retail trade sells a combined total of 122 million square feet of plastic laminates annually.* Approximately 66 percent of these sales are sheet laminates, 24 percent are post-formed tops, and 10 percent are roll laminates. Home improvement centers generate the greatest movement in all product types; they sell a total of approximately 78 million square feet of plastic laminates.

6. *The average retail prices of plastic laminates vary considerably between post-formed tops, sheet laminates, and roll laminates.* To provide uniform comparisons, we have used price per square foot as a common denominator. The price per square foot of post-formed tops varies from $1.69 in discount stores to $2.78 in lumberyards. Sheet laminates range from

TABLE 14-2. Average Annual Movement in Square Feet for Each Retail Outlet Stocking Plastic Laminates

Retail Trade Class	Post-Formed Tops	Sheet Laminates	Roll Laminates
Discount stores	3,000	2,400	4,800
Home improvement	4,200	7,800	2,700
Hardware stores	—	600	—
Lumberyards	2,100	5,400	600

Source: Estimates based on national store checks and a telephone survey.

$0.82 to $0.89, and roll laminates sell for from $0.59 to $0.74 per square foot. Table 14-3 provides a breakdown of the average prices charged by retailers for plastic laminates.

7. *Retail channels of distribution sell a combined total of $138 million (at retail prices) of plastic laminates.* Sheet laminates and post-formed tops account for the bulk of these sales, and both product categories are equally important segments of the plastic laminate business. Home improvement centers are by far the most important trade class in terms of annual retail sales. Table 14-4 provides a detailed breakdown of sales volume by product type and trade class.

8. *The average retail margin (percentage off retail) received by the trade on plastic laminates varies from 30 to 44 percent.* Although many retailers would like to receive higher margins, discounting practices tend to drive the margins down to these averages. The variances in margin between trade classes and product types are primarily a function of discounting practices. Table 14-5 provides a breakdown of retail margins by trade classes and product types.

TABLE 14-3. Average Retail Prices (per Square Foot) Received on Plastic Laminates by Retail Trade Class

Retail Trade Class	Post-Formed Tops	Sheet Laminates	Roll Laminates
Discount stores	$1.69	$0.82	$0.59
Home improvement	1.89	0.82	0.74
Hardware stores	—	0.82	—
Lumberyards	2.78	0.89	0.74

Source: Estimates based on an average of all price points obtained during national store checks.

TABLE 14-4. Plastic Laminate Sales at Retail Prices by Trade Class (000)

Retail Trade Class	Post-Formed Tops	Sheet Laminates	Roll Laminates	Total Plastic Laminates
Discount stores	$ 761	$ 114	$1,325	$ 2,200
Home improvement	41,920	38,600	6,784	87,304
Hardware stores	-0-	361	-0-	361
Lumberyards	18,473	29,754	244	48,471
Total	$61,154	$68,829	$8,353	$138,336

Source: Estimates based on a comparison of annual movement in square feet times the average retail price identified during store checks and telephone surveys, times the percentage of stores in each trade class that carry the product.

TABLE 14-5. Average Retail Margins Received by Alternative Trade Classes

Retail Trade Class	Post-Formed Tops	Sheet Laminates	Roll Laminates
Discount stores	39%	36%	30%
Home improvement	44%	36%	38%
Hardware stores	—	36%	—
Lumberyards	40%	35%	40%

Note: Margins are percentages taken off retail price received.
Source: Estimates based on telephone discussions with trade headquarters personnel and national store checks.

9. *Most plastic laminates sold by retail channels of distribution are purchased through distributors.* Approximately 90 percent of sheet laminates, 88 percent of post-formed tops, and 70 percent of roll laminates are purchased through distributors.

10. *The average margins received by distributors on plastic laminates are from 28 (percentage off wholesale) to 43 percent.* The margins charged by distributors for post-formed tops tend to be the highest, and those on roll laminates tend to be the lowest. Table 14-6 describes the margins received by distributors on plastic laminates.

11. *Retail channels of distribution generate over $59 million in factory dollar sales on plastic laminates.* These sales figures represent net dollars received by manufacturers after subtracting retail and distributor margins. Approximately 65 percent of plastic laminate sales are concentrated in the north central and southern regions of the United States. The sales concentration in each geographic region is roughly the same from one product type to another.

12. *Plastic laminate sales through retail channels of distribution are fairly evenly divided between sales to do-it-yourselfers (homeowners) and sales to professionals (contractors, builders, developers, and so on).* Sheet laminates tend to be purchased by professionals to a slightly greater degree than by do-it-yourselfers. Roll laminates are clearly a do-it-yourself

TABLE 14-6. Average Margins Received by Distributors on Alternative Types of Plastic Laminates

Plastic Laminate Type	Average Distributor Margin
Post-formed tops	43%
Sheet laminates	28%
Roll laminates	20%

Source: Estimates based on discussions with the retail trade.

item. Approximately 94 percent of all roll laminates sold through retail outlets are bought by do-it-yourselfers.

13. *Discount stores tend to cater to the do-it-yourselfer to a significantly greater degree than any other type of retail outlet.* Approximately 83 percent of plastic laminate sales through discount stores are to do-it-yourselfers. This compares to 54 percent in home improvement centers, 46 percent in hardware stores, and 41 percent in lumberyards.

14. *Approximately 20 percent of the total plastic laminate market (in terms of factory dollar sales) is sold through retail channels of distribution.* Approximately 15 percent of industry sales in square feet is sold through retail channels of distribution. The percentage of factory dollar sales through retail outlets is higher than the percentage of square feet because of slightly higher pricing in the retail segment.

15. *The market for plastic laminates sold through retail channels of distribution is increasing at the rate of 15 percent annually.* At this rate of increase, the retail market will more than double in the next five years. Factory dollar sales are expected to increase from $59.5 million in 2000 to over $119 million in 2005.

CONSUMER RESEARCH RESULTS

1. *During focus groups, consumers provided a number of different reasons for doing home improvements themselves rather than having them done for them by professionals.* Economic factors play a major role in the do-it-yourself decision. In most cases it simply costs less to do it yourself than to hire a professional. Pride and the satisfaction of doing a good job was another important reason. Some consumers felt that doing home improvements was a positive therapeutic change from their normal routine.

2. *Respondents indicated that plastic laminates are used throughout the house.* There were many examples given of consumers' use of plastic laminates. These included kitchen countertops, bathroom vanities, bar tops, table tops, children's rooms, and many other applications.

3. *Consumers listed many benefits of the use of plastic laminates.* Many respondents felt that plastic laminates were durable, chip resistant, and strong. Plastic laminates were generally

felt to be stain resistant and easy to clean. Consumers liked the fact that plastic laminates come in many colors and patterns. They also felt that plastic laminates require fairly low upkeep, are heat resistant, and will not burn easily. Plastic laminates were felt to be easy to select and purchase, and were less expensive than the items they simulated (such as wood). Consumers liked the fact that plastic laminates are waterproof and good to prepare food on. The look of plastic laminates was generally felt to be acceptable to others, and easy to match for replacement or additions.

4. *The major improvement requested by consumers was that plastic laminates be made easier to work with.* They would like plastic laminates to be easier to get home, easier to cut and install, and easier to remove and change. They would like plastic laminates to be made available in a variety of sizes, and to be more pliable and moldable. Finally they would like the manufacturer to provide "how to apply" tips to make the do-it-yourself process easier.

5. *There were several additional general improvements suggested by focus group respondents.* Many respondents asked for an adhesive that was easier to work with. Some wanted the material to be made even harder, more scratchproof, and more chipproof. Some asked for a material that was more heat resistant and easier to seam. Some respondents asked for new patterns and colors. Some wanted to see less expensive plastic laminates. An interesting request by several respondents was for a plastic laminate repair kit.

6. *In the majority of the households represented in this research, the wife typically conceived the project.* In many cases it was indicated that she was interested in developing home improvement ideas, and was willing to collect patterns, get costs, and do some of the preparation work. Many of the wives included in this research said that it took them from a month to a year to get their husband started on the project.

7. *In the households represented in these focus groups, the husband typically made the actual purchase of plastic laminate.* He typically evaluated the quality differences in products and looked for dollar savings from alternative products. In most cases he selected the actual product and sought out installation guidance.

8. *These focus groups indicated that advertising and promotions were not significant in the plastic laminate category.* Some respondents remembered advertising by the major brand, although they generally forgot the message. Advertising for other brands was not recalled.

Retailer sale advertising was remembered by some respondents. For this category, however, sales were not typically viewed as important. Many respondents were suspicious of sale merchandise and would respond to a sale only if a project was already planned.

9. *The most popular new product concept, based on this research, was a plastic laminate that would be easier to work with.* Consumers were presented with a series of alternative concepts. These included an inexpensive low-pressure laminate, compact two- by four-foot sheets, precut kits, and a purchase by mail concept. The plastic laminate concept they liked best was a product that was easier to get home, easier to cut and install, and easier to remove and change.

TRADE PRACTICES AND ATTITUDES

1. *Most retailers who carry plastic laminates believe that it is a profitable product line and an essential segment of their overall line of home improvement products.* Home improvement centers strongly believe that they must offer their customers a product that can cover countertops, kitchen cabinets, and so on. This trade class has reached a point where it feels that it must carry plastic laminates in order to be fully in the home improvement business. Those lumberyards that carry plastic laminates (45 percent) feel similarly about the product category.

2. *Most discount stores and hardware stores do not consider plastic laminates a necessary part of their product line.* Hardware stores that now carry plastic laminates (3 percent) feel that plastic laminates are simply a minor product line that they carry to satisfy a small number of their customers. Most of the discount store managers interviewed during this study had not really considered plastic laminates as a logical part of their home improvement lines. Those discount stores that do carry plastic laminates (7 percent), however, find that the product category moves very well and has found a permanent home in their stores.

3. *Most retailers who carry plastic laminates put either the product itself or samples of the product on display to enable their customers to find the correct product type and pattern for their needs.* In some cases, primarily in home improvement centers, retailers construct massive displays to create an entire plastic laminate section. In addition, these outlets will

generally also have a wallboard that contains samples of additional patterns available to the consumer.

4. *Discount stores that carry plastic laminates generally have a display with product available right on the floor.* Discount stores generally do not have an additional wallboard; however, they generally have sample chips available should the consumer desire patterns that are not available on their displays. Lumberyards follow practices similar to those of home improvement centers. Hardware stores generally have no display, but have sample chips available should their customers ask about plastic laminates. The following specific display practices apply to each different type of plastic laminate:

   A. *Sheet laminates.* Retailers prefer to sell sheet laminates by providing their customers with samples of patterns rather than actually displaying the physical product. Retailers feel that sheet laminates are difficult to handle and easily damaged, and that it is hard to predict the patterns and sizes that will meet their customers' needs. Because of this, lumberyards, hardware stores, and approximately half of the home improvement centers do not physically stock sheet laminates. Discount stores generally do stock sheet laminates because they want each sale to be a carry-out item.

   B. *Post-formed countertops.* Retailers who sell post-formed countertops normally have one or two patterns displayed on the floor in several sizes. The two most popular patterns in this category are butcher block and white with gold flakes. Retailers generally also have sample chips for custom orders.

   C. *Roll laminates.* Roll laminates, when sold, are always displayed in a special merchandiser. Retailers do not special-order roll laminates. The merchandisers are always provided by the manufacturer.

5. *The plastic laminate market through retail outlets is clearly dominated by a small number of manufacturers.* Two manufacturers account for almost all of the retail sales of low-pressure laminate rolls. Two other manufacturers account for almost half of the sales of high-pressure laminate through retail outlets. Yet another two manufacturers account for an additional 25 percent of high-pressure laminate sales through retail outlets.

6. *Most retail outlets offer several brands of high-pressure laminates and only one brand of low-pressure laminate rolls.* Retailers who stock plastic laminates will generally have one brand in stock and will offer additional brands on a special-order basis. In sum, manufactur-

ers of plastic laminate do not have exclusive distribution through retail outlets for products other than low-pressure laminate rolls.

7. *Discount stores are a notable exception to the multiple-brand policies of retail outlets.* Discount stores would prefer to sell only plastic laminates that they have in stock on a merchandiser. Discount stores do not like to special-order plastic laminates (or any other product) for their customers. Because of this, most discount stores carry only one brand of each of the different types of plastic laminates.

8. *Retailers believe that their customers generally are not loyal to a single brand of plastic laminates.* They feel that most consumers are aware of the major industry brand name. Many consumers will actually use this name as a generic term for the plastic laminate category. When actually making the purchase, however, these consumers will readily shift to whatever brand is in stock or comes in the pattern that they prefer. Consumers do not insist on any particular brand of plastic laminate.

9. *The primary functions of in-store personnel are to provide information, take orders, and assist in the actual purchase transaction.* The degree of service varies dramatically from one type of retail outlet to another. In-store personnel in home improvement centers are generally fairly knowledgeable about plastic laminates. They take the time to assist customers in selecting patterns and placing orders, and then they help in moving the merchandise out to the customer's car. Additionally, many home improvement centers will arrange for a customer to have a plastic laminate countertop actually installed in the home. Lumberyards and hardware stores will also provide customers with a fair amount of service. Discount stores provide the least amount of service to customers. These organizations are not as well staffed as the other trade classes, and their employees are not as well informed about technical products such as plastic laminates.

10. *A primary consideration for retailers selecting a supplier of plastic laminates is service.* The price offered to retailers is obviously an important consideration, and it must be competitive. A major consideration is whether the retailer believes that the manufacturer or distributor can provide quick, dependable service and a broad enough line of patterns to supply consumers' needs. Once a retailer selects a supplier of plastic laminates, that retailer is very reluctant to change suppliers as long as the service remains dependable. In sum, the retail trade is not constantly shifting suppliers to obtain the best price at any given time.

11. *Retailers frequently promote plastic laminates throughout the year.* Some promotions are used to build store traffic, which helps retailers build their volume on their other product categories. Other promotions discount a few plastic laminate items in the hope that consumers will trade up to more expensive products in the plastic laminate category. The following promotion practices are typically employed in the retail channels of distribution:

A. *Popular patterns.* Home improvement centers will frequently advertise discounts on two or three popular patterns of post-formed countertops. The objective of this promotion technique is to shift customers from these low-priced limited patterns to higher-priced special-order patterns.

B. *Remnants and cutoffs.* Home improvement centers will frequently advertise sales on a limited selection of remnants and cutoffs at prices as low as $0.29 per square foot. Because the sizes and patterns of these products are very limited, retailers are generally successful in upgrading the customer to a more expensive brand that they carry.

C. *Laminate rolls.* Home improvement centers will frequently place low-pressure laminate rolls on sale in their newspaper advertisements. Their objective is to shift customers into high-pressure laminates at a higher price and profit. Discount stores will also promote laminate rolls with the objective of building store traffic.

D. *Lumberyards and hardware stores.* These trade classes rarely participate in promotions on plastic laminates.

E. *Discount stores.* Discount stores are the most frequent promoters of plastic laminates. This trade class generally has seven sales per year, and each sale generally lasts a week. Discount stores always promote sales in their newspaper ads.

F. *Home improvement centers.* Approximately 42 percent of home improvement centers launch promotions on plastic laminates. Those outlets that do promote this category follow practices similar to those of discount stores.

CONCLUSIONS

1. *Plastic laminate sales through retail channels of distribution are an important segment of the total industry.* Approximately 20 percent of total industry sales of plastic laminates move through retail channels of distribution. This represents over $59 million in factory dollar sales. In addition, sales through retail channels tend to be more profitable for manu-

facturers than sales through the traditional channels of distribution. Finally, the retail market for plastic laminates is growing at the rate of 15 percent annually, which means that this market will more than double in the next five years.

2. *The retail segment of the plastic laminate market is a very stable business that does not fluctuate very dramatically from one selling season to another.* Sales through retail stores are made to a broad base of customers, and therefore they do not have wide fluctuations. Retailers do not tend to shift suppliers frequently, which results in fairly even sales cycles for manufacturers and distributors.

3. *It would be difficult for JPK to achieve broad-scale distribution in those outlets that are now the principal sellers of plastic laminates.* Home improvement centers and lumberyards currently dominate the sales of plastic laminates. These retail organizations are very satisfied with their current suppliers, and would be very reluctant to take on a new supplier. Their current suppliers provide them with competitive pricing and with excellent service through their large network of distributors. . . .

4. *If JPK were to be successful in gaining distribution through home improvement centers and lumberyards, this would result in only minor incremental volume.* These trade classes generally carry several brands of plastic laminates. If they were to agree to take on the New Top brand, this would be likely to be in addition to their present brand. Because of this, New Top would be forced to share the sales from these outlets with several other manufacturers, resulting in only minor increases in volume to JPK.

5. *Discount stores could provide an excellent opportunity for JPK to penetrate the retail market for plastic laminates.* We believe that although discount stores are currently a minor factor, they could rapidly become a major segment of the retail plastic laminate business. Our conclusions regarding discount stores' potential are based upon the following observations:

   A. *Discount stores are rapidly moving into the home improvement business.* During visits to discount stores throughout the United States, we noticed a number of product lines that were clearly in the home improvement area. These products included wood paneling and lighting fixtures. During discussions with headquarters personnel at a number of leading discount stores, we were told that their objective is to take on those home improvement product lines that will fit into their merchandising policies and add significantly to their profits.

B. *Most discount stores are not now in the plastic laminate business.* Only 7 percent of discount stores presently carry any plastic laminates. Over 5,900 discount stores have not yet entered the market.

C. *Those discount stores that are currently selling plastic laminates are generating excellent volume and profits.* Discount stores that now carry plastic laminates generate an annual volume at retail prices of $4,700 per store per year.

D. *The success of those discount stores that are now in the plastic laminate business could serve as an excellent example to motivate other discount stores to enter the business.* Our interviews with nonparticipating discount stores have indicated that they are simply not aware of the potential of plastic laminates for their organizations.

6. *A discount store program on plastic laminates could provide an excellent opportunity for JPK to generate substantial incremental volume and profits.* For example, if JPK were to obtain exclusive distribution in 1,500 outlets, and if each outlet generated factory dollar sales of $2,000 per store per year, this would result in incremental sales to JPK of over $3 million annually. This would seem to be a reasonable forecast because of the small percentage of stores requiring distribution and the modest annual volume projections.

7. *In order for JPK to successfully launch a discount store program for plastic laminates, it will be necessary to develop a comprehensive program for the discount store channel.* Because this channel is currently not in the plastic laminate business, it will be necessary for JPK to show them how to enter the business and to provide them with all of the products that they will need in order to be successful competitors. Specifically, the following will be necessary:

A. *Presentation of the opportunity.* JPK will need to put together a presentation that clearly demonstrates to the discount store trade the opportunity for discount stores in the plastic laminate market.

B. *Merchandising plan.* Because discount stores do not have the experience that other retail outlets in the plastic laminate market have, it will be necessary for JPK to provide them with a background of successful promotion techniques, pricing policies, and other elements of a successful merchandising program such as those employed by other retail channels of distribution.

C. *A full product line.* Discount stores will be primarily catering to do-it-yourselfers. Because of this, JPK will need to arrange for them to obtain low-pressure laminate rolls as well as high-pressure sheets and post-formed countertops.

D. *Excellent distributors.* It will be necessary for JPK to launch such a program in an area where JPK has distributors that can adequately service discount stores.

8. *A retail program launched by JPK through discount stores could serve as a basis for JPK's obtaining distribution in other types of retail outlets and through incremental distributors.* Marketing plans and experience gained by JPK in operating through discount stores could be used in developing presentations to home improvement centers and lumberyards. This could enable JPK to gradually expand its retail program. As discount store distribution is expanded across the United States, JPK could use this as a vehicle to obtain new distributors.

9. *JPK could launch a retail program through discount stores with a minimum of risk.* Such a program should be able to be launched without any large up-front expenditure (e.g., national advertising) and therefore would not require any up-front losses. Because of the concentration of this market, JPK could gradually implement and expand such a program on a chain-by-chain basis and constantly expanding geographic regions. Additionally, it should be very easy for JPK to identify whether or not such a venture would be viable simply by exploring the concept with a number of discount chains. In sum, JPK should be able to enter this market on a step-by-step, pay-as-you-go basis.

MARKETING OBJECTIVES

The primary objective of this marketing plan is to establish JPK Counter Top Corporation as a major source of plastic laminates sold through retail stores. This will be done by providing the industry with a totally new consumer product that is much easier to work with than existing products in the plastic laminate category. The following are additional specific objectives of this marketing plan:

1. *Expand the overall do-it-yourself market.* The introduction of an easier to work with plastic laminate should broaden do-it-yourself consumers' interest in the category.

2. *Provide a preemptive retail merchandising program.* The goal is to get retailers to use a merchandising system from JPK that will stimulate sales of plastic laminates to consumers.

3. *Target the thrust of the program toward discount stores.* The specific goal is to obtain distribution in 4,312 retail outlets and to generate $40 to $50 in retail sales per store per week. This will result in JPK's capturing 8 percent of the home center/discount store market.

STRATEGIC PROGRAMS

1. *A plastic laminate product line that is easier to work with should be developed.* The plastic laminate product line should be offered to consumers in two sizes: four feet by four feet and four feet by eight feet. The plastic laminate should be offered in the four most popular patterns: butcher block, white, walnut, and almond. New patterns should be rotated in periodically.

2. *New Top should be used as the brand name for the new line of plastic laminates.* This unique name has the following qualities: It is preemptive and proprietary. It is applicable to public relations and promotional activities. It was found in consumer research to be meaningful and memorable to the target market, and it is timeless. This name should be used in all references to the new product, including packaging and displays, point-of-purchase material, and sales and public relations materials.

3. *Packaging should be developed for New Top that communicates the necessary consumer information.* Specifically, the new packaging should communicate the brand name, the product size and pattern, various product applications, application instructions, and the unique advantages of New Top compared to other plastic laminates.

4. *A merchandiser should be developed to display New Top at store level.* The display should have a dramatic visual impact, and should be flexible for in-line, freestanding, or end-aisle use. The display should hold the product safely. It should include a dramatic header sign (with permanent chips) and should dispense brochures that include sample patterns. The display should have a use life of three to five years, should be affordable, and should be provided free to the trade.

5. *An extensive in-store promotion program should be launched with the program.* This should include point-of-purchase material on the display, consumer brochures with usage information, a demonstration movie for store equipment, and advertising artwork for store usage.

6. *The New Top program should be launched with a major public relations program.* The public relations program should include national press releases to generate local feature print articles, as well as local and national radio and television appearances. A demonstration movie should be created for television broadcasts.

7. *A manager should be appointed as the national program coordinator.* This individual should create and implement the annual marketing plan. He or she should interface with all marketing suppliers, hire and supervise the zone managers, and coordinate all internal efforts. This manager should also monitor the overall progress of the program and make periodic reports to senior management.

8. *Zone managers should be appointed to hire and supervise manufacturers' representatives.* These people should also line up and coordinate distributors, sell and maintain retail accounts, and implement all zone aspects of the marketing plan. They should monitor all progress within the zone and provide periodic reports to the national coordinator.

9. *Manufacturers' representatives should be used to gain initial retail account distribution.* These individuals or organizations should also maintain a constant sales effort at retail headquarters, provide frequent retail store service, and interface with JPK distributors when necessary. They should implement the district aspects of the marketing plan and should report progress in their districts to the zone manager.

10. *Distributors should receive, warehouse, and ship all New Top product from the JPK factory.* These distributors should receive all shipping orders from the JPK factory, pick-pack individual store shipments, and drop-ship all orders to retail outlets via UPS. Invoicing should be handled by the JPK factory.

11. *New Top should be launched with competitive pricing and margins.* The retail price of the large size should be $24.99, and the price of the small size should be $13.99. Retailers should be allowed a suggested 45 percent margin. There should be a 2 percent cash discount, and the product should be sold on a guaranteed sale basis for the initial order. Manufacturers' representatives should receive a 5 percent commission, and distributors should receive a 15 percent warehouse fee. The product should be consigned to distributors.

12. *A formal desktop presentation should be used to generate new accounts.* This should be a flip chart booklet telling the New Top story. There should also be leave-behind brochures for the trade. Product samples should be given to each prospective account. A display setup sample should be available when requested. A product fact sheet and press kit handouts should also be available for prospects.

13. *Sales presentations should be made by manufacturer's representatives.* These people should be assisted by zone managers and the national coordinator. The sales presentations should be made at an off-site location whenever possible, and otherwise at the buyer's facility. Presentations should be targeted to the buyer level.

14. *The New Top program should be launched according to the following timetable.* Assuming that the program is approved on March 1, 2001, the national expansion should be able to begin on January 1, 2002. Table 14-7 gives the proposed timetable for the New Top plastic laminates venture.

FINANCIAL PROJECTIONS

1. *The costs of developing the New Top venture in 2001 are projected to be $311,320.* This includes package and display design costs, the development of brochures, sell-in sales materials, and travel expenses.

2. *Sales during the first year of national expansion (2002) are forecasted to be $2.2 million.* This represents sales of 4.8 million square feet of plastic laminate. Sales are expected to increase to $5.2 million in 2003 and $5.9 million in 2004. These dollar figures are for net factory sales.

3. *The operating costs, product costs, and strategic costs for 2002 are forecasted to be $2,054,000.* These costs are expected to increase to $4,315,000 in 2003 and $4,662,000 in

TABLE 14-7. Timetable for New Top Venture

Management presentations for approval	3/1/01
Select national program coordinator	5/1/01
Finalize product design	6/1/01
Brand name legal registration	7/1/01
Finalize package construction and graphics	8/1/01
Finalize display design and graphics	9/1/01
Finalize marketing communications	10/1/01
Secure initial distribution commitments	11/1/01
Produce initial product and materials	11/1/01
Ship initial product	12/1/01
Begin national expansion	1/1/02

2004. The largest portion of these costs is the cost of the product (factory cost), followed by the distributor warehouse fees and packaging costs.

4. *Income before tax is expected to be $166,000 for the first year of national expansion.* This is forecasted to represent 7.5 percent of sales. The income before tax for 2003 is expected to be $866,000, which is forecasted to represent 16.7 percent of sales. The income before tax for 2004 is forecasted to be $1,259,000, or 21.3 percent of sales. Table 14-8 gives the forecasted three-year income statement for the New Top venture.

TABLE 14-8. Forecasted Three-Year Income Statement (in 000s)

	2002	2003	2004
Units (square feet)	4,848	11,312	12,928
Net factory sales	$2,220	$5,181	$5,921
Operating and Product Costs			
Transportation (6%)	133	311	355
Cash discount (2%)	45	104	118
Factory cost (0.14 S.F.)	679	1,584	1,810
Package cost (0.045 S.F.)	218	509	582
Product warranty (1%)	22	52	59
Compensation on sales (5%)	111	259	296
Distributor warehouse fees (15%)	333	777	888
Operating managed cost	197	252	252
Committed cost (4%)	89	207	237
Strategic Costs			
Displays & materials	127	160	65
Public relations	50	50	0
Introductory sales expense	50	50	0
Total costs	$2,054	$4,315	$4,662
Income before tax	$ 166	$ 866	$1,259
% sales	7.5%	16.7%	21.3%

Index

About the Author

Winslow "Bud" Johnson is president of the Stamford Marketing Group, a consulting firm that specializes in research and development for winning marketing plans. He has been directly involved in the development of sixty marketing plans implemented by forty-two different clients. His clients include a wide variety of *Fortune* 500 companies, including such organizations as AT&T, Bank One, Dana, Gillette, H.J. Heinz, Kimberly-Clark, and Sara Lee. He has also assisted seven major global companies, such as Brother International Corporation, and a variety of smaller organizations, including three start-ups financed by venture capital.

Johnson started his career at the Market Research Corporation of America, where he managed the West Coast Division in Los Angeles. At MRCA he worked with clients in using qualitative and quantitative marketing research to determine whether new marketing concepts work and how to make them stronger. After MRCA, Johnson spent a number of years at Glendinning Associates as a marketing consultant specializing in the development of new products. He joined the Stamford Marketing Group in 1975.

A cum laude graduate of the University of Southern California with B.S. and M.B.A. degrees, Johnson moved to Connecticut in 1972, where he still resides. He has published numerous articles in professional publications on research and development for marketing plans. Johnson is a popular keynote speaker and workshop leader. He has been a frequent guest expert on many radio and television programs, including *Good Morning America,* and his work has been quoted in the *New Yorker* magazine and other publications nationwide. If you have questions or comments about anything in this book, the author can be reached by e-mail at smgemail@aol.com or by phone at (203) 348-2356.